ACADEMIC PATHS
Career Decisions and Experiences of Psychologists

Edited by
Peter A. Keller
Mansfield University

LAWRENCE ERLBAUM ASSOCIATES, PUBLISHERS
1994   Hillsdale, New Jersey   Hove and London

Lawrence Erlbaum Associates, Inc., Publishers
365 Broadway
Hillsdale, New Jersey 07642

Cover photograph by Terry Wild; supplied courtesy of Franklin and
Marshall College

Library of Congress Cataloging-in-Publication Data

Academic paths: career decisions and experiences of psychologists /
   edited by Peter A. Keller
        p.   cm.
   Includes bibliographical references and index.
   ISBN 0-8058-1370-5 (alk paper). -- ISBN 0-8058-1371-3 (pbk. : alk. paper)
   1. Psychologists--Biography.   I. Keller, Peter A., 1945–
BF109.A1A24   1994
150′.92′273--dc20
[B]   94-34111
                                                  CIP

Books published by Lawrence Erlbaum Associates are printed on
acid-free paper, and their bindings are chosen for strength and dura-
bility.

Printed in the United States of America
10 9 8 7 6 5 4 3 2 1

Contents

Preface

This book contains the autobiographies of 13 psychologists who work in academic settings. Their experiences are as diverse as the academic institutions and organizations from which they come. However, all of the contributors have in common an infectious enthusiasm for their academic experiences and the unique opportunities provided by their careers.

The idea for this volume grew from my observation that psychology students often have only vague notions about the career experiences and personal lives of academic psychologists. Discussions with colleagues as well as graduate and undergraduate students convinced me that this was much more the rule than the exception. After all, how would they know? Although in some instances students may develop personal relationships with mentors and key instructors, they usually lack a sense of the academic life from a faculty member's perspective.

Of course, academic departments and the exposure of students to faculty vary considerably depending on the size and type of institution. And all departments have their own working climate. As often as students may experience a sense of academic community, they see fractious departments and faculty pursuing their own interests separate from colleagues and, frequently, students. My own recollections of being a graduate student at the University of Miami in the late 1960s were of frequently closed faculty office doors except during a limited number of office hours. A few faculty seemed always to have open doors and space inhabited by research assistants. I had positive experiences with Edward J. Murray who supervised my thesis and Edith Lord who guided my doctoral dissertation. A life-long friendship has even grown from a relationship with another Miami faculty member. But what of the others? Did they have the rumored hidden offices? Maybe they really spent most of their time at the backyard swimming pool? As students we knew that at times they met and talked with each other because they gave us feedback about major examinations and policy changes. What were those meetings like? How else did these people spend their careers? At that time I was training to be a clinician and really had very different career ideas in mind, but I was curious about the lives of my instructors.

My undergraduate education was at Franklin and Marshall, a selective liberal arts college that expected psychology majors to be deeply involved in laboratory research. The enthusiasm of the faculty for teaching and their interest in research were what excited my initial interest in psychology. The department maintained a stimulating and positive climate that demanded student involvement. I can still remember walking past the building that housed the department late on Sunday evenings and noticing the office lights of Ken Brookshire, one of my early mentors. College teaching must be an awfully interesting job to bring someone away from his family at that hour. Although I wasn't fully conscious of it at the time, I think that small events such as these must have ultimately influenced my decision to enter academia. Perhaps to my own family's dismay, my office lights are sometimes blazing on weekend and holiday evenings. I now know that I share Professor Brookshire's enthusiasm for the challenges and freedoms of academic life. One of my hopes is that this book will communicate the enthusiasm of others to student readers.

I have organized the chapters in this volume to help students understand more fully the diverse experiences of academic careers in psychology. I invited contributions based on a three-dimensional matrix designed to ensure some form of representation from the various areas of psychology. On one side of the matrix were the various types of institutions in which academic psychologists might work. Thus, there are contributions from psychologists at institutions that range from 2-year community colleges through doctoral-level research institutions. Another dimension was, of course, the contributors' areas of interest and expertise. Finally, I have attempted some balance in the cultural and ethnic backgrounds of the contributors.

Although this book is, in a sense, about career planning in academic settings, I make no pretense about it being a career planning guide. My goal is to give readers some sense of what motivates academic psychologists and what their lives are like. From this you may be able to gain some ideas that will help direct your career decisions.

I hope the final selection of chapters makes it clear that there is no single pathway to a successful academic career in psychology. If there is anything that the contributors have in common, it is a high level of energy and an enthusiasm for their academic discipline. One colleague commenting on the selection of chapters noted that the outstanding accomplishments and productivity of these contributors might actually intimidate some student readers. She facetiously suggested the need for a subsequent volume on more "average" careers in academia. I trust that readers will not be intimidated by the accomplishments of these authors but will be stimulated by the variety of opportunities associated with their careers in such different settings.

Peter A. Keller

Chapter 1

Career Paths in Academia: No Single Route to Success

Peter A. Keller
Mansfield University

This book describes the career paths and experiences of 13 psychologists who work in diverse academic settings. My goal in organizing the chapters was to open a personal window into the lives of academic psychologists for students contemplating careers in academia. The contributors were invited to prepare autobiographical chapters as representatives of various kinds of institutions and psychology careers in academia or closely related settings. Each was also invited because of successful experiences or important accomplishments that modeled opportunities others might follow.

I have known a few of the contributors for a decade or more through contacts in professional organizations and at conferences, or through paths crossing because of shared academic interests. I have had no previous contact with others, but I had noted some aspects of their careers through the literature in psychology. I attempted to pick contributors who would have an interesting story to tell and valuable lessons that they could share with the intended readers—primarily graduate students and upper division undergraduates in psychology.

Unlike some career options where young people may see models throughout their lives, the image of work in academia is not available to most of us at an early age. Students usually first come into contact with college professors only when they begin their postsecondary studies. Depending on the size of the institution and the climate of the departments in which they study, their contacts with faculty are often relatively distant. Only more mature and strongly motivated students are likely to cross the natural barriers between faculty and students and to observe the lives of their instructors.

In reading the autobiographies the reader will discover that each describes experiences that are in some way unique. Almost all have a number of exceptional accomplishments that distinguish their careers. All have found their academic paths rich, challenging, and fulfilling. The experiences of these authors also suggest that there is no such thing as a typical career path. Academic psychology is as varied as the people and institutions in which they work. My hope is that this book will offer insight to some who have been curious about the academic life, encouragement to some who thought they might not "qualify" for an academic career for lack of the "right" background, and a sense of how to get started for others who may be puzzled about the vicissitudes of academic life. The following section describes some of the common, and perhaps not so common, career threads of these authors.

Early Experiences Guiding Careers of Academic Psychologists

My invitation to prepare an autobiographical chapter brought a positive, but sometimes hesitant, response from most potential authors. In all, 18 invitations were extended to obtain the final 13 chapters. Although several of the invitees declined because of the time frame for completing the work, many whose chapters appear in the book were, at first, reluctant. They often asked something like, "Are you sure you want me? My career path has been quite unusual." For a moment I wondered if I had made some horrible mistake in selecting these individuals. Upon reflection, I think not.

In reconsidering the career paths of colleagues I had known fairly well over the years, as well as the group I had asked to write chapters, it became apparent that there is no typical career path in academia. Not surprisingly, there is quite a contrast among the early experiences of the contributors. Consider, for example, Ludy Benjamin who started out to be a dentist, or Samuel Cameron who was interested in a military career at first. Nancy Felipe Russo makes an important observation about her maintaining career ideas but no specific career plan until well along her academic path. Although Patricia Keith-Spiegel notes that she and most of her colleagues loved school from the early years, it is just as clear that some of the authors in this book floundered during their undergraduate and, for a few, even their early graduate careers. Nonetheless, it seems obvious that a love for learning and for the challenges of the academic environment now characterizes virtually all of these authors.

Opportunities Taken or Missed

An early career factor noted by several contributors is serendipity. Many felt that one or more chance occurrences had had a significant influence on their career paths. Academic psychologists with especially successful careers describing the role of fortuity or luck in directing their careers, especially their early paths, may seem puzzling to readers who hear about the importance of careful planning from their advisors. My own conclusion is that the role of serendipity is probably overstated by a number of the contributors.

Perhaps Robert Perloff best captures the issue in the opening part of his title "Playing the Hand That's Dealt You. . . ." In a sense, each of us makes a gamble when we set a direction for ourselves or accept a job. Yet we must choose to put ourselves at the proverbial table to receive the cards that may be dealt. And we must clearly make decisions to play our cards wisely if we are to develop a successful career. From a slightly different perspective, Gary Melton describes both the role of chance and the "constancy of perspective and goals across (his) life." For Melton and the other authors, as well as most people in the working world, there are opportunities taken or passed by almost every day. Each day also represents an opportunity to connect or to not connect with others whose interests are related to ours. These choices and connections have important implications for the opportunities that arise in our lives.

Mentoring is a related issue that helps determine career direction. Many of the authors in this book describe early mentors or advisors who helped guide them or who suggested opportunities. I believe that most competent faculty keep watch for motivated and talented students who have potential for graduate study and academic or professional careers. We especially enjoy interacting with such students and will devote extra effort to guiding them toward interesting opportunities. Indeed, it is these students that often take the initiative to seek out faculty mentors and explore graduate school and career options with them. At most institutions it is only a small fraction of the undergraduate students who will achieve a successful career at an advanced level in psychology. Faculty usually take pride in having mentored students who achieve such successes.

A Sense of Empowerment in Career Management

One characteristic of virtually all of the contributors to the book is a strong sense of empowerment. From their graduate studies forward, they often had a sense of mission. In each position taken, they attempted to accomplish some important goals. They were persistent in their efforts and not deterred by barriers to success. Although the space allocated for each chapter means that the stories are certainly incomplete, it seems that significant opportunities rarely slipped by as these authors pursued their options. Or if they did, it was intentional because some other opportunity presented itself. These authors also were not deterred by failed experiences nor afraid to move on to new opportunities or positions. Although I encouraged the authors to address negative aspects of their experiences, most offer very few complaints, even about positions they decided to leave. They are focused on growth and development and rarely lament failures or complain about frustrating aspects of their work.

Most of the authors have had relatively long tenures in just a few positions. It may be instructive for readers to note why authors elected to change positions or stay as they explore the chapters. For the most part, the changes seem related to the authors' perceptions of their ability to accomplish their goals from a particular base of operations.

Several of the authors have had significant experiences in positions that do not directly involve the traditional academic roles of teaching or research. For example, Nancy Felipe Russo, Ludy Benjamin, and Dalmas Taylor have, at one time or another, all worked in leadership positions with the American Psychological Association (APA). And Ursula Delworth held a position at the Western Interstate Commission for Higher Education. For them, professional administrative roles seemed to complement their more traditional university endeavors and to lead naturally back to academic institutions.

Other contributors have provided leadership for university initiatives aimed at public needs. At present, Gary Melton heads a Center on Children, Families, and the Law at the University of Nebraska, and he will be directing an Institute for Families in Society at the University of South Carolina by the time this book is published. Stanley Sue directs a National Research Center on Asian American Mental Health at the University of California, Los Angeles. In these instances the authors have merged their research or policy interests with other academic activities. Their pursuits reflect the potential richness of academic career paths as well as their individual commitments to particular goals.

Professional Socialization

Russo makes explicit the importance of informal professional socialization to the development of a career in academia. Although it seems that there are many resources for professional psychologists to develop perspectives on career options and plans, I believe academicians generally have had less access to such guidance. Several recent volumes (e.g., Kilburg, 1991; O'Connell & Russo, 1983, 1988; Rheingold, 1994) either describe the personal career experiences of psychologists or address career management issues. The focus in the present book is on anecdotal information that can provide valuable insights about career possibilities. Russo notes the importance of understanding the requirements of the system in which one must function. On the one hand, academia encourages, at times even demands, considerable autonomy. On the other hand, it can be very unforgiving for newer faculty who fail to discern or respond to the sometimes unwritten norms of an academic department or institution.

Often a mentor or senior faculty member can help guide psychologists entering academia. In fact, many chairpersons identify such mentoring as a critical role for themselves. Although some faculty survive or even achieve great success while operating outside the usual norms established in a department, it is always wise to assess carefully and understand the norms and expectations of the setting in which one works. Some of this assessment should take place during a job interview, but there are often many subtle expectations that are likely to be missed by an aspiring academic. Therefore, it is important to identify wise and supportive mentors and seek consultation regularly as one begins any academic position.

Selecting an Institution

By design, this book includes career experiences from a wide range of institutions. My assumption is that one may find challenging and satisfying academic careers in many different kinds of settings. Sometimes in their graduate experiences students get the sense that real academic careers virtually always take place in high-powered research institutions, that only ground-breaking research will lead to success in academia, or that lesser positions inevitably mean a sacrifice in terms of quality and integrity. Some chapters in this book may even reinforce this notion. My personal belief is that nothing could be further from the truth. I hope these are myths that this book refutes, as a number of the contributors have experienced rewarding careers and made important contributions to psychology while based at institutions that are neither known for their research nor highly selective in their student admissions.

Each department and institution has a unique climate that either enables new faculty to be effective and supports them on a route of success, or perhaps confuses them about where best to expend their efforts. Settings that support personal and professional development are much more likely to give faculty a sense of fulfillment and to recognize their accomplishments. In these settings there is an emphasis on continual re-examination of existing efforts and a move toward innovation and improvement. Such settings are, in my experience, more likely to encourage collaborative work and to build a sense of community that supports both individual and group efforts. New faculty would be wise to assess for such qualities by asking appropriate questions and scanning the environment as they look for positions.

There is also the important issue of person–institution fit. Personal temperament, academic goals, and appropriate skills must be considered in light of institutional qualities. Well-functioning institutions and departments typically have a clearly defined mission and goals. Unfortunately, at many institutions faculty receive conflicting messages about important role issues such as teaching, advising, research, university service, and so on. Anyone examining career possibilities should assess their own goals in relation to their expertise and the possible fit with different kinds of institutions.

Students consulting with their present faculty may hear different stories about career possibilities in academic settings. In my experience, it is usually best to consult with several faculty about career planning. It is important to assess natural biases each may have as a consequence of their own undergraduate and graduate training as well as other institutions at which they may have worked. If possible, I would suggest consulting with psychologists who have regular experiences visiting other academic institutions. If you can identify such individuals and discuss their observations in depth, you are more likely to be able to discern the kinds of institutional settings in which you will have the most probability for success.

Although I think that many young academics have the potential to develop satisfying careers at a variety of institutions, there are certain matches that should be avoided. This also means coming to grips with realistic career aspirations. I have seen a number of instances where faculty perceived to be failing at one institution have been able to thrive at another which has a different mission or a more supportive climate. The chapters that follow should allow readers to compare career experiences in a variety of academic settings.

Primarily Undergraduate Teaching and Research Careers

Several of the autobiographies in this book describe career experiences in undergraduate teaching and research. The authors of these chapters have in common their excitement about shaping students' thinking and their love for the process of learning. Consider, for example, the work of Ann Garrett Robinson in an urban community college that provided her an opportunity to innovate, and to reach out and address student and community needs. Note, too, from her experiences that not all interests in scholarly writing necessarily require one to produce a widely recognized text or a series of research papers in refereed journals. Indeed, for some whose main interest is teaching and who savor contacts with students, the community college offers rewarding career opportunities. Yet it may preclude the chance to develop a significant research program or to obtain certain kinds of grants because the demands of a heavy teaching load and the limitations of institutional mission will not support such efforts. Still, the setting allows one to teach with enthusiasm and to work with students who might not otherwise have the chance for college study.

Several contributors to the book work at institutions focused primarily on 4-year undergraduate education. For example, Stephen Davis describes the rich rewards of a career at a modest sized state university. His career has included teaching, an active student-oriented research program, as well as serving as chair of a 17-member department. Before his present position at Emporia State University in Kansas, he taught at two other institutions. At his second position he came to value the role of research in training students. Critical factors in accepting his present position were the collegiality of the faculty and the community in which the university was located. His energy and enthusiasm contributed to the development of the department as well as organizations to support the efforts of students. As his career at Emporia developed, he accepted leadership positions in regional and national organizations, including the APA Division on the Teaching of Psychology.

After a brief "false start" in a position at a Caribbean medical school, Antonio Puente took a position at the University of North Carolina at Wilmington in 1981. Like Stephen Davis he has involved his undergraduate students in research and found this enterprise rewarding. He, too, has been active in providing leadership to state and national organizations. For example, he has chaired important committees within the APA and served on high-level task forces in the rapidly growing area of neuropsychology. Through sabbatical opportunities and contacts with others in the field, he has even developed a program of research in collaboration with world renowned scholars. In addition, he has managed to maintain an active independent practice in neuropsychology.

From these two examples there can be little doubt about the possibility of significant accomplishments from a multipurpose state university as a base of operations. Readers will, however, take note of the high energy levels of the two authors. Obviously, not all faculty in regional public institutions are so productive. It also seems important to note the ways in which these authors have built at least some of their research programs around their students.

Samuel Cameron, by contrast, has done his teaching at a small private college in a metropolitan area. After his false start at a large medical institution proved to be a disappointing match, he obtained a position at Beaver College where he has remained for three decades. His position at Beaver has allowed him to teach, conduct research, and engage in clinical service. One of his most interesting accomplishments has been to extend opportunities for study in psychology to high school students via a National Science Foundation grant. Like other authors in the book, he has also been active in providing leadership for regional and national organizations from his base at a smaller institution.

Ludy Benjamin's career experiences could fit under several different categories. After 8 years at Nebraska Wesleyan, a private Midwestern college where undergraduate students were the priority focus of faculty activities, he obtained a position as director of the APA's Office of Educational Affairs. From there Benjamin moved to Texas A&M, a large state university. Although Texas A&M is an active research university, he has taught undergraduates, pursued his research interests in the history of psychology, served on university committees, and made a broad range of national contributions. His chapter includes valuable personal insights about the different roles academic psychologists may fill and the settings in which they may work, especially in relation to the contrast between a small college and a large research institution. Benjamin also describes some of the expectations of an academic life in a way that readers should find useful. The description of his work schedules provides special insight into the academic life.

Baron Perlman describes "the rhythms and serendipity" of his academic life at the University of Wisconsin, Oshkosh, a thriving state university of 11,000 students. His department supports both bachelor's and master's degree programs. An active instructor, he has engaged in grant-supported research and also played a dynamic role in the development of faculty across the university. His efforts in this regard reflect the new emphasis that universities are placing on the improvement of undergraduate teaching. Perlman's chapter captures the many, often conflicting, forces that pull on most university faculty. He describes missing opportunities to be an "academic cosmopolitan" more involved in events at a national level. Perlman's chapter also describes how he has grown more interested in undergraduate teaching as his career matures, and how he has recognized for himself the importance of relationships with others in the university community.

Patricia Keith-Spiegel's career has been focused on teaching, and she provides perspectives from two different university settings. Before accepting her present position in an endowed professorship at Ball State University, she spent 25 years on the faculty of another comprehensive state university—California State University, North Ridge. The previous position offered limited resources and little sense of community in its academic setting. Her recent move to Ball State University in Indiana brought her to a more cohesive setting that values the quality of teaching. In fact, her professorship is designed to encourage an emphasis on teaching, and she heads the Office of Teaching Resources in Psychology, which is supported by the APA Division on the Teaching of Psychology and located at Ball State University. She describes an array of interesting activities and important achievements that have enriched her career. Keith-Spiegel writes about the roles of wife, mother, and professor during the era in which the women's movement developed. She also reflects on important qualities of the academic environment, such as connections with other faculty, that can enhance or detract from the quality of life as a professor.

Primarily Graduate Teaching and Research Careers

The authors described in this section have spent their careers mainly at research-oriented, doctoral degree-granting institutions. There is certainly some overlap between the missions of their universities and the ones previously described, as well as the roles in which the authors have engaged, but these individuals have, for the most part, focused their careers more on scholarship and research, and less on teaching. This is obviously a risky generalization, for they too have played an important role in mentoring students, but there is a different quality to the focus of their efforts. In some instances there has also been a significant emphasis on academic leadership. For example, both Stanley Sue and Dalmas Taylor have held administrative positions at major research institutions.

Ursula Delworth is a faculty member in a doctoral counseling program in the School of Education at the University of Iowa. Her early career visions of studying law first gave way to a master's degree and work in school counseling, followed by doctoral study in counseling psychology. Delworth's first postdoctoral experience was at the Colorado State University counseling center, where she discovered her love of scholarship and developed innovative programs to train students as paraprofessionals. Before moving to her present university she also worked as a grant director for the Western Interstate Commission for Higher Education. At the University of Iowa she obtained a position that offered the opportunity for work in the counseling center as well as an academic department. Delworth describes clearly some of the midcareer choices she had to address and the demands of editing the APA journal *Professional Psychology: Research and Practice*. Her insights into the personal challenges we face across ours careers provides a special dimension to her chapter.

In the next chapter Nancy Felipe Russo describes her many roles in academia. Before assuming her position as professor of psychology and women's studies at Arizona State University, she taught at American University, Richmond College of the City University of New York, and served on the staff of the APA's Educational Affairs Office. While working with APA in the late 1970s and early 1980s, she became involved in a wide range of activities including efforts to address women's issues. Russo has written extensively about women's concerns, including collaboration on several collections of autobiographies of important women in psychology (e.g., O'Connell & Russo, 1983, 1988). She also became active in supporting the needs of Hispanic women in psychology. Russo's chapter describes the strenuous demands of working as an administrator, teacher, researcher, author, and committee member within a large university. Among other things, she advises developing psychologists to "be clear on your values. . .then live your life in service of your values." Her experiences and recommendations concerning the importance of mentoring may be especially important for those with goals in academia.

Among other accomplishments in his distinguished career, Robert Perloff has served on the faculty of both psychology departments and a business school at major universities. He is a past president of the APA and a professor emeritus at the University of Pittsburgh where he first joined the Graduate School of Business faculty, as Director of the Management Research Center, in 1969. He subsequently held other administrative positions while teaching a variety of courses at the interface between psychology and business. Perloff's autobiography reveals a rich career of leadership opportunities taken in professional organizations and in consulting as well as his academic accomplishments. He addresses the differences between teaching in a psychology department and a business school. He also reflects on the many challenges of his eminent career and concludes with sage advice to others. Perloff is convinced that to be successful one must learn to cope with adversity that he believes enhances one's resolve.

Gary Melton has for more than a decade headed the Center on Children, Families, and the Law at the University of Nebraska, Lincoln. His interests are in the area of public policy, and he has been nationally recognized as a scholar and advocate working for the interests of children and families. He describes a long-standing preoccupation with politics as well as public policy issues, and his career has merged interests in psychology and the law. He left his first position at a regional university because the demands of teaching 15 credit hours per semester interfered with his scholarly pursuits. Since then he has served at the Institute of Law, Psychiatry, and Public Policy at the University of Virginia and then at the University of Nebraska. Melton notes the importance of an interdisciplinary setting to his training and present work. In contrast to the authors in the previous section, teaching is not a primary focus for Melton who has used the academic setting as a platform to study public policy and to advocate for social change.

Stanley Sue, who teaches at the University of California, Los Angeles, developed his attraction to psychology after his early experiences in a technical high school. Interestingly, he is part of a family generation of psychologists. Sue discovered an interest in ethnic research out of his observations of the turmoil that many U.S. universities experienced in the late 1960s. At the time he assumed his first position at the University of Washington there was resistance to recognizing ethnic research as a legitimate area for psychologists. But with the help of the persistence he describes in his chapter, support for this kind of research grew. In 1981, Sue joined the faculty of UCLA, which offered more opportunities for his studies. Later he established the National Research Center on Asian American Mental Health and served as an associate dean for the graduate division. Sue's chapter describes the various aspects of his life at a large research university and comments on some of the personal experiences that affect him.

Dalmas Taylor is a social psychologist who has served in administrative roles at three different universities. In the past he has been a researcher in both academic and nonacademic settings. Taylor describes the link between his interests in psychology and his early experiences as an African American growing up in Detroit and in a pre-affirmative action United States. He shows how the social context shaped his passions and perspectives. Taylor was the first director of the APA Minority Fellowship Program, which is designed to encourage doctoral study in psychology for people of color. Since the late 1970s he has served as a dean and then as a vice president and senior vice president at two major universities. From these vantage points he provides a unique perspective on academia that others may never see directly.

Other Considerations in Career Planning

As already noted, the authors of the chapters in this book bring a diversity of personal and professional perspectives to their chapters. They also raise a number of interesting career considerations. Several of the more important issues are discussed briefly here.

The Multiple Roles of Academic Work

Many of us who work in academia, and who love learning and the opportunities that come from a setting designed to foster scholarship, find universities to be full of exciting opportunities. For virtually all of the contributors to this book, academia has involved many different roles. Most of the contributors seem committed to several directions at once, and their autobiographies suggest that they must indeed work very hard to meet their many obligations. Thus their work is as demanding as it is rewarding.

Not surprisingly, teaching has been an important role for all but of a few of the contributors. In fact, several have decided to renew their efforts directed toward teaching and development of the students with whom they work as they make mid-career adjustments. For faculty at undergraduate institutions, teaching demands the majority effort, and as evidenced by the pursuits of Keith-Spiegel, there is currently a renewed interest in the quality of college teaching across the nation.

Research and scholarship are activities in which most all of the contributors to this book contribute a considerable amount of effort. However, they go about their pursuits in remarkably different ways. For example, contributors such as Davis and Puente regularly involve their undergraduate students in a variety of research projects, many of which are publishable. Others energetically pursue scholarship through national networks of colleagues with similar interests or through specially funded centers with nationally recognized goals and accomplishments.

Several of the authors are involved in various forms of special service to their departments and universities. Indeed there is often a pull to serve universities through a myriad of committees that address everything from curriculum development and interdisciplinary initiatives to student admissions and retention. In many institutions there is an expectation that faculty provide a certain amount of committee service. Some of the committee work can be quite rewarding as new programs develop and important tasks are completed. Committee work can also contribute to the development of valued relationships and the sense of collegiality mentioned by several authors. For Perlman, scholarship has grown directly from his university efforts to help other faculty develop their talents. At the same time, this kind of work can require an exceptional amount of time that may not be fully recognized when tenure and promotion are at issue. For new academics, in particular, this issue must be carefully assessed in the context of each institution and the kinds of effort it rewards.

Melton observes that it is common for faculty to have contracts or understandings about how they will divide time among the primary activities of research, teaching, and community or clinical service, with the portion determined by the type of institution. This seems to me extremely important. Yet it is my observation that many newer faculty members are confused by the multiple role demands of their universities. Beyond seeking a match for his or her talents, one of the most important thing a new academic can do is reach a clear understanding about role expectations. Recently tenured or promoted colleagues as well as the chairperson, and in some institutions, the dean, should be consulted to develop the necessary perspective. It is on the basis of this understanding that some kind of plan for managing time can be established.

Tme Management in Academia

As Perloff notes in his chapter, time is a zero-sum game. Choices made to direct career efforts in one direction inevitably preclude other accomplishments. Although many career choices clearly determine in advance how one will spend a majority of his or her time, one of the advantages and challenges of the academic life is the wide range of possible choices for career effort and the accompanying recognition that one can only accomplish so much.

While observing the flexibility that one has in scheduling his or her academic life, Benjamin also estimates that successful academics work 60 or more hours per week, a number consistent with my personal experiences and observations. However, Perlman notes how prone to interruption one's schedule is in an academic setting. Students, other faculty, and administrators may all have sudden needs that contribute to unplanned meetings or tasks that must be addressed on short notice. For example, its not unusual to be asked to prepare several letters of recommendation or quickly review someone else's grant proposal within a few days. Ironically, the more productive a faculty member is, the more likely he or she is to be called upon to render such assistance. These and other more predictable tasks all contribute to the briefcase full of work that some authors noted they routinely take home.

In addition to being energetic, successful academicians must be well disciplined in organizing their work. Recognizing that being in one's office invites interruption, some work at home routinely or have alternate work areas in which they are protected from intrusions. However, in institutions that emphasize teaching and advising, there will be pressures to make oneself readily available to students. Some faculty rise early or stay up late, depending on their personal preferences, to complete their many obligations. The life of unusual flexibility and the ability to, on occasion, get away from the office obviously has its price in terms of the high expectations successful academicians set for themselves.

Outside Organizational Service

Many of the contributors to this volume have provided exceptional organizational service that runs beyond the usual expectations of academia. For them, the service appears to have afforded special rewards in a number of dimensions. One can learn about many things to which one would not have been exposed in one's own setting. Outside service is often a source of special recognition for one's talents, and it provides the opportunity to offer leadership and encourage improvements for the discipline at a higher level. Perloff also notes the opportunity to enhance the credibility of psychology through contributions to organizations. Outside participation and leadership in organizations are also important avenues for learning about the intriguing political realities of one's profession. There are, of course, many personal benefits to outside involvement as well.

Such participation can lead to a range of new personal as well as professional relationships. It is also through such connections that one realizes the importance of networking in accomplishing professional goals and that one becomes positioned for new opportunities that otherwise would almost surely never arise. Perloff describes candidly some of the tangible benefits to outside organizational involvement including the opportunity to "live well" through involvement with high-level organizational efforts.

Still, some who choose academic positions are more timid or uncomfortable with the foray into such directions or feel limited with the amount of time available given their other commitments. Such decisions are often based on personal needs and proclivities as well as more practical considerations. In my view this is an area that requires careful thought and certainly some risk-taking for successful involvement. Obviously, many academics find considerable reward and make valuable contributions through their outside organizational involvement.

Networking Strategies

Networking involves efforts to contact, learn from, and at times collaborate with others who share common interests. It is an important strategy in most professional fields of endeavor, including academia. Over the 20 years of my own academic career I have had occasion to contact hundreds of psychologists from whom I wanted information or whose assistance I needed with some project. Sometimes the contacts have been brief; in other instances they have led to shared projects and long-term relationships built around personal as well as scholarly concerns. Often networks begin in graduate school through contacts with faculty, whose existing networks one may join, and expand as we pursue our own research or writing. Such contacts have a way of expanding exponentially and leading to other productive interactions. For many academics some of their most valued and stimulating interactions come with colleagues from other institutions. The rewards of such networking are available to those willing to take small risks to expand their world of interactions.

Melton provides a specific example of how networking, or seeking consultation in reference to one project, led to a new job opportunity that might otherwise not have occurred. In fact, many of the career opportunities described in this book came through networks of contacts with strategically placed colleagues. Like others, academicians must make important choices about how far to develop their networks. Suffice it to say, a more or less conscious strategy of connecting with others can play a critical role in determining one's future experiences and accomplishments.

Understanding the Quality of One's Work Environment

As mentioned in the introduction to this chapter, different academic settings may offer distinctively different qualities of life. In my estimation too little attention in psychology has been given to issues such as the sense of community and the quality of relationships that accompany a position. In a commentary on community in academia, an English professor at a research university (Tompkins, 1992) observed that "the dynamic intellectual exchange one might have imagined taking place among distinguished scholars frequently fails to occur because everyone is too busy doing his or her own work" (p. 15). In our discipline, psychologists are often trained to be independently productive and to function autonomously. In fact, formal reward systems usually provide less credit for collaborative than individually directed projects. As often as not these tendencies and the competitive reward systems of academia lead to acrimonious departments that afford little cooperation and fairly defensive or self-protective work strategies.

I encouraged the contributors to this book to reflect on the qualities of their work and personal lives. Several made sensitive observations in this regard. For example, Benjamin compares the sense of community he experienced at a small liberal arts college with that at a large research university. Keith-Spiegel also contrasts the impersonal quality of life at one university with that obtained in her new position that allowed for more personal contacts both within the university and its smaller supporting community. Among the other authors, there is a sense that some place considerable importance on the quality of their relationships with students and other faculty, whereas others seem to place much more emphasis on their individual scholarly goals. These are issues that each person seeking an academic position must assess in terms of his or her potential fit with job expectations. When one recognizes that he or she may spend the better part of a lifetime working with academic colleagues, the quality of relationships and how much effort one wishes to invest in this direction are important considerations.

There are, of course, many other lessons to be learned from the experiences of these authors. Each offers a unique and personal perspective on the potential richness of the academic pathway. Only by reading the individual chapters will you be able to discover the insights these authors offer on careers in academia. It is, however, clear that academia offers many rewarding opportunities with no single path to success.

References

Kilburg, R. R. (Ed.). (1991). *How to manage your career in psychology.* Washington, D.C.: American Psychological Association.

O'Connell, A. N., & Russo, N. F. (1983). *Models of achievement: Reflections of eminent women in psychology.* New York: Columbia University Press

O'Connell, A. N., & Russo, N. F. (1988). *Models of achievement: Reflections of eminent women in psychology* (Vol. 2). New York: Columbia University Press

Rheingold, H. L. (1994). *The psychologist's guide to an academic career.* Washington, DC: American Psychological Association.

Tompkins, J. (1992, November/December). The way we live now. *Change,* pp. 13–19.

Chapter 2

Psychology and Community College Teaching: Helping People in Context

Ann E. Garrett Robinson
Gateway Community-Technical College

My Community College Context

I am a full-time professor of psychology at Gateway Community-Technical College, a state institution in New Haven, Connecticut. I first joined the faculty in 1972, when I left a position with the New Haven Board of Education. Before explaining more about my experiences, I describe the community college context that I have experienced.

Connecticut came late to state-sponsored education. The community college system was established in 1968. When I accepted the offer to come to the new South Central Community College (its original name), I felt like a missionary entering unsettled but promising educational territory. I would be the only instructor in psychology and the assistant chair of the social science department. My immediate mission was to develop a psychology curriculum responsive to local needs.

Social sciences where I am located included 10 full-time faculty at first. We taught on the premises of New Haven's Wilbur Cross High School after the regular school day was over. Faculty headquarters, the library, and a center for remedial work were located across town in a vacated state armory that had just previously been a shelter for horses. (And damp weather always brought this history lesson involuntarily to all who worked there!)

The salient characteristic of community colleges is that they are open to all, in contrast to the selective winnowing imposed by traditional colleges and universities. The defining characteristic of community colleges is that they are accredited to award the associate in arts or sciences as their highest degree, after a 2-year course of study. Community colleges are also sometimes called "2-year colleges," and before World War II, when most operated under private auspices, they were most often called "junior colleges."

Community colleges these days are usually funded by state, county, or city government, and they are mandated to respond to local needs. They may offer vocational training. They may also offer courses such as English as a second language (ESL) and curricula that support adult continuing education.

This much I knew, but the nuts and bolts of community college teaching was terra incognita to me as I started out. A little research made me aware of a vast theoretical literature concerning community colleges. Because I did not intend to reinvent the wheel, I took the bull by the horns and enrolled in the off-campus doctoral program offered by Nova University, in Florida, which specialized in this area of academic interest.

Putting the theory I learned at Nova immediately to the test, I applied for and received a federal grant (from the ACTION special volunteer program) that enabled me to develop community service laboratories at South Central. Some 250 students eventually participated, and we provided service to 20 city and state agencies.

Three years after I arrived, South Central found a permanent home—a reconditioned warehouse in the new Long Wharf industrial park in New Haven. This location was a political compromise between two competing factions, representing the city of New Haven, on the one hand, and greater or metropolitan New Haven (minus New Haven proper), on the other. The Long Wharf location was next to the junction of north–south and east–west interstate highways, thus allowing easy driving access from the surrounding area. The city has access to Long Wharf both by car and via the city bus system.

This nascent polarization between the city and the surrounding region reflected, among other things, changing ethnic proportions, most notably among Whites, African Americans, and, today, Hispanics. Since World War II, African Americans have been moving into the big Connecticut cities, but not as fast as Whites have been moving out. The 1960s saw the fastest increase for the African American population. In the 1990s, Hispanics are the group increasing fastest in the city.

The city-region polarization became overt at the time of the New Haven racial riots of 1967 and the incidents of 1970 associated with the (federal) trial of Black Panther members. To contrast city and suburbs became a polite or coded way to allude to African American versus White. The ostensible debate over where to permanently locate South Central often became acrimonious when participants were in fact covertly expressing allegiances to competing ethnic and economic interests.

Internally as well, the college was undergoing traumatic changes in those early days. Between 1969 and 1979, for instance, South Central had three presidents, three interim presidents, four academic deans, three acting academic deans, two deans of students, and four community service directors.

We moved into our new, state-of-the-art Long Wharf quarters in 1975. Each classroom was carpeted. The green chalkboard could be covered with a ceiling-mounted projection screen. Each classroom contained a television monitor with dial access to our in-house television studio. I began to produce my own psychology videotapes and to assign television production projects to students in lieu of traditional term papers.

The central space in the building was designed as a library/media center. The center housed (in 1992) some 36,000 bound volumes, 330 titles on microfilm, 322 periodical subscriptions, and almost 1,100 tapes, records, and compact disks. There are spaces for individual study and a small community art gallery.

Our remodeled warehouse also contains a cafetorium (a combined auditorium and cafeteria) and undeveloped areas that could one day serve the performing arts. Like most community colleges, we have no dormitory facilities.

In 1992, the community college and technical college systems in Connecticut were merged, in large part to save money. The New Haven area merger produced Gateway Community-Technical College with a campus in New Haven that was the former South Central community college and a campus in North Haven that was the former Greater New Haven technical college.

The new college has 5,207 students, four-fifths of them at the Long Wharf campus in New Haven. Approximately 98% of the students are Connecticut residents (as of 1992); the remaining 2 percent come from three other states and 26 other countries. Some 60% are women. Almost 75% study part time, and 55% are at least 25 years old.

The ethnic composition of the student body is 17% African American, 6% Hispanic, and 2% Asian. By contrast, the city of New Haven (as of 1990) is 36% African American, 13% Hispanic, and 2% Asian; whereas greater New Haven (without the city) is 5% African American, 5% Hispanic, and 1% Asian. I include these figures to give the reader a basis for understanding who is served by the college relative to potential needs in the areas served. Gateway has 259 faculty members, 30% of whom are full time. Our student–faculty ratio is 22:1.

The Connecticut community college system is unionized. Our faculty workload and working conditions are specified in a statewide collective bargaining agreement. The union contract defines our teaching duties and additional responsibilities. The contractual "additional responsibilities" amount to 9 hours a week. Examples of additional responsibilities include participation in community service activities that are consistent with the mission of the college; development of new instructional techniques, course offerings or programs, or major revisions of courses or programs; and advising student organizations and activities.

My Professional Activities

Presently, I teach introductory psychology, social psychology, industrial psychology, and cultural anthropology. At one time or another I have taught almost all the psychology courses listed in our yearly catalogs. On Mondays I teach three courses:

a morning class that begins at 10 a.m., an afternoon class, and an evening class that ends at 10 p.m. On Tuesdays I have a morning class followed by office hours. On Wednesdays I have two classes; on Thursdays, one class.

My additional responsibilities include advising the psychology club and sponsoring the local chapter of Psi Beta, the national honor society in psychology for community colleges. I have also served as national president of Psi Beta for 3 years, during which time we affiliated with the American Psychological Association (APA).

Outside the campus I have established a community presence. I regularly perform excerpts from my four-act musical play *Clowns and Clouds of Destiny: Antietam, Antietam, Antietam.* I am a charter contributor to the "As I See It" column of the daily *New Haven Register.* I am a deaconess in my church. I have analyzed life histories of influential (but relatively unrecognized) religious personages of the African diaspora. I have researched the lives of women at work—particularly women under slavery in the West Indies and women in hairdressing occupations in this country. I have brought to public attention the contributions of the three wives of Booker T. Washington. Finally, I have also done fieldwork projects with children in Nairobi, Kenya at Kenya Christian Homes, which serves children in difficult circumstances.

Always, my students come first in my career. I try to be there for all of them. I have organized breakfast meetings for students who needed extra help and participated in recreational programs with students. At Thanksgiving I open my home to international students who have no place to enjoy the holiday, sometimes cooking and serving as many as 75 meals. I have formed ESL seminars and have been given special awards for helping, by Hispanic and Swedish students. I emphasize culture-conscious teaching that takes into account the backgrounds of all of our students, as I reported in the September 1989 issue of the *National Journal of Community-Technical Colleges.*

"Ann, you love working here," a colleague of mine observed some 10 years ago, at one of those moments when I was regretting there were too few hours in the day. I hesitated before responding, "Yes, I do. This is my advice, which is a kind of Booker T. Washingtonian advice. People should try and find a career that gives dignity to labor and that can become a labor of love."

The capstone of my professional career took place in 1992 when, at the APA convention in Washington, DC, I received the Division on the Teaching of Psychology award, 2-year college category, for "teacher of the year in psychology."

My Career Journey

My career was launched in January 1957, when I received my master's degree in clinical psychology from Wayne State University in Detroit, Michigan. Before I finally came to Gateway Community-Technical College in New Haven, my work took me to juvenile correctional institutions in North Carolina, to psychiatric hospitals in Maine and Indiana, and to a public school system and a private 4-year college in Connecticut.

I clearly recall the moment my career decision crystallized. I was completing my senior year (1949–1950) at C. M. Eppes High School in Greenville, North Carolina. A notice about opportunities in psychology appeared on the high school bulletin board and as I studied the notice—it was from the Veterans Administration—I suddenly knew with a certainty what I was going to be. "Yes, this is it," I said to myself. "I am going to become a psychologist."

I had been thinking about the humanities, or some of the performing arts, or law, or maybe medicine. My teachers took my aspirations seriously. I was spoken of as "a library child" because of the time I spent at the George Washington Carver library with my aunt, who was the city's Colored librarian.

I think it was the idea of service that focused my vocational interest. During World War II, which had ended just 4 years earlier, we youngsters had been impressed with the importance given to patriotism by parents, our school teachers, and the tight-knit agricultural community in which we lived. Patriotism meant service to country. Like many of my classmates, I had uncles who were honored and respected for having been "in the service," as participation in the military was called. Now, the bulletin board notice informed me, there was a need to serve those who had served.

So I majored in psychology at North Carolina Central University in Durham, although I was also careful to minor in biology just in case I might want to apply to medical school later. Through the influence of interesting classes, encouraging teachers, and a group of psychology majors who helped each other, I grew firm in the notion that I was indeed on the right track.

Our little group of psychology majors shared books, knowledge, notes, and an enthusiasm for our chosen academic discipline. We considered ourselves special by virtue of our declared major, and we were, in fact, held in deference by our classmates for the same reason. We did not hesitate to pontificate about hypnotism, neurosis, and any other esoteric matter our friends thought a psychology student should know about.

The four of us—all women—were guided by two dedicated and caring professors, George Kyle and Carol Bowie. Both were retirees who joined the full-time university faculty after having practiced clinical psychology in psychiatric hospitals. Professor Kyle was a gentle, easy-going man. "I enjoyed working in psychiatric hospitals but discovered that I would be more satisfied teaching," he would often say. He cautioned us to avoid what would later be called burn-out, by reminding us of the diverse career possibilities open to us in psychology. In future years, he believed, we African Americans would be able to work in many more settings without the severe barriers engendered by race.

Dr. Kyle's privately spoken concerns about the restricted occupational opportunities then open to African Americans were shared by others. At that time, it would have been job-threatening, not to say life-threatening, to speak of such matters in public. This was still the era of segregated schooling in the South, and the academy was a microcosm of the wider society. Later, in the wake of the U.S. Supreme Court's Brown versus Board of Education decision and the broad civil rights movement, a new and freer spirit of expression allowed academicians and psychologists to address important career and occupational issues, both on their own campuses and with colleagues in their professional associations. In summary, George Kyle's hopeful vision was true. I have certainly found that career possibilities in psychology are diverse and rich with opportunities.

Carol Bowie, our other professor, was an unusual person in many ways. In the 1950s it was rare enough to meet an African-American woman who had practiced clinical psychology. It was even more unusual to meet an African-American woman who was a licensed airplane pilot. Not once, however, did she mention gender in the context of her career as a psychologist. Instead, she repeatedly spoke about her love of flying and the problems that had posed. "I always wanted to control a large mechanical object," she said with her slight lisp. "I got my license, but it was difficult." Determination and persistence will see you through, was the message we got. As I look back, I think this tall, slender woman was also using her experiences in becoming a pilot to prepare us for the gender challenges we would face in our future careers in psychology.

By the time I graduated in 1954 there was no more thought of just possibly becoming a physician. Racial barriers, nonetheless, reduced to nil my prospects for graduate study in psychology in North Carolina. I would study out of state. My parents were encouraging and used their resources to supplement the compensation offered by the state of North Carolina to residents who were prevented by reason of race from graduate study within the state.

During my first semester "up North," at Wayne State University in Detroit, I underwent culture shock. Wayne was interracial. Whites and African Americans sat together in the classroom and often sat side by side. Wayne was mainly a commuter college, although a limited number of students—both men and women, myself included—were housed on campus on the upper floors of a multipurpose building that also included office quarters and a cafeteria.

Although graduate schools of that era did not routinely use admissions tests to select students, a faculty had its ways to assess a student's readiness. I was asked to "volunteer" to take an intelligence test (the Wechsler Scales) by an advanced graduate student whose quality of performance was much respected by the faculty. Shortly after the test, I was invited, much to my delight, to work as a graduate assistant in the clinical psychology department, a position I held until I completed my course work at Wayne.

I then devoted myself full time to a study of the effects of congenital and adventitious deafness on the adjustment of deaf children, research supervised by my major professor, Harold Powell. After passing the comprehensive examination, I was awarded a master's degree in clinical psychology in January 1957. I was now a psychologist. What would I do?

Nostalgia, I think, and a sense of obligation brought me back to North Carolina and a position in the correctional institutions for male and female juvenile offenders. My job turned out to be administering Stanford-Binets from sunup to sundown. I routinely scored the tests and wrote brief reports for the purpose of screening those students who needed placement in special education classes. I recall only long, monotonous, and boring days. This was not the work of which I had dreamed.

Within a few months, I accepted a position as a clinical psychology intern in Augusta, Maine, and once more headed north. Augusta was a tidy city with immaculately swept streets. Augusta State Hospital sparkled with perfectly polished oak floors. I loved the beauty of the setting and the remarkably blue skies when the whole world outside was blanketed in sparkling white snow.

I joined two other interns in a department with three senior psychologists. Each intern was assigned to two clinical supervisors, one senior psychologist supervising psychodiagnostic testing and the other supervising individual psychotherapy. Under the strictest supervision we administered, scored, and made interpretations of test protocols that always included the Rorschach.

My first client in psychotherapy was of French-Canadian descent, a short, red-haired man in his 30s, who believed himself to be Jesus the Christ. Our sessions were cordial so long as there was no hint of uncovering his belief system or addressing his emotional concerns. The sessions were taped and presented at the Friday afternoon supervisory seminars. "Why did you say that, Ann?" or "Why not try this approach?" We clinical interns were subjected to close scrutiny and developed appropriate Rogerian, Adlerian, or Freudian techniques. "Cures" were not expected for these long-term residents of the hospital. When I departed the hospital, my first client remained. I have often wondered what became of him.

At the end of the year, I accepted the first clinical job I was offered. I could have easily found a teaching position in a historically African-American college, but I was determined to work as a clinician. I found my new job through an employment opportunities bulletin that listed job openings in psychology throughout the nation. Among the positions I applied for was one as a clinical psychologist of LaRue Carter Hospital in Indianapolis. The chief psychologist there responded to my inquiries and set up an interview with me in Brooklyn, New York, which was his hometown. I was delighted later to receive an appointment letter.

I was placed, at first, on a probationary work status, pending the results of my performance on a state civil service test for psychologists. Having passed the test—which could only be taken once—I thought I was finally on my way to the kind of career in psychology of which I had dreamed.

New doors of opportunity opened once again. I transferred to Central State Hospital in Indianapolis, where I gained additional opportunities to practice. There, I administered complete assessment protocols, saw clients in individual psychotherapy, and made ward rounds with a psychiatrist at the Farm Colony. The patients at the Farm Colony had been diagnosed as chronically ill, and many had been hospitalized for more than 20 years. The doors at the Farm Colony were not locked, and the patients were free to move throughout the farm compound during the daytime. The Farm Colony was their home, a peaceful place where many were kept busy as agricultural workers during the summer and left sedentary during the cold winter months.

I studied psychodrama at workshops led by Adelaide Starr, who had been trained by J. L. Moreno, the founder of psychodrama. I used my acting skills through this medium and found that Farm Colony patients were willing participants in our theatrical forum, particularly during the winter months. A community volunteer with acting talents served as my co-leader. The small psychodrama theater we created received positive feedback from the patient-participants.

On weekdays when I was not at the Farm Colony, I worked on the "main grounds" of the state hospital. There I functioned in more traditional ways: conducting individual psychotherapy, administering psychological tests, and attending team meetings where newly admitted patients were diagnosed. On the days I was on the main grounds I joined my colleagues each morning in the chief's office. There we sat around the chief's desk and discussed our different clinical activities, affirmed weekly assignments, and bonded as a group struggling to compete with medical personnel for rank and status in this psychiatric institution. It was in these circumstances that I learned about the connection of APA activities to the quality of our work lives.

A most important event in my life happened at Central Hospital. While working there, I met and married Charles E. Robinson, a psychiatric social worker. I continued to work at Central Hospital for 3 more years before taking maternity leave. When I returned, I served briefly as a psychological consultant and matriculated for graduate courses at Indiana University, where I had been accepted into their doctoral program.

Then my husband was offered and accepted a promising position in psychiatric social work on the clinical faculty of Yale University School of Medicine and we all moved to New Haven, Connecticut. Our second and last child was born there the next year. We have remained in New Haven where I have worked as both a psychologist and college instructor.

My New Haven Experiences Leading to Community College Teaching

I have frequently been asked by my students how I came to teach in a community college rather than returning to clinical work. In response, I tell them about my first 3 years in Connecticut, working for the New Haven Board of Education and how I became interested in the interrelated connections between schools and community.

At first, as a psychological examiner, I routinely administered intelligence tests to children being considered for placement in special education classes. After one semester, however, I joined a crisis team of social workers and educators who attempted to resolve school–student–community conflicts in a middle school. It was my job was to observe children identified as manifesting behavioral problems. In the course of this work, I soon came to see I needed to study the whole culture of the school to make sense of the behaviors of individual children. Of course I continued to carry out my literal job assignment of observing children having school problems. But, at every appropriate opportunity and without upsetting school styles of operating, I discreetly tried to learn "what is going on in this place" from different groups and different individuals, listening to many sides.

In this way I learned about the significance of the classroom in the age-based tasks that the children were expected to complete. At the end of the year, I prepared a report on the children and their developmental progression and their expressed needs. I made this available first to the school principal and his administrative staff and next to the board of education. It was my considered view that effective intervention with troubled and troubling children required working knowledge not just of the children but of their classrooms and teachers, their homes and families, and the distinctive community setting.

Following my report, I was assigned, as school psychologist, to a study team sponsored jointly by the New Haven Board of Education and the Yale Child Study Center. The team originally included an anthropologist, an educator, a child development specialist, a school social worker, and a school psychologist (myself). The team was headed by James Comer, a social psychiatrist, who was known to place importance on the emotional climate in the classroom and who advocated parental involvement in the daily life of the school. In our working meetings we explored the effectiveness of various intervention strategies in urban schools and tried to formulate the right questions to be asked about racial considerations in the development of school programs. Who, for instance, should be acknowledged as speaking for the populations the school serves? When is it useful to speak of a "culture of poverty," and what kind of reality does it imply?

My third and final job assignment within the New Haven Board of Education was as coordinator of research with focus on Grades K through 3. I supervised the administration, scoring, and interpretations of achievement testing in 17 inner-city schools. I traveled regularly to each of the schools, visited classrooms, talked with teachers, and listened to accounts of their daily struggle to do effective work while subjected to many conflicting forces such as government officials, school administration, parents, and their students. Discipline was a frequent theme, and so was the question of when and whether children should be trained for work instead of being given a well-rounded curriculum. Always more questions than answers.

I left the public school system to take a position as assistant professor of community psychology at Trinity College in Hartford, Connecticut, about an hour's driving time from where we lived in New Haven. After 2 years I was again ready to break new ground and came to the community college setting where I have now worked more than 20 years. Here I was close to my home and my children. Here I was better able to assist my husband in our newly established consulting business. Also, here I was closer to working with students as a part of their community context.

Looking Ahead

Only recently have I begun to appreciate that my stint as a community college teacher will have an end just as it had a beginning. Twenty plus years in the trenches is surely honorable service. Time to hand on the torch? It isn't that many years before I will be eligible for a state pension.

Only recently have I begun to appreciate that there are new issues of urban unrest I may not be prepared to cope with. We came to New Haven in time to witness the riots of 1967 and the spectacle of the National Guard on the village green during the Black Panther trial a few years later. This highlighted incidents against a background of routine city living. We have stayed here long enough to see the exception become the rule. Youth gangs and drug dealers rule whole streets and even neighborhoods. Random drive-by shootings are a fact of life. Members of my family must carefully plan how we will get on and off public transportation. I have myself recently been the object of urban violence.

The public schools were open to all when we came here a quarter century ago; today there is something close to de facto segregation in the primary and secondary schools. African Americans—some 36% of the city population—now make up 85% of city school students. Affluent White students are sent to private schools. New Haven has come to rank among the dozen poorest cities in the nation, whereas the state of Connecticut as a whole continues to boast one of the highest per capita incomes in the nation. New Haven has the most AIDS cases in the state and the highest infant morality rate in the nation.

The words of George Kyle, my professor at North Carolina Central, come back. He warned against burn-out. And he implied a solution when he noted that a psychologist can do many things. Soon I intend to complete the master's degree in anthropology and education I started at Columbia University's Teachers College. I have twice been a research fellow at Yale and would be open to a similar appointment either here or abroad to complete my work on student volunteer programs. And before I turn in my blackboard, I want to teach in the areas of cross-cultural psychology and women's studies.

My words of advice to those contemplating a career in psychology today? You know who you are. Be persistent in pursuing your goals. Psychology offers a rich selection of career choices including the noble opportunity to serve others in many different settings.

Chapter 3

You Take the High Road, I'll Take the Low Road: A Satisfying Career at a Small State University

Stephen F. Davis
Emporia State University

As this chapter is being written, I am 8 months deep into the process of adjusting to being a full-time teaching faculty once again. For the past 13 years my responsibilities, in addition to teaching and working with students on research projects, included serving as chair of the 17-member department at Emporia State University (ESU).

Located midway between Wichita, Kansas, and Kansas City, ESU is a regional state university having an enrollment of approximately 6,000. Besides the traditional undergraduate psychology major, ESU also offers the master of science (MS) degree with specializations in clinical, industrial, experimental, and school psychology. An MS in art therapy also is offered. This diversity of offerings reflects the functional roots of our department. Many of the early faculty were trained by G. Stanley Hall at Clark University or at the University of Chicago. The eclecticism and tolerance that characterized functionalism in the early 1900s persists into the 1990s psychology program at ESU. However, I am getting ahead of my story; I return to ESU presently.

Undergraduate Training: Southern Methodist University

My boyhood days were spent in Lexington, Kentucky. For some reason, I dreamed of attending college at Southern Methodist University (SMU) in Dallas, Texas. Imagine my delight when my father accepted a position in Dallas! Following graduation from high school, I rather naively applied to only one college, SMU. Luck was with me; I was admitted. Luck is an appropriate descriptor when talking about my admission to SMU. I was not an especially diligent student during my high school career. My senior annual suggests that I was destined to make my mark in the world of drag racing and auto mechanics. My fascination with building and racing cars persisted into my freshman and sophomore years in college. These activities, plus the "responsibilities" associated with being a fraternity member, were not especially congruent with academics. In a word, I nearly flunked out of SMU! My first semester grade point average of 2.25 slipped to 1.25 the next semester. Then it fell to 1.00. The dean was poised to expel me. Then I made a 2.00 and was allowed to stay in school.

The summer following my sophomore year at SMU was a turning point for my career in psychology. I traveled to Wisconsin to visit relatives, took a job, and stayed the entire summer. My summer job was on the dish crew at a summer conference center. All of the employees were college students; many of them were psychology majors. Even though I was a psychology major and had taken several psychology courses, my co-workers that summer spoke something akin to a foreign language when they talked about psychology! My errant study habits, missed classes, and frequent "dozing" finally caught up with me. I came face to face with the realization that my future in this field was in serious jeopardy. I returned to SMU with a new sense of purpose and academic direction. The result, to the amazement of my teachers and the dean, was the first in a series of straight A semesters.

It would be a nice and tidy ending to the story if I could indicate that I graduated at the end of my senior year and then went on for graduate training. However, life simply is not like that; when one records several D and F grades, there are penalties to be paid. It took me an extra semester to complete my BA degree.

I would be remiss not to mention the support, guidance, and encouragement of three SMU psychology faculty during my final five semesters as an undergraduate. Virginia Chancey, Al North, and Jack Strange provided encouragement, gave support, and opened more than one door of opportunity as I struggled to regain academic credibility.

Graduate School I: The Master's Degree

Completion of my BA degree brought a new challenge: graduate school. My recent academic successes at SMU prompted me to remain there for the MA degree, a wise decision, indeed. Under the patient guidance of Al North, my last two semesters as an undergraduate had been filled with an addictive activity—research. The MA program offered an opportunity to continue activities that I found to be highly rewarding.

During my MA program I was awarded an assistantship and worked for both Drs. Strange and North. Strange, whose forte was abnormal psychology (he used to joke about his last name and his chosen area), was writing a text on that subject. I was given the task of preparing the instructor's manual to accompany this text. I was deemed worthy of authorship on this project and my first publication saw the light of day.

Under Al North's patient tutelage the intricacies of Hullian theory and Amsel's frustration theory became understandable. Numerous rat studies were conducted to ascertain the effects of reward magnitude and shifts in reward magnitude. The experimental psychology bug had bitten me; I was a confirmed rat runner. Our research went quite well and additional publications began to make their appearance. Dr. North also gave me my first opportunity to attend a professional convention. The 1965 Psychonomic Society meeting in St. Louis was an experience I will never forget!

Graduate School II: The PhD Degree

Beginning my MA program at midyear resulted in its completion at midyear. Thus, another hurdle presented itself: finding a doctoral program that would accept a new student at the start of the second semester. Once again, I naively assumed that an opening and financial support would be there. Texas Christian University (TCU) admitted me and even offered me an assistantship.

My wife Kathleen and I made the trek from Dallas to Fort Worth in January 1967. At TCU my fledgling research skills were honed by Dr. H. Wayne Ludvigson, a student of the famed learning theorist, Kenneth Spence.

A few days following the end of my first semester at TCU, I happened to be riding the elevator with Department Chair, Dr. Malcolm Arnoult. Dr. Arnoult asked how my first semester had gone; I responded "outstanding!" Following a few more pleasantries, Dr. Arnoult dropped what was akin to an atomic bomb on me. My duties for the summer would be to teach a class. When did summer school start? In 2 days! What class would I be teaching? Statistics!! I had served as a teaching assistant at SMU and had enjoyed this responsibility quite a bit. However, teaching statistics was an entirely different story.

With my copy of *Basic Statistical Methods* by Downey and Heath in hand, a friendly pat on the back, and an encouraging "go get 'em," the 1967 summer statistics class was in my hands. My lecture notes were carefully prepared and written in large letters on every other line of sheets from a legal pad so that I would not overlook anything. I stayed exactly 1 day ahead of the class and prayed that no eager students would read ahead. Teaching the statistics class proved to be a major event in the evolution of my career. Despite my apprehensions, the students actually seemed to learn something about statistics and I fell passionately in love with teaching. My remaining 2 years at TCU were filled with additional research, classes to take, and, thankfully, more classes to teach.

The King College Years

In the spring of 1969 I began to entertain visions of leaving TCU to establish my own career. Since the academic turn around that occurred during my undergraduate days at SMU, I had unquestioningly assumed that my future revolved around being a psychologist at a college or university; the diversity of career choices open to psychologists today simply did not exist in the late 1960s. Such considerations as size of institution, research or teaching orientation, private liberal arts college or state university never entered my mind. I started looking through the APA Employment Bulletin. Two jobs of potential interest appeared: one in Tennessee, one in Texas. Following interviews, and subsequent offers from both institutions, I accepted the position at King College, a small, Presbyterian college located in Bristol, Tennessee, on the Tennessee–Virginia border. ("Small" really is an understatement. There were 302 students enrolled at King College when I began my duties in the fall of 1969. However, we graduated a Rhodes Scholar that year!) For the next 3 years, I was part of a two-person psychology department and truly learned the meaning of the term *generalist*.

In addition to perpetuating and enhancing my love of teaching, the King College years spawned other activities that would become integral components of my professional life. These activities included research collaboration with students and taking students to conventions to learn about psychology and to present their own papers.

Establishing a research laboratory at King College provided unique challenges. When I interviewed for the position, an old dormitory that was being remodeled was to house the psychology offices and classrooms. I was told that I would have laboratory space in the basement. Unfortunately, my understanding of the term *renovation* did not coincide with that of those in charge of the construction. Hence, my first "lab" consisted of a coal bin that had been cleaned, painted, and (thankfully) supplied with electricity.

After several weeks of intensive work, the lab was deemed ready and a small animal colony was begun. Having never been exposed to research, the students were eager to collect data and thrilled to be part of a convention presentation. Their amazement and pride to see their names on the journal articles published during this period provided meaningful reinforcement for this neophyte academic.

The Austin Peay Years

The lure of a larger institution and the prospect of being able to teach graduate students resulted in my acceptance of a position at Austin Peay State University (APSU) in Clarksville, Tennessee, in the fall of 1972. The 7 years at APSU did much to mold my approach to academia and the training of students.

Even though we were relegated to a storage closet and the back of a classroom, it took less time to establish a laboratory at APSU than it had at King College. In fact, several animal studies were completed during my first quarter on campus. At that time my students and I were diligently investigating olfactory communication in animal maze learning, and I could see myself pursuing this topic for many years to come. However, change was in the wind.

The impetus for this change originated with the graduate students. I soon found that all graduate students did not want to do rat studies for their master's thesis, and those who did could not be counted on to share my burning interest in olfactory communication in animal maze learning. Hence, students started proposing some of the "strangest" (at least to an old-time rat runner) research I had ever heard of.

Thankfully, I had the presence of mind to give these unorthodox research ideas a fair hearing. We began to follow through on some of them. Thesis topics such as "personality characteristics of civilian and military policemen," "an analysis of the size of human figure drawings and level of self-esteem in school-age children," and "death anxiety in military couples" began to reach fruition. At first I was more than just a little skeptical of these new avenues of scientific endeavor; after all, I had been trained in a rather strict Hull–Spence tradition. However, as more of these atypical projects were proposed and completed, I found that they had considerable interest and appeal.

So, more than 20 years ago, I found my research focus beginning to shift. To the dismay of Dr. Ludvigson, my dissertation director, all of those hours that were invested in teaching me the importance of programmatic research seemed wasted. In some ways he probably was right. I had come to the realization that my laboratory and research interests did not exist for any specific type of research; they existed for the training of quality students. I would like to think that this realization came more as a "program shift," rather than the abandonment of programmatic research.

The shift in focus of my research activities had additional ramifications. Now that many of the problems were being proposed by the students themselves, more students started coming around to suggest potential research ideas. Thus, more projects were undertaken. In turn, the increased number of projects resulted in more papers to present. Hence, we started attending the annual spring conventions of the Southern Society for Philosophy and Psychology and the Southwestern Psychological Association. The newly formed Middle Tennessee Psychological Association provided an excellent forum for fall presentations.

Another dimension to the training of research skills in my students also began to emerge during this time. Because research efforts were conducted on a year-round basis, new students could join the "lab group" (as it came to be called) at different times during the year. Hence, varying degrees of skill and expertise were present. Having read Bill McKeachie's fine text, *Teaching Tips* (McKeachie, 1986), I was aware of the potential benefits of peer teaching. The lab group offered an excellent setting to put this technique to work. The more experienced student researchers would act as mentors to the neophytes. For example, the first assignment for a student working on a project using human subjects may consist of coding responses or entering data into a computer data bank. Similarly, a neophyte working in the animal laboratory will begin his or her research by learning the techniques of good animal care. As projects are completed, new ones that involve increased involvement, input, and responsibility are undertaken. I have found that my student researchers frequently are capable of making significant contributions to the design of an experiment by the time they are working on their second or third project. By the time the second or third project is completed, I have a good idea whether the student has the potential to assume additional responsibilities. I prefer to call this variant of the familiar teacher–scholar model the "junior colleague" model. From my perspective, it has been quite successful over the years.

In my "spare" time I began serving as a reviewer for several book publishers. Although publishers do not offer a lofty honorarium for such work, the experience is excellent and, as I explain later, such activities may lead to other opportunities. However, if you do agree to serve as an editorial consultant, you are encouraged to make your reviews compulsively thorough and incisive; reviews should be returned promptly.

Although the APSU years were enjoyable and influential in molding my approach to research and the training of students, they were not without a problem or two. The major issue I confronted was advancement; the longer I remained at APSU, the clearer it became that opportunities for advancement were rather limited. Much of my frustration centered around the the merit system that was in place at the time. Under this system everyone was assured of a certain percentage increase in their salary each year. To obtain a merit increase, an application and supporting documents had to be prepared and submitted. The problem was that there were a fixed number of merit steps for each rank. Unfortunately (from my perspective) merit steps could overlap between ranks. Hence, by the time my promotion to associate professor was approved, I was already at the first merit step in the full professor rank. That situation left me with only three additional merit steps to be achieved during my entire career at APSU. Although money has never been the impetus for any of my career decisions, it was depressing to think that I could be meritorious only three more times during my entire professional career.

Such considerations prompted thoughts of securing another position offering greater growth potential. In discussing this situation with a colleague, the possibility of seeking an appointment as a department chair was suggested. Having never been enamored with administrative responsibilities, this option was not high on my list of possibilities. However, in the fall of 1978 two chair openings presented themselves and I applied. One opening was at a major state university that offered PhD programs in clinical and experimental psychology. The second opening was at a regional state university located "somewhere in Kansas" that only offered bachelor's and master's degrees.

The Emporia Years

Following the interview process, contracts were offered by both schools. The collegiality of the psychology faculty and friendliness of the town swung the decision toward the smaller, less prestigious Kansas school—in retrospect, another wise decision. The fall of 1979 found me beginning my first year as chair at Emporia State University.

Many of my colleagues tried to convince me that by becoming a department chair my research activities and student involvement would drop to a near-zero level. Thankfully, these pronouncements were not trapped in the empty recesses of my mind! In fact, as I started my new position I made a concerted effort to perform all aspects of my job (chair duties, teaching, research, and student involvement) to the very best of my abilities.

When we arrived in Emporia the atmosphere and environment at ESU were perfect for program growth and the development of student research and involvement and related activities. Coincident with my arrival on campus, the psychology department was moving into a new, multimillion dollar building. Unlike their previous quarters, the new building had a full complement of animal and human laboratories, observation rooms with one-way mirrors, and computer facilities. An air of excitement was shown by faculty and students alike. Hence, my role as chair was to help channel these energies into productive avenues. As my leadership style is one of leading by example, this role suited me perfectly.

For the third time in my career I was faced with the task of completely developing a new laboratory. The third time must be a charm; everything fell into place quite smoothly. There was even a small amount of money to help purchase equipment! By the end of the first semester the lab was sufficiently functional to allow us to gather data for presentation at the SWPA convention to be held in Oklahoma City the following spring (1980). Once again, student involvement was underway; as is seen here, its boundaries have yet to be determined.

In addition to stimulating research, the new psychology quarters also prompted the inception of an invited speakers series. (Lack of pride in facilities that were housed in a building that was condemned 30 years before it was vacated had precluded visitors being invited to the ESU campus in earlier years.) The speakers series proved to be successful. Such notables as Frank Beach (the noted comparative psychologist and an ESU alumnus), social psychologist Lawrence Wrightsman, former SWPA President Roger Mellgren, APA President Frank Farley, Charles L. Brewer (Editor, *Teaching of Psychology*), and two American Psychological Foundation National Teaching Award winners, Wilbert J. McKeachie and Ludy T. Benjamin, Jr., have made the trip to Emporia to speak to interested groups of students and faculty. The fact that students and faculty from neighboring institutions also were invited to attend these presentations proved fortuitous.

A faculty member from Sterling College (Sterling, Kansas) brought several students to the first invited lecture. Following the presentation, ESU students conducted a tour of the new facilities for the Sterling College students. As my Sterling College colleague and I watched the interaction between the two student groups, the same idea occurred to us simultaneously: Why not establish a yearly conference where students could have the experiences of presenting papers in an nonthreatening atmosphere and interacting with their peers from other schools in the area?

The first such convention was held at ESU in the spring of 1981. For the first few years this annual event was held on our campus. More recently, it has begun to rotate among several schools in Kansas, Missouri, and Nebraska. Currently, the Great Plains Students' Psychology Convention attracts more than 200 student papers and 300 attendees annually. My association with the founding and yearly staging of this highly successful event has been one of the high points of my career. The convention also has provided a viable outlet for many of my students to make their first professional presentation.

As if helping to establish one organization was not sufficient, the fall of 1980 found myself and a Wichita State University (WSU) colleague (in fact, a former master's student from APSU) discussing the need for a broad-based, statewide association whose annual meeting would feature research papers presented by faculty and advanced students. The Association for Psychological and Educational Research in Kansas (PERK) was born in the summer of 1981 and its first convention was held at WSU that fall. This annual fall event also has provided excellent professional experiences for many of my aspirant students.

Oddly enough, decorating our new departmental office in the fall of 1979 also facilitated student involvement. As we were unpacking various pictures and documents from the old quarters, the ESU Psi Chi charter emerged. As the chapter had been dormant for a number of years, its existence had been forgotten; the need for reactivation was evident. A reactivated Psi Chi chapter would provide a needed organization, as well as encouragement, for academically outstanding psychology students. What about those students who were not among the academically elite; shouldn't they also have an organization? A resounding "yes" to the latter question prompted the re-establishment of the ESU Psychology Club. (The original Psychology Club was founded in 1904 by Norman Triplett. However, it also had been dormant for many years.)

Psi Chi and the Psychology Club quickly became very popular. Because I served as faculty advisor for both groups, knowledge of the role and function of such organizations on our campus was acquired. It became apparent that both groups were entitled to request budgets from the Associated Student Government (ASG). Here was a source of funds that could be used to help support student travel to professional conventions. These funds, supplemented by various fundraisers, enabled even larger groups of students to attend psychological conventions. In fact, it has become common place to see a group of 30 or more ESU psychology students, many presenting papers, at the PERK, Great Plains, SWPA, and Southern Society conventions.

My involvement with the ESU Psi Chi chapter and the Great Plains convention had other, unanticipated effects on my career. Through the Great Plains convention I made the acquaintance of Joe Palladino, founder of the Mid-America Undergraduate Student Research Conference. Joe's involvement with student conferences prompted him to develop a symposium on this topic for the 1984 APA meeting in Toronto. The decision to attend that APA meeting and participate in the symposium were major events in my professional life.

In addition to participating in an enjoyable symposium, I was introduced to several of Joe's friends who were enthusiastic members of APA Division Two (Teaching of Psychology). I soon found that several of my colleagues also were members. Here was a group of professionals who were actively pursuing their interests in my most cherished professional activity—teaching! By the end of the convention I knew that involvement with APA Division Two was destined to become a major part of my professional activities.

The 1984 APA convention also resulted in greater involvement with Psi Chi, especially on the national level. Two of my students, one the 1983 Psi Chi/J. P. Guilford National Undergraduate Research Award winner, accompanied me to Toronto. Consequently, we attended several Psi Chi functions and were introduced to such notables as Ruth Cousins, the executive director of Psi Chi, and B. F. Skinner, who conducted a special session for Psi Chi students. These were exciting times! My students and I returned to Emporia with a mission: to make our Psi Chi chapter one of the best in the nation. I returned with a second mission: to begin taking students to the APA Convention on a regular basis. Both goals have been met.

Whether one uses a quantitative or qualitative barometer, the Emporia Years have been especially good in terms of student growth and development. Between the fall of 1979 and the spring of 1993, 123 journal articles having student co-authors were published. During this same time period, 236 student papers were presented at professional society meetings. Moreover, students have presented 122 papers at various student conventions. That 55 of these papers received awards at the Great Plains Students Convention, the Association for Psychological and Educational Research in Kansas, and the Southwestern Psychological Association attests to their quality. Such student accomplishments have provided a major source of reinforcement for my professional activities.

Facilitating the growth of the ESU psychology program and its faculty also have provided a significant source of reinforcement. When asked to characterize my leadership style, I always answer that "I lead by example." From my perspective, this approach resulted in a harmonious and unified department that had a common goal: to be the best psychology department possible. As the ESU MS program was ranked among the top programs of its kind in the United States (Gordon, 1990), I feel that we have been successful in achieving this objective. Moreover, this atmosphere of cooperative productivity produced several individual success stories. One success concerns a faculty member who was being denied promotion to full professor because he had never conducted research and published. Initially he firmly resisted the new orientation of the department. Finally, he came to my office and wanted to know how he could "get involved with that research stuff," because he wanted to be promoted. I was thrilled; this request represented a major step forward! We decided on a research program that coincided with his teaching interests and a project was started. I was consulted at every step and even assisted in the preparation of the research report. A task that initially was distasteful and arduous gradually became fun. The "big reinforcer" was delivered—his first publication was accepted. The rest is history. Numerous publications and convention presentations followed. Even though promotion to full professor was achieved in 1985, the zest for research has not subsided and this faculty member continues to be one of the most productive scholars in the entire university.

Unexpected Recognition

Up to this point (the early 1980s), I was perfectly content with a career that revolved around conducting research, mentoring of students, and trying to be a good department chair. However, as the 1980s progressed, my career began to undergo some unexpected changes.

First my students and colleagues began to place my name in nomination for rather lofty offices in various professional associations. Much to my surprise, I was elected to several of these positions. Initially, there was the Presidency of the Association for Psychological and Educational Research in Kansas. Then, I was elected Secretary of the Southern Society for Philosophy and Psychology (SSPP). Having been a Southern Society member for many years and having prepared numerous students to give their first papers at SSPP meetings made this election very meaningful. My involvement with APA Division Two led to my election as Chair of the Membership Committee. Then, within a 3-year period (1987–1989) I was elected President of SSPP, SWPA, and APA Division Two. For a teacher from a relatively unknown institution "somewhere in the middle of Kansas" such lofty positions seem beyond one's imagination; that I have actually occupied them still boggles my mind.

The receipt of several awards marked a second development in my career that occurred during the 1980s. First, the ESU Psi Chi students voted me Psychology Teacher of the Year in 1982. Then in 1984 my ESU colleagues nominated me for the annual Roe R. Cross Distinguished Professor award. As this award is the highest honor an Emporia State faculty member can receive, and because I had been at ESU for only 5 years, I felt that my chances of receiving it were very slim. To me, the real award was being nominated. My colleagues felt otherwise; they were correct.

In 1987, the Psi Chi/Florence L. Denmark National Faculty Advisor Award was established. The ESU Psi Chi Chapter placed my name in nomination to be the first recipient of this annual award. I was certain that there were many others who were more deserving of this recognition; the students disagreed. They were correct.

From 1983 to 1985 I represented APA Division Two on the selection committee for the prestigious American Psychological Foundation (APF) Distinguished Teaching in Psychology Award. The annual trek to Washington, DC, to decide the recipient of this award was inspirational, to say the least. I was able to see and discuss the credentials of the best teachers in our discipline. During my service on this committee, such notables as Ben James Winer, David Cole, Wilbert McKeachie, and Frank Beach were selected to receive the APF award. Then in 1988, my colleague and graduate school friend, Ludy Benjamin, proposed that I be nominated. I agreed, knowing full well that this competition was beyond my capabilities; Benjamin disagreed. He was correct. Sitting on the stage at the 1988 APA Convention in Atlanta, Georgia with such notables as Nobel Laureate Herbert Simon to receive this award represents one of the peak experiences of my career.

The following year (1989) I was nominated for, and won, the APA Division Two Award for Teaching Excellence. This award always will be very special because it was given by my peers in Division Two. Many of these awards call attention to my involvement with students. To me it seems unusual to receive an award or be elected to an office in recognition of doing what should be a routine part of one's job. I prefer to attribute such recognition to working hard and having been in the right spot at the right time.

Lessons Learned From My Experiences

I have been content to allow my career to wander as it sees fit, rather than plotting specific timelines and courses. Nonetheless, this question is somewhat difficult to answer. There do seem to be several consistent threads that tie the pieces together.

First, whether one considers conducting research, taking students to conventions, presenting papers, publishing articles, serving as a journal/book reviewer, installing Psi Chi chapters, or writing textbooks, high levels of activity have characterized all aspects of my career. For example, the spring 1993 "lab group" consists of 36 students who are working on 11 different projects. Additionally, my students and I are scheduled to present 19 papers at various conventions this spring. The ability to maintain high levels of activity and productivity in these areas at an institution such as ESU involves a reward system that is different from those typically found at larger, research oriented schools. For me, a considerable portion of my professional reinforcement comes from interaction with my students. In his description of former APF Teaching Award recipients, David Pittenger (1992) eloquently and correctly summarized my situation as follows:

> It should be noted that Davis teaches at a state school that does not have a competitive admission policy, a prestigious history, a national reputation, or a comfortable endowment, and that does not view itself as a research institution. Hence, Davis's level of activity appears to have been maintained by the reinforcing value of his continued interaction with his students. (p. 165)

Second, if you aspire to such levels of activity, it will help if you are very compulsive and slightly anal-retentive. When carried to extremes, such traits can be detrimental to activity and productivity. However, I have found these attributes to be beneficial in helping me deal with such recurrent tasks as organizing student trips to conventions, planning where to present various research papers over the next one or two years, meeting the myriad of deadlines that one encounters in academia, and so on. Such organization plays a major role in my day-to-day activities.

During a typical day I am up and ready to start working at 6:30 a.m. (I tend to be a Type A morning person.) Usually, I spend 3 or more hours working at home before going to the office. (The lack of interruptions at home allows me to complete a great deal of work.) A brisk, 1-mile walk to the office provides needed exercise. The 2 hours in the office before lunch are spent meeting with students, answering correspondence, and preparing for afternoon classes. Following classes, additional time is devoted to meeting with students, discussing research projects, and preparing various manuscripts. I typically leave the office at 6 p.m. Following dinner, an additional 1 or 2 hours is devoted to those items that have come home for attention. Yes, organization does help!

Third, it would be misleading not to indicate that some sacrifices have been made along the way. From my perspective the greatest demand has been upon my time. As just noted, work invariably comes home from the office every evening. Likewise, a healthy portion of each Saturday and Sunday is devoted to the completion of psychology related tasks. Although such demands have decreased the amount of free time that I have (or might like to have), I do not view myself as a unidimensional individual; I do have hobbies, a family life, and even find a few hours now and then to sleep. For example, I am a passionate collector of old phonograph records, baseball cards, Doctor Who videos, belt buckles, and old psychology books. Additionally, I have edited a quarterly journal on old-time fiddle music for the past 26 years. My wife and I enjoy bird watching, going to zoos, and canoeing. In short, I am a busy, perhaps slightly Type A, person.

Fourth, my family really deserves equal credit for the accomplishments that have been made during my career. In all instances my wife, Kathleen, and daughter, Jennifer, have supported and encouraged all of my professional activities. Without such a positive and understanding support system, I am convinced that my career would not have developed to its present proportions.

Fifth, do not say that you will "never" do something; you probably are mistaken. I was. At various points in my career I staunchly vowed that I would never: (a) go into administration, (b) attend APA conventions because they were too large and impersonal, or (c) write textbooks. You already know the fate of Vows a and b; I was department chair for 13 years and have been faithful in my attendance at the APA convention since 1984. With regard to writing textbooks, do you recall those book reviews I started doing while I was at APSU? In 1989 one of the publishers I had reviewed for began suggesting that I write a book. For a year I steadfastly resisted, then in 1990 I gave in and agreed to write an introductory psychology text. In the fall of 1992 a contract to write an experimental psychology text for the same publisher was signed. Don't ever say never.

Sixth, a willingness to accept opportunities when they are offered has characterized my career. If you are an active professional, opportunities will come your way. Even though you may be busy (opportunities do not present themselves when you have nothing to do), try to accept as many of these opportunities as possible. For example, when asked to serve as a journal reviewer during a rather demanding semester, you will be tempted to say no. If you can work this activity into your schedule without creating too much turmoil, do it; such a request may not be made again if you decline. Currently, I review 50 or more journal submissions a year and serve (or have served) as a consulting editor for three journals. However, I am quick to add that each opportunity must be attended to and fulfilled to the best of your ability.

Finally, the vast majority of this chapter can be boiled down to one sentence. You can have a very rewarding career and even achieve a modicum of professional stature "at a state school that does not have a competitive admission policy, a prestigious history, a national reputation, or a comfortable endowment, and that does not view itself as a research institution" (Pittenger, 1992, p. 165). Although the salaries may not be as high as they are at the more prestigious schools, there are more opportunities to interact with students and facilitate their professional growth. In this regard I have already enjoyed a career that has taken me far beyond my wildest expectations. As I am prone to say to my students, "If I can do it, so can you!"

References

Gordon, R. A. (1990). Research productivity in master's-level psychology programs. *Professional Psychology: Research and Practice, 21*, 33–36.

McKeachie, W. J. (1986). *Teaching tips* (8th ed.). Lexington, MA: D. C. Heath.

Pittenger, D. J. (1992). A brief history of the American Psychological Foundation's Award for distinguished teachers of psychology. In A. E. Puente, J. R. Matthews, & C. L. Brewer (Eds), *Teaching psychology in America: A history* (pp. 153–170). Washington, DC: American Psychological Association.

Chapter 4

An Unconventional Career Path in Teaching and Neuropsychology

Antonio E. Puente
University of North Carolina at Wilmington

This chapter was an extremely challenging endeavor for two reasons. First, I find it difficult to write about myself. Second, my approach to a career in psychology has followed an unconventional path. I believed as a young person that the methods commonly used to understand behavior were at best insufficient, at worst incorrect. Then, and even now, the path to addressing questions about behavior seemed to me muddled and insufficient. However, since thinking about the mind was a primary motive in my life, I was forced to pursue a previously uncharted road.

Early Years

In order to explain the present, a reconstruction of some of the past would be useful. I was born to an aristocratic and powerful family in Habana, Cuba. My paternal grandfather accrued wealth in the sugar business, and my maternal grandfather was president of the Bar Association of Cuba. My parents enrolled me in the most prestigious private school in the capital where I excelled in academics, earning the top ranking in each of the grades (as rankings superseded numerical scores). I was driven to school in a limousine and taken care of at home by my nanny. Leisure times were spent at the Habana Yacht Club where one of my grandfathers was, commodore. My mother, who had attended boarding school in Philadelphia, married into another prominent family. My father lost both his father and the anticipated inheritance unexpectedly in a mysterious fire. However, he was to eventually rise through the management of International Harvester of Cuba to a managerial position of significance. Little did anyone expect that more demanding problems for my family were yet to come.

In 1959, Fidel Castro, a disenfranchised student and lawyer, successfully overthrew the corrupt yet relatively stable government of Fulgensio Batista. Within a year, "democracy" had been replaced with the totalitarian regime that to this day continues torturing the human mind and spirit. For our family everything was lost including material acquisitions, freedom, and opportunity. With no knowledge of the English language nor of the U.S. culture, excluding my mother, and only a change of clothes and a total of $50, we landed in Miami facing an uncertain future. My immediate family crowded into a one bedroom apartment in Miami Beach with my aunt, uncle, and their four children. The disorienting experiences continued when I was placed in a third-grade class with no other Spanish-speaking children. Because no one, even the teacher, understood Spanish, I translated my name to Anthony Bridge. The only thing I did not have to translate, my name, was the only thing I could because I had no knowledge of English.

After struggling in that setting, my parents moved to San Antonio, Texas, where International Harvester had given my father a commissioned job as a salesman. This proved to be an impossible situation because my father had never been a salesman and did not know English. Our total monetary assets had been reduced to a mere 9¢. My father contemplated homelessness before Catholic Charities and several generous U.S. families intervened. Fortunately, my mother began teaching at St. Peter's Catholic School where my brother and I enjoyed tuition-free education for 2 years. Eventually, my parents decided that if we were to be miserable, the best we could do was go back to Florida where a stronger social support existed.

Family friends located a bookkeeping position for my father with a prosperous heavy equipment company in Jacksonville, Florida. Of course, numbers extend beyond language barriers and my father was able to succeed despite his still limited knowledge of English. Unfortunately, he experienced a decade of serious medical illnesses including tuberculosis (requiring a year's stay at a sanitarium), lower extremity paralysis (after an unsuccessful operation), and finally a heart attack. My mother held the family together financially and emotionally while working once more as a Catholic school teacher. My brother and I continued with a parochial school education trying as much as possible to learn the language, the culture, and this incomprehensible situation into which our family had been thrust.

High school years were spent studying, reading (especially biographies of individuals who seemed to have persevered in the face of adversity; I recall vividly the stories of Edison and Lincoln), surfing, and testing the limits of my parents' patience and society's tolerance to my persevering questioning. In those days, tolerance was not a common societal value and individuals from nonmajority group cultures were not widely accepted.

College Experience

My parents encouraged me to pursue further education although resources were simply not there. Interestingly, my high school counselor and most teachers had suggested a vocational track, presumably because of my difficulties with the language, culture, and standardized tests. One particular problem I recall was being bypassed for "honors" classes due to my low scores on intelligence and achievement tests. Indeed my first intelligence test was administered when I did not know English. In an attempt to be courteous, I smiled a great deal when the "psychologist" posed questions I did not understand. To this day I imagine that the diagnosis must have been "moron but friendly."

I attended Florida Junior College at Jacksonville, inexpensive and accessible, while working evenings. During my first semester there, one of my Hispanic friends encouraged me to sign up for a psychology course taught by Dan Hadwin, a consummate humanist. Hadwin offered not only an academic introduction to the fascinating world of the mind, but provided much needed emotional support and eventual career advising. For example, he gave my parents financial information about careers in psychology that to this day I believe was optimistically flawed. I finished the requirements for an Associate in Arts degree in 1½ years and was fortunate to receive a scholarship for further education.

Seizing on the excitement about the study of the mind and the possibility of financial assistance, I decided to pursue studies in psychology at what I thought was the best university in Florida, the University of Florida. The problem was that I did not have a scholarship to Florida. My mother, probably using all the psychology that she could muster, was able to convince my father to support my choice of universities. Due to late decisions, I chanced on enrolling for Donald Dewsbury's Animal Behavior class during my first semester. I was extremely fortunate to have spent my time at Florida working in his laboratory and being tutored both by him and his hard-working graduate students. To this day, I maintain a close professional relationship with Dewsbury. After graduating from Florida in another 1½ years, I took 1 year off to determine what, if anything, I could do with a degree in psychology. I came to realize that further education was highly desirable. Once more, however, no resources were available.

My time during that year was divided among surfing and playing tennis (both of which I still do regularly), working the night shift as a psychiatric technician, and auditing psychology courses at the University of North Florida. I also decided to read everything Freud and Darwin had written since they seemed to be two good resources for answering questions about behavior and the mind. The basic questions about human nature were fascinating, and my life had been a panorama of psychological challenges. Ultimately, I could not think of anything more interesting and exciting than to pursue a career in psychology. My conclusion was that one could actually receive a salary for thinking about the issues that had consumed my life and thoughts.

Unfortunately, plans for further study did not seem to match the realistic possibilities. For example, my GRE scores totaled only about 1,000, which hampered my entrance into doctoral programs. In the early 1970s ethnic minority concerns were mainly restricted to African Americans, and even then, in the most narrow fashion. Also, my father, presumably wanting to keep our family together under adversity, had initially discouraged me from pursuing graduate school in psychology. He believed psychology was a discipline for and about the middle class, something we had not and probably could never attain in this country. Again my mother intervened, convincing him that I should be allowed to pursue my chosen interests. He acquiesced to the idea of further education and compromised with "no study outside the state of Florida." Hence, applications were limited to Florida schools, although one application was covertly sent to the University of Georgia where there seemed to be good clinical and biopsychology training. Furthermore, Georgia was heavily involved with the Yerkes Primate Research Laboratory, originally founded in Orange Park, Florida (a place that I had become acquainted with during undergraduate years at the University of Florida). I was somewhat uncertain about specific career paths. However, the brain, abnormal behavior, and the adaptability to adversity were fascinating subjects awaiting further study.

Graduate School

Georgia accepted me into their biopsychology program, but I worked in both the clinical and biopsychology programs. Indeed, I basically pursued parallel educational tracks. My master's thesis was supervised by Irving Beiman, a clinician interested in studying abnormal nervous system function, whereas my doctoral dissertation was directed by Lelon J. Peacock, a biopsychologist well versed in both the nervous system and the history of psychology. If there was ever a "schizophrenic" existence, this was it. I would perform EEGs on volunteers from the psychology clinic during the day and perform septal lesions on hamsters during the evening at the psychology department's animal laboratory. Needless to say, the parallel tracks caused a great deal of concern among the faculty and my peers alike, especially because the two programs were at the time not on speaking terms. My goal was to study clinical neuropsychology and "minor" in philosophy. How naive I was because neuropsychology as a career track did not exist; philosophy had no place in psychology during the 1970s; and, of course, I was still having problems with the English language and my finances.

I was stunned after my first year of training not to receive financial support from the program to continue studies at Georgia (none was available the first year either). In retrospect, I should have not been surprised. I had just finished receiving a B triple minus (one could not really obtain a lower grade) in sensory physiology from a professor who had begun to date my girlfriend of the time. In addition, my statistics professor had assigned me an incomplete in the first course of a three-course sequence. He very gently encouraged me to pursue another career after my presumably abysmal performance on the final exam. One of the lowest points in my life came when my advisor at the time, Bradford Bunnell, consulted with other faculty members about the decision not to fund my second year. One late Friday afternoon after the spring quarter exams, he uncomfortably told me that "The faculty believe that you do not have what it takes to obtain a doctorate in psychology. . .among other things your command of the English language is not acceptable." I spent the summer months back in Jacksonville, Florida, working the night shift as a psychiatric technician trying to determine what options, if any, were still available. This situation could not be discussed with my parents who were struggling to support me, nor with my peers, as the entire spectacle was embarrassing and humiliating. Perhaps my father had been right about psychology. I was confused and depressed.

The solution to the predicament seemed to come from nowhere while working one of those never-ending night shifts. I decided that the professors at Georgia did not understand me and worse yet didn't comprehend the important questions of the mind. I inquired from the graduate school at Georgia how quickly one could complete MS and PhD degrees; 3 years I was told. I proceeded to do what ever was necessary to finish in the minimum time, and in 3 calendar years both graduate degrees were obtained. Not only was I financially destitute, but the support from my parents was shaky, and my own emotional strength was buoyed by what I considered, at the time, to be questionable foundations. This was a matter of survival, nothing else.

My master's thesis (clinical) was defended on January 6, 1978, and my doctoral dissertation (biopsychology) was defended the following Friday, the 13th. Along the way, I had established a relationship with a New Jersey-born, Florida-raised nurse who somehow always supported the unusual plans and ideas I had learned to harbor secretly. I had come to the conclusion that it was best not to share such thoughts because, at the very least, they were considered odd, and at the very worst, unattainable. Toward the end of my graduate education, I think she was the only person who believed in me. I doubted anything left to doubt. In the midst of all this turmoil we were married, and slowly plans for the future began to materialize.

Early Career Experiences

On January 16, the Monday after defending my dissertation, I was scheduled to begin teaching functional neuroanatomy at St. George's University School of Medicine in Grenada, West Indies. So after a going away party, we embarked on a journey from hell. After stopping on what seemed every island in the Caribbean, we finally landed in Trinidad late Sunday night, with only minutes to spare for our commuter plane to take us to our final destination in neighboring Grenada. Unfortunately, our dog was impounded at the Trinidad airport, despite prior arrangements with the government's veterinarian. To aggravate matters, I was arrested because of my Cuban citizenship, despite verifiable residence status in the U.S. An intoxicated soldier guarded our makeshift jail while I tried to figure out an "escape" so I could teach the following day in Grenada. We eventually left the compound under the cover of darkness and walked to the airport where we were able to retrieve our dog and depart on another commuter flight, without proper authorization, of course.

The Grenada airport at the time amounted to no more than a small building with a gasoline powered generator to allow for radio contact with incoming airplanes. Culture shock was only beginning. We traveled through the jungle, noticing poverty, despair, and the fact that everyone was Black. After arriving early, following our immigration ordeal in Trinidad, I went to teach, leaving my wife at our rented house overlooking the ocean. The house had no walls, allowing the sea breeze to enter. The classroom's main access was from the beach; the students were older than I; and "behavior" was not a welcomed word in the medical school curriculum. The year was spent once more reliving how it felt not to fit in. I also spent the year building a neuroanatomy laboratory, and, eventually, an entire medical library. In the latter two cases, it was my responsibility to work with the "architect" and the construction foreman to oversee the actual design and construction of the buildings. Later, the responsibility shifted to acquiring furniture, books, journals, and other materials. The experience was out of a novel, maybe science fiction. I was trying to establish a career in what seemed to me circumstances and a country from another planet. The truth of the matter was that I was close to being correct. During my tenure in Grenada, the prime minister had actually requested funds from the United Nations to establish a permanent landing site for UFOs on top of the island's inactive volcano. Voodoo was much more effective than public relations in running campaigns, marriage was not common, refrigeration was not available, running water was essentially nonexistent, and communication with "civilization" was sparse. Our regular contact with the outside world was via short wave radio.

Just as we were getting adjusted to this unusual existence, Cuban troops began infiltrating the island. I was at best minimally assured by the U.S. ambassador to Barbados that, as a U.S. resident married to a U.S. citizen, I would be safeguarded if indeed the political climate deteriorated, which eventually it did. With such "assurances," my wife left for the United States as quickly as possible while I finished the semester in the midst of a crumbling government, eventually departing to the United States in December 1978. Unfortunately, my entry papers were not in order, and my green card was so old it actually was blue. The custom officials at St. Thomas, being in the holiday spirit, played with the dog and did not check my outdated documents, allowing me to illegally re-enter the United States.

Such scrimmages had left me numb, and I decided that I was going to settle down, have children, and try to have a normal career and life. Among other things, I applied to become a U.S. citizen. The limits had too often and too aggressively been stretched. We settled at the beach, and I began my work at Northeast Florida State Hospital, a position my parents had secured through the Cuban psychiatric community. Here the patients spoke English and the psychiatrists Spanish, and here is where I added the "clinical" to neuropsychology, although largely self-taught. The state hospital was a wonderful place to work with a wide range of psychopathology, especially brain-damaged individuals. However, the serious questions about the mind were replaced with demanding clinical responsibilities. During the evenings I taught undergraduate and graduate courses in psychology at the University of North Florida where I had audited courses several years earlier. However, I was not well integrated into the department. All in all, the positions were not a good fit with my goals.

Obtaining a Permanent University Position

After applying to more than 70 academic positions, mostly on the east coast, I finally received invitations to three interviews along the eastern seaboard. I decided against an offer in Miami because it was not clear that the position would be tenure track and, further, I did not want to be known as an Hispanic psychologist from Miami. As far as I was concerned, there were more important issues to consider, and I did not want to focus solely on ethnic minority issues. An opening in New England proved to be more personally challenging. When I questioned the chairman at this prestigious university as to why they were interested in me, he simply said that it was an affirmative action hire. I took this to mean that my ethnicity was substantially more important than my abilities and interests. It was horribly cold outside (February) as well as inside. The University of North Carolina at Wilmington (UNC-W) was, in contrast, a new university located on the coast. I was appointed visiting assistant professor in 1981. I gradually rose through the ranks with a great degree of difficulty and, I believe, misunderstanding, to become a full professor in 1990. The misunderstanding was probably a cultural, possibly intellectual, maybe even personal, misalignment with some of the senior colleagues. It is important to note, however, that two other senior colleagues did "mentor" me and assisted in working around these invisible barriers. I sincerely doubt I would have eventually become tenured if it was not for these two understanding colleagues. One of them, Lee A. Jackson, went on to become our department chair.

UNC-W is a regional university with a strong classic liberal arts focus, both in terms of the mission and student body. The current emphasis appears to be marine and international studies. Of the approximately 8,300 students, 400 are undergraduate psychology majors. Until recently, the Department of Psychology's focus has been exclusively undergraduate, but in 1994 a master's program was begun. The department has expanded to include 22 tenure track professors with several more part-time lecturers from the private practice community. Overall, the university has doubled in size since my arrival in the early 1980s, but resources have become increasingly limited. Nevertheless, our department is highly regarded because of its commitment to both teaching and research.

During my tenure at Wilmington, the focus has clearly been on attempting to establish myself as a credible psychologist with a specialty in clinical neuropsychology, who happened to be an Hispanic. To accomplish this goal, I decided on a three-prong approach focused on teaching, research, and service. I would attempt to establish myself as a very interesting and involved professor who required students to do much more work than usual, with an emphasis on critical thinking skills. Upper level courses would also be introduced to research and writing skills with students having to complete an original study. My own research required the establishment of both a research program and a reputation for doing unique studies involving questions of the mind, often having philosophical foundations. For me, service would be defined in a broad perspective. Finally, I have emphasized service to the profession rather than to the university.

Teaching Psychology

Teaching, for me, has been dichotomized into two types of courses—the introductory course to psychology and everything else. I chose to teach Introduction to Psychology for several reasons: (a) I enjoy turning students on to psychology; (b) The course forces me to keep abreast with the entire field, and (c) A general course forces me to focus on basic questions about the mind that are often forgotten when one specializes. To this date, some of my best professional moments have come from discussions with first year students about basic psychological questions. My upper level courses always revolve around two topics—disordered behavior (with an emphasis on physical/neural problems) and the history and theories of psychology. The history course provides a forum for the more philosophical questions about psychology within a scholarly and historical context. The other courses allow me to pursue a strong biopsychosocial approach to understanding human behavior, especially abnormal behavior. I have always taken great pride in teaching outside the classroom, including the laboratory and clinic. All my research students, whether undergraduate, graduate, or postdoctoral, have published with me. In my experience, the laboratory is a unique place for further learning and the stimulation for additional education. Additionally, all research students have pursued advanced careers in such areas as law, medicine, biology, and psychology. These students have always been my colleagues as I relied on them much more than they will ever imagine. To this day, their criticism and collegiality remain important to me.

Research Opportunities

My research has focused on understanding how biologlcal, psychological, and cultural factors play a role in mediating human brain function. After exploring several measurement variables, my focus shifted to biological factors, namely antipsychotic or neuroleptic medications. The psychological issues I have typically emphasized have been the effects of perception and awareness in mediating the control of higher cortical functions, such as problem solving. These two lines of research required the use not only of "normal" subjects but clinical ones as well. The need for clinical subjects presents challenges in a university liberal arts setting. Finally, cultural issues have been important in my research. For example, I have been interested in how culture, especially the Hispanic culture, modulates the expression of brain function and dysfunction.

To pursue this line of research I needed the assistance of colleagues with larger populations of Hispanics. Fortunately, I was able to secure visiting professorships at the Universidad de Madrid and also of Grenada, in Spain. I had previously been unsuccessful in establishing research collaborations in Puerto Rico, through the American Psychological Association's Visiting Psychologist Program, and Argentina, through a Fulbright Scholar award. These colleagues were more interested in pursuing behavioral and psychodynamic interests.

My research career has always focused on the presentation and eventual publication of research studies. To date, I have presented numerous studies at professional and scientific meetings in North America and abroad and over 100 of my articles, 48 chapters, and 6 books have been published, mostly in English. Also, I co-established Plenum Publishing Corporation's book series in neuropsychology (15 to date) with Cecil Reynolds of Texas A & M University, and the journal *Neuropsychology Review* (4 volumes to date) with Gerald Goldstein from the University of Pittsburgh.

In recent years, questions of mind and brain have become very important to me. Clearly, the most unusual opportunity to answer such questions has come in the form of working with Roger Sperry, psychology's only Nobel Laureate. Between 1992 and his death in 1994, I worked closely with Sperry in his emphasis on the study of consciousness and values. To accomplish this we stayed in close contact via telephone and fax, and I visited him at the California Institute of Technology in Pasadena every 3 to 4 months. Currently, I am assembling a festschrift of his former doctoral and postdoctoral students. At the 1994 meeting of the American Psychological Association (APA) to be held in Los Angeles, approximately 45 collaborators from nine different countries and spanning five decades of teaching and research will present research that has been spawned by Sperry's ideas.

Service to the Profession

My service has been directed toward the profession of psychology, in general, and clinical neuropsychology in particular, although I have pursued both in parallel tracks. For psychology, I chose to participate at the state level where I began my involvement as a member of the Program Committee of the North Carolina Psychological Association. After agreeing to co-chair the committee several years later, my co-chair moved to the South Pacific and left me with the formidable task of developing the conference by myself. After chairing several successful conferences I was elected president of the organization. With the able assistance of Sally Cameron, executive director, several changes were instituted including the establishment of the North Carolina Psychological Foundation. I went on to serve as its Founding President and also to acquire a building and a permanent home for both organizations through the acquisition of a $350,000 gift.

I have also become involved with the APA in several capacities, mostly in education and minority issues. Within education, I served on and later chaired the Committees for Undergraduate Education (establishing the St. Mary's conference; see McGovern, 1993), and Continuing Education (formulating the concept of mandatory education for licensed psychologists). I was later elected to and eventually chaired the Board of Convention Affairs (and APA's 101st convention in Toronto). In Minority Affairs, I served as chair of the Awards Committee for the Minority Fellowship Program, directed by James Jones. In addition, I served on the Board of Directors for Division Two (Teaching of Psychology) of APA by chairing its Undergraduate, Ethnic Minority Affairs, and later the Fellows Committees. In Division 40 (Clinical Neuropsychology), I served as a Member-at-Large and Ethnic Minority Liaison to APA. Additionally, I was also involved in the issue of prescription privileges by participating on APA's Board of Directors' Task Force on Psychopharmacology and chairing another related task force, for the National Institute of Mental Health. Finally, I served the National Academy of Neuropsychology as chair of the annual conventions during the late 1980s and eventually became the organization's 12th president.

Clinical Service

Interspersed with these academic pursuits, I have been fortunate to develop a successful practice in clinical neuropsychology. Initially I ventured alone, later joining a neurologist, and then settling for about 7 years with a gregarious group of doctoral-level psychologists. Recently, I merged my practice with a large multidisciplinary medical practice as the only nonphysician doctoral-level health provider. The practice formed a department of neuropsychology that is currently being expanded. Both in and outpatient services to neurologically impaired individuals are provided alongside board certified physicians in a very collegial fashion.

One unique aspect of the practice has been the focus on research. Patients have for a long time comprised a rich source for ideas as well as research volunteers. Further, several of my more able undergraduate students (e.g., Heather Griffith) have worked as technicians in the practice after graduation and prior to entering graduate school. As an outgrowth of our discipline's difficulties with reimbursement and scope of practice, I eventually became involved with the process of coding clinical services. Recently, I was invited to join the American Medical Association's Advisory Committee for the Current Procedural System—the first time a psychologist has been involved in this process. Further, I have been working with the Health Care Financing Administration, a federal agency that establishes guidelines for health care in the United States, to insure that a greater understanding and acceptance of psychology and neuropsychology is achieved by the health-care community.

Conclusion

Although my career journey is not over, and although there is more to reveal, I have tried to present the highlights of my unorthodox approach to psychology. A basic assumption has been that my professional development is but a reflection of my personal life. Teaching, research, and service to psychology have been the basic pillars in my quest for understanding the mind. The obvious direction for me has been to understand behavior better by studying brain disorders within a biopsychosocial context. Underlying this approach is the question of consciousness and adaptability.

I believe not only that I have chosen an unconventional career path, but the outcomes have, at times, been difficult to handle. Also, I have chosen to focus on my family that now includes three children, a difficult task alongside an active career. Further, my base of operations has been a regional university not typically geared for a professional life such as mine. Hence, one may wonder how all of this could have happened. My accomplishments are probably due to a combination of factors. My family has always been extremely supportive, and I believe that the university has allowed me unusual flexibility, including the opportunity to develop a private practice. Earlier in my career I thought that establishing myself at a regional, and then relatively small, university would be detrimental, and it was never my intention to stay at UNC-Wilmington for more than 3 to 5 years. However, as my career developed, the base of operations seemed to become much less important than other factors such as quality of life and flexibility. Also, being a political refugee from another country encourages one to work extremely hard and take very, very little for granted. Finally, I have tried to develop a creative, energetic, and sustained plan to accomplish my goals.

Surprisingly, many of my initial goals have been accomplished and success and notoriety have followed, something I have been totally unprepared to handle. As a consequence, for the last 2 years my focus has been on an intellectual and personal re-charting of the unconventional path I began many years ago. Having established myself, both professionally in psychology and personally in the United States, has freed me to pursue the important questions about the mind that I began considering as a young person.

I chose a career that would reflect my life and fulfill my intellectual curiosity. My questions about the mind appear unanswerable, but the process of questioning has been exciting. The rewards have been immeasurable. I can only hope that when it is all said and done, I can satisfactorily answer the question Roger Sperry always asked, "Have I made a difference?".

Reference

Mc Govern, T. V. (Ed.). (1993). *Handbook for enhancing undergraduate education in psychology.* Washington, DC: American Psychological Association.

Chapter 5

Reflections on the Richness of a Small College Career

Samuel M. Cameron
Beaver College

How frequently is career development a series of planned orderly transitions and how frequently a series of fortuitous events? As I review my career, I realize how little was due to planning and how much was due to chance. Although chance played a role in presenting opportunities, my background and training allowed me to take advantage of these opportunities and, through hard work and application, turn them into achievements. I also realize how much I owe to the good advice and mentorship of others who had confidence in me and offered me many of these opportunities.

I first became interested in psychology in high school. I was fascinated by the field of para-psychology and tried to read everything I could find on it in our branch of the Philadelphia Library. Rhine's work on ESP was a particular focus and my best friend, Bob Boritz, and I spent hours running trials with the Rhine deck, only to find that we, at least, had absolutely no ESP powers. Eventually, my reading led me to a book by Adolph Huxley entitled *The Devils of Loudon*. Huxley explained the supernatural phenomena described in the book on natural grounds suggesting that the individuals involved were hysterical personalities. Huxley referred to Freud's work on hysteria in defending his thesis. Freud's *Psychopathology of Every Day Life* was the next book I checked out of the library. However, in high school, I did not know about careers in psychology. My goal was a career in the military or medicine.

I was in the honors section at Northeast High School, an inner-city school in Philadelphia. Everyone in the honors section was planning to go to college. However, most of us were from poor working-class families and had no money to pay for college. My college plans depended on finding scholarship money. As I was interested in a military career, I applied to West Point, but only won alternate status. My back-up plans were nonexistent.

I had recently read two books that suggested a plan of action. The books were Steinbeck's *The Grapes of Wrath* and Kerouac's *On the Road.* I thought I would hitchhike to California, pick grapes for a year while establishing residency, and go to UCLA for free. In the interim I won a state scholarship that could only be used at the University of Pennsylvania. The school principal, Dr. Young, was a bit dismayed when he called me into his office to share this good news only to learn that I had not applied to Penn. He immediately got on the phone to their admissions office and somehow got me accepted on the spot. My college course was set, but not through any active decision of my own.

Finding My Way in Higher Education

When I entered Penn I was still interested in a military career, but I was also interested in medicine. So I signed up for ROTC and declared as a pre-med student. ROTC was an unanticipated experience. I was a member of Pershing Rifles and, eventually, earned the status of potential distinguished honorary military student. In the spring of my sophomore year, a general from the 5th Army Corp was scheduled to inspect our unit. During each drill for months ahead the Corp had to practice passing in review before the reviewing stands. We practiced it so many times that we were better than perfect at presenting arms, and so on. The week before the inspection, there was a torrential downpour during drill. Even though we were better than perfect, the entire Corp still had to practice passing in review over and over again throughout the rainy drill period. As I was a commuter and wore my woolen uniform to school each drill day, I went to the rest of my classes in heavy sodden clothes and caught a cold. I decided that if the Army didn't know enough to come in out of the rain, I wanted no part of the Army. The colonel had a very hard time understanding why a potential distinguished honorary military student refused to sign up for advanced ROTC. My career choices were reduced to medicine.

Although I was getting straight As in military classes, I was getting straight Cs in chemistry. I finally came to the difficult realization that my chances of admission to medical school, let alone obtaining a scholarship , were nil. It was the second semester of sophomore year and I had to declare a major. When I thought of the courses that I had taken as possible major areas I realized that I had been most interested in psychology and philosophy. As I could not envision making a living as a philosopher, I decided to major in psychology.

In my senior year I was given an undergraduate research assistantship in the department. I believe that I was the first or among the first undergraduates at the University of Pennsylvania to be given such an appointment. I worked with Dr. Harold Rankin who was doing animal research on schedules of reinforcement. During my senior year, one of my psychology professors who was also the Dean of Students, Dr. Miles Murphy, asked me if I planned to go on to graduate school. I said that I would like to, but because I had no money I had not applied. I was still thinking that maybe I would move to California, establish residency, and go to UCLA. Dr. Murphy urged me to apply to Penn. As the GREs were not required at that time, the application was easily completed. It was my only application to graduate school. I not only gained admission, but also was awarded a graduate assistantship in the department. I later found that Dr. Murphy was chair of the admissions committee. I was stunned when, a year later, my mentor had a heart attack and dropped dead in College Hall.

At the University of Pennsylvania, for departmental honors, students had to undergo an oral examination. We were called in, three at a time, and faced a formidable array of full professors. One, whom I had never had for a class, but knew of, was Dr. Julius Wishner, head of the clinical program. Toward the end of the oral exam he asked me to describe my career goals in psychology. I answered that I would like a job where I could teach, do research, and be engaged in clinical practice. He burst out laughing and said,"Wouldn't we all, Sam; wouldn't we all." Well, of course that was exactly what he was doing and what I ultimately ended up doing as well. Dr. Wishner eventually became my dissertation supervisor and my mentor.

Although I was identified as being in the clinical program, Penn's curriculum made very little differentiation between clinical students and other psychology graduate students, particularly in the first year. Their purpose was to turn out research-oriented psychologists, whatever their area of focus. I knew little about actual clinical practice and found experimental psychology to be fascinating. I was particularly intrigued by experimental psychopathology and read extensively in the animal literature. My interest led me to submit a proposal for a Public Health Research Fellowship grant to use stress reduction as a negative reinforcement for eating behaviors in rats. I hypothesized that I might be able to make obese rats like some of my fellow graduate students were producing through neurosurgical procedures in Dr. Teitlebaum's laboratory. I was never successful in developing obese rats, but did develop a severe allergic response to the animals. As I was not allergic to humans, I finally resolved the approach–approach conflict in the direction of clinical psychology.

In 1962–1963, I did my internship at Norristown State Hospital, located just outside of Philadelphia. My supervisors were Dr. Mortimer Lipton, chairman of the psychology department, and Dr. Powell Lawton. Lipton involved me in group therapy with chronic schizophrenics, starting a lifelong interest in schizophrenia. Lawton involved me in group therapy with young male adolescents who had a variety of problems, some of a forensic nature.

Academic Positions and Related Work

My first academic position was at UCLA in the Neuropsychiatric Institute. I had finally made it to UCLA and California! I obtained the position through the "old boys network." Dr. Ivan Mensch, The Neuropsychiatric Institute's Director of Psychology, was a classmate of my dissertation supervisor, Dr. Julius Wishner. He wrote to Wishner inquiring if he had any worthy candidates for a clinical position at the Institute. I was interviewed at the annual meeting of the Eastern Psychological Association in Atlantic City and got the job. Although the position (and its responsibilities) was primarily clinical, it also carried the academic title of instructor in medical psychology. The academic responsibilities involved working with third-year medical students and first-year psychiatric residents in informal clinical settings.

I was at UCLA for only 1 year. My wife and I were unhappy on the west coast as we were separated from our family and our new daughter Diane was separated from her grandparents. I had written on several occasions to my former internship supervisors at Norristown State Hospital and one of them, Lawton, heard of an opening at Beaver College for someone to do counseling with the students and to teach in the psychology department. He notified Dr. Bernard Mausner, Beaver College's department chairman, of my availability and he, in turn, invited me to apply. I immediately responded and was fortunate enough to win the appointment. I have been there ever since and am now a full professor of psychology.

When Lipton, who had previously supervised my internship, heard that I would be returning to the area, he offered me a part-time position as the clinical psychologist in Norristown State Hospital's newly opened partial hospital unit. As I was taking a salary cut to go to Beaver College, the extra income was welcome. I also have found that over the years the continued involvement in clinical work with severely disturbed populations has enriched not only my counseling of mildly disturbed college students, but also my teaching at both the undergraduate and graduate levels. I later became a family therapist working with young schizophrenics and was also assigned to the Juvenile Forensic Unit. Thus, two main interests during my internship became the focus of my later clinical work.

I now found myself in the ideal position I had described during my undergraduate oral exams; I was teaching, doing counseling at the college, clinical work at the hospital, and research on the antecedents of aggression in children. A typical day found me spending some time on all these activities. I also found that many days involved some sort of academic committee meeting, faculty meeting, or departmental meeting. Success in academia demands that almost as much time be spent on these activities as in the classroom. The demands of teaching, college governance, counseling, and my clinical involvement at the hospital were so great that it was a constant struggle to find time for research or other professional activities, but I was able to do both. As time went on, I found myself increasingly involved in a variety of professional activities only indirectly related to my training in clinical psychology.

In the late 1960s, Beaver College was approached by our next door neighbor, Cheltenham High School, to develop some opportunities for their students to study psychology. The result was a grant request to the National Science Foundation (NSF) for a summer program in psychology for high school students from surrounding school districts. The program would have had the students learn operant conditioning in our labs at the college and spend their afternoons working in a token economy ward at Norristown State Hospital. The NSF review panel did not like the idea of high school students working at the state hospital and rejected the proposal 2 years in a row. I was discouraged but not defeated.

Dr. Arthur Breyer, Beaver College's chairman of the chemistry department had a long series of successful NSF grants to train high school chemistry teachers under NSF's Teacher Enhancement Program. He suggested that if I couldn't get a grant for the high school students, perhaps I could get one for their teachers. I took his advice and wrote a proposal to NSF to train high school psychology teachers.

The grant proposal was successful and started the part of my career that has been devoted to the improvement of the teaching of psychology at the high school level. I have subsequently had eight NSF funded projects in the teaching of psychology and am currently funded to conduct two more. Through my work with high school psychology teachers, I was appointed to the American Psychological Association's Committee on Psychology in the Secondary Schools, which I chaired from 1983 to 1984. One of our goals, initiated by Dr. Richard A. Kasschau when he was chair of the committee, was to encourage The College Board to develop an Advanced Placement (AP) Examination in Psychology. Those of us who shared this goal believed that the AP exam would play a major role in improving and setting standards for the high school psychology course. In 1986, The College Board finally convened a task force to study the feasibility of such an exam. Actual approval and development of the exam was started in 1990 and the first AP Examination in Psychology was administered in May 1992. I had the distinct pleasure of serving as table leader and reader for the first grading of the exam that spring at Clemson University.

Roles in Professional Organizations

My involvement in the Eastern Psychological Association (EPA) began when I was a graduate student. Dr. William Shaw, an experimental psychologist who taught the mandatory first-year pro-seminar, each year would exhort his students to attend EPA's annual convention. We listened and we obeyed; attendance at EPA became an annual rite of spring. I became a member in 1964, right after receiving my doctorate. Dr. Jean Smith, who taught at Pennsylvania State University–Ogontz, and part time at Beaver College, was Treasurer of EPA. One year she was sick and I took over her classes in experimental psychology at Beaver College for most of the semester. She must have been impressed by my willingness to take on extra work, because she nominated me to serve as local arrangements chair for the 1974 annual meeting in Philadelphia. I repeated that chore for the 1979 and 1983 annual meetings. I also served as program chair for the 1978 annual meeting. Then in 1989, I was elected treasurer of the EPA.

While a long-time member of the American Psychological Association's Division on the Teaching of Psychology (Division Two), I was not active in the Division's governance until 1985. Dr. Barbara Nodine, a colleague at Beaver College, was very involved in Division Two and served as President in 1982. Simultaneously, Richard A. Kasschau and Ludy T. Benjamin, Jr., with whom I had worked on various high school teaching projects, also were very involved in Division Two governance. Through the influence of these individuals (I am not sure who to blame) I was appointed to a 3-year position as the program chair for Division Two's portion of the American Psychological Association's annual convention. Upon finishing that responsibility, I was appointed to a 3-year position as chair of the Division's Teaching Awards Committee. These activities in Division Two's governance and my efforts in promoting the teaching of psychology at the high school level, eventually resulted in my election in 1986 as a Fellow of Division Two and the American Psychological Association. In 1992 I was elected President of Division Two, assuming that office in 1993.

Career Reflections

I have worked in a variety of settings: a large university, a psychiatric hospital, a community mental health center, and a small private liberal arts college. Of all of these settings I much prefer the small college. The size allows for more collegial relationships, both with other professors and with students. The expectations of publication and professional activity, although still present, are less onerous than at a large university. The disadvantages are the heavier teaching load and the smaller salaries. As I love teaching and don't require lavish living, it has always seemed a fair trade-off.

In 1989 I experienced a major illness that caused me to re-evaluate my lifestyle. I decided that I was doing too many things and needed to cut back. I discovered that, after twenty-five years, I was eligible to retire from Norristown State Hospital and I did so in 1990. In 1991, I relinquished my counseling responsibilities at the college, reverting to a full-time teaching/administration position. I now teach two courses each semester and administer our department's master's program in counseling psychology. A large part of each day is devoted to advising students and administering the graduate program. My days are less stressful, but I do miss the challenge and excitement of clinical practice.

I am now, in many respects, at the apex of my career. I am a full professor of psychology, director of a graduate program, a fellow of the American Psychological Association, treasurer of the Eastern Psychological Association, enjoy a national reputation in the improvement of the teaching of psychology at the high school level, and have just served as president of Division Two. I also was just named the Council for Advancement and Support of Education (CASE) Professor of the Year at Beaver College. Although I have worked hard to gain these achievements, I cannot truly say that any were the result of prior planning. Rather they were the result of capitalizing upon chance opportunities presented by friends and mentors. I sort of stumbled into college, into a major in psychology, and even into graduate school.

A young person starting a career in psychology today must be much more self-directed then I was. The field is now much more competitive. However, chance will continue to play a major role in anyone's career. Opportunities will present themselves and the young professional must be ready to take advantage of such opportunities and follow through with hard work and application. My advice is to never pass up an opportunity. As you complete each task to the best of your abilities, you will develop a reputation for hard work and competence. This will lead mentors and colleagues to think of you when the next task is at hand. Each task successfully completed will lead to other opportunities for career advancement.

Chapter 6

An Academic Odyssey: Experiences in a Small College and a Major Research University

Ludy T. Benjamin, Jr.
Texas A&M University

I was 16 years old and in my first year at the University of Texas and my principal worry—not unique to me—was what I was going to do with the rest of my life. It seemed obvious that I would not be able to stay in college forever. Yet that is exactly what I have done.

Undergraduate Experiences and Influences

Like most new college students I was unsure of a major, and even less sure of what I wanted for a lifelong career. I had enrolled as a pre-dental student, a decision born of thoughtful compromise. At 16, the most important thing in my life was playing golf. Although I fantasized about a life on the pro tour, my sense of reality assured me that would not happen. So I needed to find another career that would afford a decent wage but still allow plenty of time on the fairways. My father had wanted me to be a physician, perhaps to fulfill his own unrealized dream. Although I was aware that physicians made a lot of money, it was also clear that they worked long hours, and could have their lives regularly interrupted by medical emergencies. I certainly did not want to be two over par on the 15th hole and have to abandon such a round for someone's belligerent gall bladder. So I decided to be a dentist. They earned an adequate wage, people called them "doctor," and they seemed to be more in control of their hours. I reasoned that I would see patients only in the morning hours so that I could be on the first tee shortly after lunch.

This career plan lasted for about a semester. I admit that my chemistry course caused me to reconsider my pre-dental major; however, I also thought about what

57

it would be like to spend the rest of my life peering into mouths—mouths filled with decaying teeth and diseased gums. In looking around for another career (and a major), I did not have to look far—college professor. As a high school student, I had thought about teaching at the secondary school level, but dismissed it because of the long hours for little pay, not to mention the many students who seemed so uninterested in learning. Yet college teaching was clearly different. These people made a comfortable living and they didn't have to work very hard for it. They came to work at 10 a.m., taught a class, played handball, went to lunch, worked in their office for another hour or so, and were gone by 2 p.m. What sealed this choice was the realization that these people were also called "doctor." And so for 21 of the past 23 years I have been a college professor. And during that time I have played golf about six times. Clearly something went wrong somewhere.

I misjudged the nature of college teaching, but the decision to enter that profession is one of the best I have ever made. As an undergraduate I was enamored with life on a college campus, both the social and intellectual activities, and unfortunately in that order. Its magic has remained for me now that I am on the other side of the lectern. I rejoice daily in the richness of life that college offers me, and I am truly thankful that I have the opportunity to work in a rewarding environment that brings me so much pleasure and satisfaction. In recent years, partly stimulated by reports on how few students come to college planning to pursue a career as a college teacher, I have begun to tell each of my classes about my job and the multiple satisfactions that I derive from it—about the blending of scholarship and teaching, about the richness of culture, about the joy of learning for a living. A college campus is a place of excitement and diversity, of art and athletics, and, most important, of new ideas. For someone interested in lifelong learning, there could be no better place. Indeed, I give thanks daily that I am privileged to work at a job that brings me so much intellectual stimulation, pleasure, and satisfaction.

In truth, it was no surprise to me that few students come to college with thoughts of becoming a college professor. After all, they have never seen one before, unless they happen to be related to one. And professors are not often the subject of television dramas. So for most people, college offers the first exposure of this career option, the first real look at what college professors are like. And one quickly learns that they are not all the same.

In my own case there are two instructors who stand out in my undergraduate memories. One was a full professor in anthropology, only a few years away from retirement. He was the consummate master lecturer who without notes spoke in complete paragraphs, who was filled with passion for his subject, who on occasion moved his students to tears, and whose awe-inspiring lectures forced his students to challenge their own beliefs and values. The other was a new assistant professor of psychology in his first year of teaching. He was not an especially gifted lecturer, but I looked forward to every meeting of his perception class because of the demonstrations that were a part of each class period. Some demonstrations lasted only a few minutes, others might take most of the class period. But they were a predictable part of every class. The teacher was always quite enthusiastic about these demonstrations and his students got caught up in the excitement of discovery and new understanding that they generated. Today we recognize this kind of hands-on activity as "active learning." Both of these valued teachers, although very different, were partly responsible for my decision to be an academic.

As an undergraduate I had many interests. In terms of my classes I especially liked anthropology, biology, English, history, and psychology. And I chose the latter as my major probably because it seemed to contain elements of the other disciplines. But not all of my interests were academic. I enjoyed going to parties, playing basketball at midnight, and eating pizza and playing cards at 2 a.m. I did not take many of my classes very seriously in my first 2 years of college and found myself on academic probation for several semesters. My parents continued to support me even though they surely knew I was not working hard. Then in the middle of my junior year the university informed me that because of my academic record, I would not be eligible to return the following semester. So I left college at the age of 18 and I married a young woman of 20 who believed that I might actually amount to something. Nine months later we were back at the university to begin the final year toward our degrees.

Graduate School

One has extra responsibilities in a marriage and doing well in college seemed like one of mine. My academic record as a senior bore little resemblance to my earlier work. But even a year and a summer of excellent work couldn't do much to salvage my miserable grade point average. Although I graduated with my baccalaureate in psychology, my credentials for graduate school were pretty meager. And most of the schools to which I applied for doctoral work acknowledged that by sending me their letters of rejection. However, Auburn University took pity on me and I was able to begin graduate work there in psychology. In beginning graduate school I was now a father of a baby girl—more responsibilities. I had hoped to specialize in the psychology of perception, a subject that I had enjoyed as an undergraduate, but Auburn did not have a perception psychologist. I reasoned that it did not matter, I wanted to teach psychology and my specialty seemed irrelevant; I just needed to get my degree so that I could begin my career.

At the beginning of my third quarter, the registrar received complaints from a number of undergraduates about being closed out of all sections of the introductory psychology course. Because all the more advanced graduate students already had teaching assignments, the department head looked to the first-year students and tapped me as the instructor for a newly opened section of the course. I could not have been more excited nor more terrified. Here I was teaching some college students whose educational experience nearly matched mine, and some were even older than I at 21 years of age. Mostly I lectured, about what I can't remember, and I used what few demonstrations I knew to involve my students in the excitement I had felt in my perception class. I am not sure that my students learned much, but the experience was a most enjoyable one for me. And the fact that the students gave me good evaluations gave me confidence that I could be a decent college teacher.

My department was pleased and offered me the opportunity to teach two classes in the coming fall term, an offer that I eagerly accepted.

Some turns in life come most unexpectedly. In the summer I got a call from a friend from college days who was in the doctoral psychology program at Texas Christian University (TCU). He told me that another student there had dropped out and that his fellowship was available if I wanted it. The opportunity was to begin work immediately in a doctoral program, the financial support was more than double what I was receiving, and there was the chance to work with one of several faculty specializing in perception. It was too good to pass up, but I still felt guilty about abandoning Auburn which had taken me in when no one else was interested. To their credit, my professors urged me to pursue the TCU opportunity; they felt it was in my best interest. I have not forgotten their support and encouragement, and I continue to have a warm spot in my heart for Auburn University.

At TCU I pursued a degree in experimental psychology with a specialty in perception. The coursework was enjoyable but I was not interested in doing research. I got involved in research because it was expected, but I certainly felt no passion for it. And it was difficult for me to come up with original research ideas. It seemed that every important idea had already been thought of before I got there. Some of my fellow graduate students were clearly excited about what they were doing. But what I wanted to do was teach, and at TCU (at that time) graduate students in psychology were not allowed to do that.

It bothered me that I did not seem more passionate about psychology. For awhile I thought about changing to some other discipline; however, I felt that with the responsibilities of a family (a second daughter had arrived) I did not have the luxury for such exploration. There had been one course that was particularly interesting, a course on the history of psychology, but that was clearly not a viable career field. So I stayed with perception, collecting my dissertation data at the end of my third year, just before leaving for my first job at Nebraska Wesleyan University in Lincoln.

Experiences in a Small Liberal Arts College

It was not a difficult choice to decide to go to Nebraska. It was my only job interview and the only offer that I had. And so in the fall of 1970 I joined a four-person psychology department at a small liberal arts college on the gently rolling plains of southeastern Nebraska. The college was smaller than anything in my experience, 1,100 students, and undergoing some financial difficulties in the 1970s due to declining enrollments. My salary was meager, providing me with only $20 more a month in take-home pay than I earned my final year at TCU.

I taught four classes in the fall semester: two sections of introductory psychology, learning, and history of psychology. In the spring I again taught two sections of the introductory course, plus motivation and emotion, and perception. In the summer I taught two more classes including a new preparation in child psychology. And somehow during that first year I managed to write my dissertation, which I defended at TCU in the summer of 1971. That meant my rank was advanced from instructor to assistant professor and my pay increased by $500 for the year. When I think of how much time it takes to prepare to teach a new course, I am amazed that I survived that first year. And yet my memories of it—accurate, I believe—are of a year with more free time than I have enjoyed at any other time since becoming an academic.

I spent 8 good years at Nebraska Wesleyan. I began my tenure there as an arrogant youngster, believing I deserved to be somewhere more prestigious, like Harvard University. But I grew to appreciate the opportunities at that kind of college and it has proven to be the most important influence on my values as a college professor (both of our daughters would later graduate from liberal arts colleges). And my department head, Clifford Fawl, a man 15 years my senior, was chiefly responsible for my development as a teacher, scholar, and departmental citizen. He was the academic mentor that I had never really had. We remain close friends today.

Being an academic at Nebraska Wesleyan was a rich experience. Departments were small enough that one was forced to make friendships in other disciplines. I had coffee regularly with colleagues in art, biology, English, music, and philosophy. We discussed what we were reading and what we were teaching, we attended one another's colloquia speakers, we team taught courses, we attended the college's theater productions (and the theater director knew if you missed one), and we supported the various athletic teams, which contained no students on scholarships except for the academic variety.

As faculty we attended baccalaureate services, marched in the commencement procession, and attended the functions for alumni and for parents of current students. We added laboratory and community experiences to our classes, often without any extra teaching credit, which added considerably to the time we spent with students individually or in small groups. We assisted in the recruiting of prospective students. And we spent untold hours in individual meetings with students on matters of classwork, family, career, and so forth. At commencement each spring, the faculty sat on the auditorium stage wearing our academic regalia and, like most of my colleagues, I would know two thirds of the graduating seniors on a first name basis. I felt close to many of those students. Some of the psychology majors might have been students in as many as six courses with me. I often knew their mothers and fathers and siblings from advising experiences or from attendance at annual "parent's day" functions. Having been an undergraduate at a university of 26,000 students, I always marveled at the opportunities Nebraska Wesleyan students had for interaction with faculty, for special experiences in courses, and for the closeness they enjoyed as members of a small graduating class. And it made me feel that I had been cheated by my own education in a large research university.

At Nebraska Wesleyan, students were the focus of our activities. Teaching (including preparation for classes and labs and grading papers) and advising duties occupied most of my time, leaving little time for scholarly work such as research and writing. All senior students engaged in some kind of scholarly project as part of their graduation requirement, so faculty spent a lot of time supervising those projects. However, faculty research, when it occurred, was usually a product of summers or the winter break between semesters.

I never did any research in perception at Nebraska Wesleyan. I told myself and others that it was because we did not have any of the complex and expensive equipment that I had had as a graduate student. But in reality I didn't have any research ideas. Actually I was doing research—although I didn't know to call it that—as I sought to prepare lectures for my history of psychology course. By accident I had learned that one of Wilhelm Wundt's U.S. students had founded a psychology laboratory in Nebraska in the late 19th century. My search for information about him led me to some local archives and to the discovery of other famous psychologists whose origins or careers were in Nebraska. What began as work for one of my classes soon became a passion. Within a couple of years I had published several journal articles based on this history work.

For the first time in my academic career I was truly excited about a field. In 1974 I presented some of my history work at the annual meeting of the American Psychological Association (APA). There I met the co-directors of the Archives of the History of American Psychology (located at the University of Akron) who made possible my first visit to that important facility the following summer. It was the first of many trips to Akron that have been important for my research.

I served my last 4 years at Nebraska Wesleyan as psychology department head. However, in 1978 I left the college. My departure was largely motivated by a change in the upper administration whose goals for the college seemed contrary to mine. And I suspect that because my interest in research and writing had grown, I longed for an environment that provided more time for that. Yet I accepted a new job that was wholly administrative, one that I saw as a stepping stone to a college dean's position.

An Administrative Job in Washington, DC

In the summer of 1978 I went to work for the APA in Washington, DC. I was hired by Charles Keisler, APA's chief executive officer and the best manager I have ever known, to direct APA's Office of Educational Affairs. My office was involved with education in psychology at all levels from psychology teaching in the secondary schools to postdoctoral training and continuing education. It was a tremendous learning experience for me because I knew little about psychology education beyond the undergraduate level. I stayed at APA for 2 years where I learned a great deal about the breadth of psychology as a discipline and about the policy and advocacy roles of a national organization in Washington. I managed an office staff of 11 and worked with numerous boards and committees, spending most of my time in meetings. And then one day, in a flash of awareness, it occurred to me that I disliked meetings. Thus, it seemed obvious that I should leave that job and also that I should consider some career other than one in college administration where I would also endure hours of meetings.

My interest in history remained as what I enjoyed most. I had been at APA for only about 6 months when I realized how much I missed being part of college life. While at APA I made a few visits to universities, typically to give talks on the history of psychology, and those occasions reminded me of what I had given up. So at the end of my first year at APA I began to look for an opportunity to be a faculty member once more.

A Return to Academia: A Research University

I left APA in the summer of 1980 to join the psychology department at Texas A&M University. The student body of 32,000 and the 20-member psychology department were indicators that this setting was clearly different than Nebraska Wesleyan. I arrived at Texas A&M in the beginning of a period of incredible growth for psychology. In the next 10 years the university's enrollment increased to 42,000, the psychology department faculty doubled, doctoral programs were added in six psychology specialties, and the psychology department moved into a new building that nearly tripled our space.

Now in my 13th year at Texas A&M, I find that my life as an academic is very different. Texas A&M is a research university that regularly ranks among the top 10 universities in the United States in terms of the external dollars (grants) its faculty brings in for research. As a research university, the emphasis is not only on dispensing knowledge through the teaching process but also on the generation of knowledge through original research. Whereas faculty were largely judged at Nebraska Wesleyan for their contributions to teaching and student advising, faculty at Texas A&M are principally rewarded for quality research and publication and for securing external funds to support research. Further, at Nebraska Wesleyan, undergraduate students were the sole focus of faculty attention; however, at Texas A&M, graduate students are more likely to be the focus of that attention. In essence the expectations of these two institutions of higher education are very different, and a differential reward structure exists to facilitate those expectations.

In the beginning I had some difficulty in adjusting to the new set of demands. I had learned to be a professor in a small college where I knew all of the faculty and most of the students; I now found myself teaching classes so large that I couldn't learn all of the students' names, and of the several thousand faculty members at Texas A&M, I knew few who were outside of my department.

My introductory sections contained 250 students, and even the upper level undergraduate courses, like "history of psychology," might have 80 or more students. It was rare that a student would have me as a professor for more than one course. And I found that the only ones with whom I spent much time were those who were having trouble with my classes. The students who made 90s on every exam typically never visited my office. At the end of the semester, as I was assigning grades, I often could not picture these students. There were exceptions, but not many. Without contact with these students, without the chance to get to know students well through labs and multiple small classes, I soon realized that my undergraduate classes were less rewarding for me. And so it was easy to focus more time on my graduate classes, which were much smaller, and on my research and writing.

At Texas A&M I was able to find much more time—teaching two classes per semester—and support for my research in history. For several years I did research in human sleep, an interest that began during Nebraska Wesleyan days as the result of a summer spent working in a sleep research laboratory at a Texas medical school. The psychology of sleep interested me considerably, and I enjoyed teaching an undergraduate course on sleep and dreaming; however, the research was particularly time consuming, and I never really felt the excitement for that work that I felt for history. I thought often about abandoning the sleep research and devoting full time to work in history. However, I was reluctant to do that, afraid to give up what I saw as my last ties to the experimental psychology in which I was trained. Would my psychology colleagues appreciate a historian in their midst, a colleague who no longer did experimental work?

There are ages when people are known to re-evaluate their lives, and at age 40 I did just that. I decided to stop masquerading as an experimental psychologist and to devote my scholarly energies fully to the field that I loved so much. So I announced to my department head that I was closing my sleep lab, to specialize fully in history research. To my mild surprise he was very supportive of my decision and encouraged me to pursue what I valued most. And the decision is one that I have never regretted.

At the time of this writing I would say that I am roughly at the midpoint of my professional career. I have worked for 23 years and at the age of 47 expect to work at least that many more. Although I feel that I have enjoyed my work in the past two decades, the last few years have been the best. And it is quite probable that I will continue for some time to do what I do now. In earning tenure, the rank of professor, and some measure of professional standing in psychology, I have a great deal of freedom in choosing the things that I do as an educator and psychologist. This freedom has ensured tremendous diversity in my job. For almost all of my career I have looked forward every day to going to school ("work"). Knowing what surveys tell us about most people's job satisfaction, I feel extremely fortunate to have found a career that affords me so much pleasure.

Perspectives on My Current Work

As I have indicated, the nature of my work has varied during my career, largely dictated by the nature of my work setting. To this point I have described my early preparation to be a college professor, the nature of my academic life in a small liberal arts college, a little about my 2 years in full-time administrative work at the APA, and, finally, a brief overview of academic life at a large research university. What I want to do in the last few pages of this account is to give the reader a somewhat detailed account of the nature of my present job by describing a typical semester. In part this account is detailed in order to illustrate the diversity of my job.

In a typical semester I teach two classes, usually one undergraduate and one graduate course. The undergraduate course might be the introductory course or the history course, whereas the graduate courses would be history and a course on the teaching of psychology. I enjoy teaching all of those and have for a number of years. With fewer preparations (than the 10 different courses that I taught at Nebraska Wesleyan) I have been able to be more familiar with the course subject matter and, I hope, thus a better informed teacher. My favorite course is the graduate course in the history of psychology, largely because of the major papers that the students research and write for that class. A lot of my time in that class is spent working with students one on one, helping them decide on a research topic and helping them find the necessary resources.

On occasion I work with a few undergraduate students in my research. Usually I invite them to work with me after they have taken my history course. In the past 5 years I have published several articles and one book with undergraduate students as co-authors. However, graduate students are more likely to play the role of research assistant. I enjoy involving students in my research, yet most psychology majors and graduate students are interested in working with faculty to learn about experimentation. So my research is not usually as appealing as that of my colleagues who work in social or cognitive psychology, for example.

I also work with graduate students as a member of their master's or doctoral committees. In a typical semester I will have two to three such meetings. Because of my interests in teaching, I also meet with graduate teaching assistants on an informal basis, usually because they have come to me with a problem of class discipline, suspected cheating, and so forth.

In addition to teaching and research, one of the duties of an academic is "service." Although there are many ways to serve one's department, committee service is a standard avenue. I serve on a minimum number of departmental committees (for reasons that I have already explained). My involvement is in those whose subject interests me the most (e.g., undergraduate education, library) or in those for which my membership is required because of my professorial rank (e.g., promotion and tenure). There are peaks and valleys in committee work, but for me I spend an average of 2 to 4 hours each week either in meetings or doing work associated with those meetings. Committee work is one of those necessities of academic life; still I would be willing to be relieved of all of those duties.

I spend as many hours in service activities beyond my campus as I do here. I serve on several national committees, for example for the APA and for the Educational Testing Service (ETS). These duties result in about two to three meetings each semester. The APA meetings are always in Washington, DC, and the ETS meetings are held in various cities from Boston to San Diego. My expenses in attending those meetings are paid for by the agencies and not by me nor by my university.

Another service activity that I particularly enjoy is doing program reviews of other psychology departments, which I have done for the past 12 years. Usually I do one to two of these each semester at the invitation of a department. Sometimes I am part of a team, as in the case of a review of a clinical psychology doctoral program for the APA Accreditation Program. And sometimes I am the lone reviewer at a small college psychology department or perhaps a larger state university with a master's degree program. Prior to the date of the visit I am sent materials (sometimes substantial) describing the program. The visit usually lasts 2 days, and I am then responsible for submitting a written report (or contributing to one) based on my perceptions of the program. I have always been interested in the undergraduate curriculum in particular, and I learned long ago that there are many ways to teach students about psychology. I consider myself a student of the curriculum, thus I always enjoy seeing how other colleges and universities function. Over the years these reviews have taken me from California to New York, and from Manitoba to

Alabama. In doing them I have met a number of interesting people and always feel that I learn more from them than they do from me.

Another kind of service to the profession of psychology is in the form of journal work as an editor or reviewer. For the past 10 years I have been an associate editor of the *American Psychologist*, APA's principal journal. My duties involve contracting for obituaries of distinguished psychologists—I handle about 10 of those in a semester—and serving as editor for submissions on the history of psychology. I also serve as a reviewer or consulting editor for other journals, principally on articles either in history or the teaching of psychology. Such activity can be quite time consuming, yet as one whose publications have benefited from the reviews of numerous other scholars, it is a duty I would not shirk. And I learn a lot in the process, about topics in which I have considerable interest.

I have saved my favorite activity for last, and that is research. As a historian of psychology I spend some of my time each year in one or more archives, looking at original manuscripts, letters, laboratory notebooks, and other unpublished materials. This past year, for example, I made two trips to the Boston Public Library to use the papers of Hugo Münsterberg (1863–1916), an early pioneer in industrial psychology. Those documents are important because of a book I am working on about the history of U.S. psychology's involvement in business and industry.

I also collect information via oral histories by interviewing individuals who may have information important to my research. This summer I will visit a man in California who worked with Harry Hollingworth (1880–1956) in the 1930s and 1940s. Like Münsterberg, Hollingworth was an important figure in psychology's involvement with business.

The nature of my work is such that projects are sometimes ongoing for several years. In fact I recently published a book that I worked on for 20 years and a journal article that was in the works for 15 years. Some projects take that long because the work continues until I feel that I have sufficient information to tell the story. History research is like detective work and one isn't done until all leads have been followed and all rocks turned over. Based on movies and novels, I always thought detective work was pretty exciting—and so is history research. It's about curiosity and discovery, and discovery is always exciting.

Obviously I would publish very little if I worked on only one project at a time. But in fact I typically have 6 to 10 projects going at any one time. In the past 12 years I have written or edited 11 books and nearly 50 journal articles. More than half of those are on the history of psychology and most of the others relate to the teaching of psychology. So you can see that writing is something that I do every semester, but especially so in the summer. There is great pleasure involved in bringing a project to completion, especially if you have lived with the topic for a long time. And there is pleasure in feeling that you have contributed some new understanding to psychology, in my case, that people may now think differently about some issue in the history of psychology because of my work.

In addition to publishing my research, I have the opportunity to present that work in public presentations. Normally I will make one to three presentations in a semester. Some of these are at professional meetings, such as the annual meeting of the Southwestern Psychological Association. Sometimes I submit my papers to the program committees for their review and, I hope, acceptance. And sometimes they invite me to give an address at their convention. Other presentations are at colleges or universities. Needless to say, it is very flattering to be invited by other colleagues to present one's work.

Although most of my presentations are about my history work, I also give a number of talks on the teaching of psychology, particularly on the subject of active learning, that is, the involvement of students in hands-on and minds-on learning. In recent years I have been especially involved in working with high school psychology teachers who are preparing to teach a college equivalency psychology course in the high school. Currently, I have a 4-year grant from the National Science Foundation to assist these teachers through the conduct of month-long summer workshops on my campus. Working with these teachers has been a particularly rewarding experience.

One of the chief advantages of an academic life is flexibility of scheduling. Other than class hours and office hours, there are very few times when my presence is mandated. So I could leave school during the day to attend a school performance of one of my children, take an extended lunch hour with colleagues, or even stay home for a day of uninterrupted writing. Academics could typically fulfill their contractual obligations in a minimum number of hours, certainly within a 40-hour week. However, like most jobs, this one is open-ended and you can put in as much time as you want. My experience indicates that a 60-hour work week (or more) is typical for those who are successful. That has never seemed a problem for me because the work has always been so enjoyable, and because I am able to schedule most of those hours to meet my own preferences.

A typical work week for me would be as follows. I spend 4 days at the university, usually arriving at 7:30 a.m. and leaving around 5 p.m. One day each week I will stay home to write, or I may spend that day out of town on one of my professional trips. In the evenings I usually work another 4 to 5 hours. I do not usually work on Friday evening nor on Saturday, but I often work another 4 to 5 hours on Sunday. I am fortunate in that I need less sleep than the average person—typically 5 to 6 hours each night—so I have more leisure time than one might think.

Another advantage of an academic life are the frequent breaks from the academic schedule, and some of those breaks are quite long. On a typical semester system I would have a month off between semesters, another week in the spring for "spring break," and another 3 to 3½ months off in the summer. Vacation has always been important in my family and we have taken numerous trips since our daughters (now grown) were small. Because my wife is an elementary school librarian our academic calendars match so that we usually have free time together. We have always taken a 3-week vacation each summer, and usually we go for shorter trips in December and during spring break. In the past 20 years we have visited 46 states, most of the provinces of Canada, and more than a dozen countries in Europe. And most of those trips have included our daughters as well.

Like many academics, I have typically taught for 4 to 6 weeks during the summer. Occasionally I receive invitations to teach in summer school at other colleges and universities. On one of those visits my wife and I recently spent 6 weeks in the upper peninsula of Michigan where I taught one section of introductory psychology 4 days a week. There was plenty of time to enjoy the cool summer weather, do some fishing, and explore the beauty and history of that interesting region. Such opportunities combine vacation and work, although mostly we avoid mixing the two. Some summers I have chosen not to teach and have spent my time divided between vacation and research or writing.

Final Reflections on an Academic Life

If you are reading the academic profiles in this book, it is likely that you are contemplating the possibility of a career as a college professor. I hope that this brief account has led you to understand the multiple reasons for my considerable satisfaction with this profession. Were I to live my life over I would not change much of it (other than working harder as an undergraduate student). The three jobs that I have held have all taught me a lot about my profession and about myself. In my present job I miss the close contact that I had with undergraduate students at Nebraska Wesleyan, the sense of identity that I had with that small college, and the cross-fertilization of ideas that resulted from frequent contact with colleagues in other disciplines. Yet I enjoy greater professional opportunities in my current setting and more job diversity. The scholarly activity expected at a research university has become the most rewarding part of my job, and my happiest hours are spent in doing archival research and writing. I still greatly enjoy teaching and believe that my courses are better than ever. As an active scholar in history and the teaching of psychology, I am forced to keep current in those content domains. And that currency, as well as my own research, significantly enriches my courses.

As I reflect on this academic odyssey, I believe that there are facets of my life and career that are common to many individuals, both in and out of academic life. I remind the reader that many careers likely involved failures along with the successes. In looking at successful individuals, it is sometimes easy to forget that fact of life.

Further, I am struck by the nonlinear paths that careers follow. Job changes are not always predictable, nor does one job setting necessarily follow from another. In reality there are probably few careers that are planned out from the beginning. Serendipity, experiences (often ones that might seem unrelated to career interests), and the demands of different settings affect our careers in ways that we could not have predicted.

I cannot say that this academic job is right for everyone. However, as I look around at people I know in other professions I cannot find one of them with whom I would exchange jobs, unless of course Jack Nicklaus wants to leave the senior pro golf tour and become a college professor. I wish you insightful thinking in your career decisions and a personal and professional life of worth and happiness.

Chapter 7

The Rhythms and Serendipity of an Academic Life

Baron Perlman
University of Wisconsin Oshkosh

> *So sometimes things are ahead and sometimes they are behind;*
> *Sometimes breathing is hard, sometimes it comes easily;*
> *Sometimes there is strength and sometimes weakness;*
> *Sometimes one is up and sometimes down.*
>
> —From Tao Te Ching 29

I am a full professor at the University of Wisconsin Oshkosh (UWO), a public, regional university with a century long heritage as a state teachers' college. It grew from an enrollment of 2,500 in the early 1960s to 11,000 students in the late 1960s and early 1970s. It continues to struggle in the 1990s to define its identity, values, and future.

I work in a department of psychology with 12 colleagues. Their professional identities vary from clinicians (I am a clinical psychologist) to experimentalists, cognitive psychologist to generalists. The department has 300 undergraduate majors. Our courses fulfill general education requirements as liberal arts subject matter for a liberal arts major, and as preprofessional and preapplied education. Until 3 years ago I taught four courses a semester; I now teach three. In some institutions a teaching load of three courses per semester is considered heavy; at other institutions it is a light load.

My department offers an MS degree in psychology with industrial/organizational, general-experimental, and clinical emphases. I have worked in the latter for 18 years. The applied master's training program in the clinical area is one reason I came to UWO, and it has provided me with much satisfaction.

In the Beginning

My career has been driven by fate and serendipity. I have found that this style of decision making is a better one for me than setting goals or 2- or 5-year plans.

I obtained my undergraduate education at Lawrence University, a small liberal arts school in Appleton, Wisconsin. It was a wonderful school in which I discovered that I loved ideas and the academic setting. I had no special interest in psychology when I began; I explored the liberal arts. My first psychology course was large by Lawrence's standards—30 students—and if memory serves, it was boring. But I took more psychology and got to know two caring faculty (Drs. Bucklew and Hill). Their attention and support, more than the subject matter, led me to choose psychology as a major.

Having decided on a major, I became fascinated by the subject matter and scientific inquiry of psychology. I spent three summers working in psychology and mental health preparing for graduate school admission, although I had little idea of what graduate school entailed: I spent one summer as a social work trainee on Chicago's Skid Row; I did research on a National Science Foundation (NSF) grant at the University of Illinois a second year, and I worked at a 5,000-patient state mental hospital in Manteno,Illinois a third summer. Most of all, I enjoyed being a Lawrence upperclassman with a major I liked and a sense of purpose. I enjoyed running rats in the laboratory, working on courses, my senior project, and hanging out in the psychology department.

I chose to apply to doctoral programs because I had no other viable career plans. In retrospect, I realize that I chose clinical psychology because I wanted to make sense of who I was and who I wanted to be. At the time of application, I had no awareness of my needs for personal discovery, growth, and maturity. I was accepted to two of the six doctoral programs to which I had applied, the University of Illinois and Michigan State University (MSU). I chose MSU primarily because I knew a few students there.

Graduate School

MSU turned out to be an excellent choice for me. Its practicum experiences allowed me to work with clients and to connect with sensitive caring people who helped me to grow and learn. Of particular note are Bob Zucker, my mentor and now a friend; Marsha Worby, a clinical supervisor, and Dozier Thornton, my dissertation chair.

I am a baby boomer, and the Vietnam war had a major effect on my interest in and commitment to psychology. During my first year at MSU I was drafted. Five days after I obtained my master's degree I was a private in the U.S. Army. I completed both basic and advanced infantry training and it took a great deal of effort and luck to obtain a military occupation specialty—a "social work–psychology specialist"—related to my graduate training. I spent a year at Fort Polk in Louisiana doing therapy, assessments and consultation outreach. The clinical experience was valuable; the setting depressing.

I then spent 9 months in Vietnam attached to two different infantry divisions, where I worked in mental health clinics at their base camps. I had to decide if soldiers, after complaining they "could not take it anymore," were returned to the field or removed from combat situations. I had to make the same decisions for soldiers who had experienced prolonged combat and/or traumatic events who stated that they were "fine" when in fact their abilities to do their jobs had eroded. I also ran a drug treatment program and did crisis work with issues ranging from deaths in the family back home to "Dear John" letters. I was almost killed once: talking a U.S. soldier out of a locked and loaded M-16. He was angry with his psychiatrist and found me, instead, at the clinic. The military taught me the critical importance of being empathetic with clients and understanding how they live.

I was confused when I returned to MSU, but I was open to change. When the automatic coping mechanisms that kept me going in the military were no longer functioning, I fell apart. But my growth continued. Clinical practica, and faculty and peers, gently prodded me, and I finally had the courage to begin my own psychotherapy. I was accepted for local clinical internships and worked with expert clinical supervisors. After the military, hard work was relative; the coursework was easy compared to Vietnam. With my dissertation nearly done, I needed a job. Fate intervened.

At that time, the job market was extremely tight. I declined an offer of a position at a maximum security prison in Wisconsin. This was not the work I wanted to do. In the spring of 1974, my major professor asked if I wanted to apply for a temporary assignment at MSU. Three faculty were going on sabbatical and the department needed a teacher and clinical supervisor. I jumped at the chance. (I may be one of the few clinicians in the country ever to have an "academic" postdoctoral experience.) For a year I taught and wrote. I had one committee assignment and was protected from the politics of academe. I loved the work! My office, which I still remember fondly, had high ceilings and several bookcases and tables. I could leave manuscripts, stacks of books, and papers lying around for convenient perusal. The importance of having one's ideas out in plain sight cannot be overemphasized.

I learned more in that first year of my professional life than in any year that was to follow. I started to learn how to teach. My first course was an undergraduate summer school class in abnormal psychology with 150 students. I was to teach abnormal again, do clinical supervision of graduate students, and teach an applied undergraduate practica for seniors (which I will teach again next year for the first time in 20 years).

I wrote. The interest in ideas was internal and compelling. I did not do data-based research, but wrote several descriptive manuscripts.

The year went by far too quickly and I needed to find another job. At least I knew what kind of job I wanted—to be an academician. I wanted a job in a doctoral institution such as MSU, but the job market was still tight. I found a job at a regional university—University of Wisconsin Oshkosh; it offered the graduate program and graduate teaching I wanted.

Leaving MSU was one of the most painful experiences in my life. Michigan State and East Lansing had become my home. I left fond memories, good friends and a gorgeous campus. Should I have left? I do not know. Had I stayed, I probably would not be an academician. I probably would have worked as a clinician in an area mental health center, established a private psychotherapy and clinical consulting practice, and done ad hoc teaching for MSU and other educational institutions. I will never know if I made the right choice.

The Early Years at UWO, 1975–1979

I began at UWO in September 1975; my salary was $14,300, and I was ecstatic to have a job. I was graduate coordinator and director of clinical training. I had no experience with the terminal master's degree in psychology and had never talked with anyone who had training in such a program.

I have kept my yearly schedule books since 1975 and reread them for the first time when I began writing about my academic life. I am flabbergasted at those first few years. There was so much to do and learn.

Academe was a cacophony of students; ideas; teaching assignments; service to the department and university; developing courses, fine- tuning them, tearing them apart; learning and more learning. This was a time of doing, not of quiet academic contemplation. I taught three courses per semester and received release time for my administrative work. I developed four graduate courses in my first year. In my first 2 years at UWO I served on 13 thesis committees, chairing 9, for which I received no teaching credit. This was before the days of personal computers, and all the administrative correspondence was done by typewriter. I loved all of it.

My MSU experience served me well in all aspects but one. At MSU I had done conceptual writing but no databased research; now I had to develop a research program and publish to earn tenure. But hard work and luck often go hand in hand. My interest in job satisfaction in mental health work settings dovetailed with the interests and expertise of a recently hired colleague. In 1979, Al Hartman and I received a $168,000, 3-year, National Institute of Mental Health (NIMH) research grant to study rural mental health administrators. It was one of the largest research grants ever awarded to the university.

In 1979, just 4 years after I came to UWO, three major threads were being interwoven that would carry me to 1986 and beyond: the rural administrator grant, work in a terminal master's program with clinical training, and faculty development.

UWO is different from a first-tier research or land grant doctoral institution in many ways. With its roots as a teachers' college, it struggles to develop an intellectual climate. Compared with many campuses I have been on and heard about, it is physically less attractive. The physical plant and grounds do not sustain one in day-to-day work, nor are there any symbols (no statue of Sparty like at MSU, no laboratory where a Nobel or other prize was won, etc.) to do so. Yet it is small enough so that one can make a difference, if one so strives. My forum was a nascent universitywide faculty development program.

Teaching is urgent on a campus. Students must be taught and classes must be held; these basic activities provide the visible fabric of the university. But for many faculty the pursuit of ideas is vital. In its transition from a small teachers' college to a regional university, UWO developed a faculty development program to support scholarship and administered by the faculty. One year after I came to UWO, Graduate Dean Betty Fitzgerald, who had worked at MSU, asked me to be her representative on this board. I agreed, not knowing what this meant for me.

The Early Years Continue, 1979–1986

In 1979, with 3 years of service on the UWO Faculty Development Board behind me, I began work on the NIMH grant. This point marked the beginning of my academic work in earnest. These years (1979–1986) make up a distinct chapter in my academic life. The grant provided relationships and experiences that endure. For example, this chapter grew out of my 1979 grant-related correspondence with the editor of this book. Al and I traveled to three states to interview 312 mental health administrators. We presented papers at every rural mental health and rural psychology forum in the country. We wrote a second grant proposal in 1982; it was more substantive and based on the first, and was accepted but not funded because federal grant monies had decreased in this area of mental health. We published journal articles and analyzed data for several more years, but we never wrote a book based on our grant research, nor did we seriously consider developing a consulting business to assist mental health administrators. Either course of action would have been a logical next step, either decision would have sent us in a new direction. Al and I probably know as much about rural mental health administration and work today as anyone in the country. Work on that grant taught me that I engaged in scholarship because I enjoyed pursuing ideas, and getting to meet and know people. These provide the real satisfaction and give meaning to my work.

Regional universities usually focus more on teaching than tier one campuses. While doing the grant work, I taught two courses each semester and continued with extensive service to UWO. The time and culture did not support my becoming an academic cosmopolitan. I had no role models among colleagues at UWO such as I had at MSU: persons off campus spending a great deal of time active in national organizations. I was a local who wanted to be a cosmopolitan, a tension that I have never resolved.

The grant provided me with an opportunity for scholarship, and in 1982 I was awarded tenure. I had been anxious about obtaining tenure for years but once I had earned it, I found myself working harder instead of slowing down. I could now do what I chose; tenure provided a sense of freedom.

The other two threads in my academic life continued to influence me. I began a second research program to understand terminal clinical master's training. I felt uncomfortable recruiting students and asking them to commit to a training program and career that I did not understand. I undertook a series of research projects about the terminal master's clinical degree, and, in doing so, became a national expert in this area of training. The data supported the worth and work of our students and I felt comfortable in doing this graduate training.

The third thread in these years was faculty development. Doing this work fulfilled many of my needs. The Faculty Development Board elicited and reviewed faculty proposals for work on and off campus in research/scholarship and teaching; being on this board allowed me to champion faculty and help them gain support for their work. I had a marvelous teacher in administration at UWO, Jim Gueths, the best administrator with whom I have ever worked; I also worked with colleagues I respected and liked from all areas of the university.

When Jim left the board to pursue other administrative responsibilities at UWO, I became the first faculty chair to serve without his guidance. The board had a budget of $400,000, more discretionary money than all five academic deans on campus had at their disposal. For 3½ years I chaired the board, taught half time, and continued my research. In 1986, after 10 years of service, I decided it was time to move on and resigned from the board. I did not know what would provide focus and meaning for me in the future. As fate would have it, as one door closed, another opened.

I had worked in academia for 11 years, 10 of them at UWO. I had tenure, was a full professor, and had been awarded a prestigious Rosebush Professorship in recognition of my teaching and scholarship. I was keenly committed to graduate training and felt a deep sense of loss in leaving faculty development.

1986–1994

What was I to do once my formal role with faculty development had ended? I felt a need to understand what I had devoted my life to for a decade. It seemed to involve helping faculty be entrepreneurs; their new products were ideas and scholarly projects. Jim Gueths and Don Weber, the university grants office and a friend who had been on the board for years, and I wrote a prospectus and eventually published a book titled *The Academic Intrapreneur*.

My belief in organizational structure, culture, and leadership making a difference for organizational members grew out of the work I had done with faculty development. I wrote a text on *Organizational Entrepreneurship* with a colleague and a friend in the College of Business, Jeff Cornwall. These two books were written over a 3- year period. I arose at 4 a.m. and wrote until just before classes at 8 a.m. I had never immersed myself so totally in a set of ideas before. Both books made me enough money for a weekend vacation for my family, but I learned that unless one is lucky, books do not produce much income. I write because I have ideas I want to see clearly set down on paper.

One of the biggest challenges that faculty face is the use of time. Time is finite, and working on one project means other work or ideas go unexplored. The risks I took to write these two books were worthwhile. I have no regrets and continue to be proud of what we said and how well it was written. But in looking back, I know I also wrote the books because it was a way to fill time and to delay resolving who I was as an academician.

As the 1980s ended and the 1990s began, unconsciously and without planning nor strategy, I began to focus more on my teaching. Service to faculty development was now in the past. I understood the issues, the programs, and the nitty gritty of making it work, and I had worked through the sense of loss about leaving it.

I was less interested in researching terminal master's training. As fate would have it, my expertise was recognized and the recognition brought a sense of closure. I was asked to be the keynote speaker at a June 1990, national conference on Applied Master's Training in Psychology that was held at the University of Oklahoma. Four days at the conference allowed me to share my ideas and, most important, meet many people interested in and involved with applied master's training in psychology.

After 18 years of doing applied graduate work in psychology I was burning out and losing my focus. The difficult work of applied terminal master's training was becoming less attractive. Because of a limited number of training faculty I have been intensely involved for 18 years, devoting much summer time to students' theses. I have served on 77 thesis committees, yet UWO provides no teaching credit for thesis work. The program allows 2 years to educate students to become competent to work with clients. The amount that needs to be taught is enormous; the time is short. I was tired and wanted to change my academic work and have more time for myself.

At present, admissions to the graduate clinical emphasis are suspended pending a decisions on whether the training will be continued. The prospect of teaching only undergraduates appeals to me. It is time to move on.

An Average Day, Week, and Semester

Before I go further let me describe an average day, week, and semester, none of which has changed much over the years. The sentience of academic life for me has been the absence of "think houses," quiet places to be and contemplate. Time for thought and intellectual pursuits is hard won.

I am a morning person, so I am at work by 6:45 or 7 a.m.; if I want to reduce stress, I am here earlier. My office is located on a long corridor. I have no gatekeeper; anyone who wants my attention need only knock at my door. This physical arrangement makes it impossible to do sustained intellectual work on campus. By coming early I get an hour or more of quiet time before the hubbub begins. I use this time to write, or when I have an 8 a.m. class to go over the day's assignment and lecture notes. Sometimes I use a small desk lamp and lock my door so no one knows I am at work. A "Do Not Disturb" sign on my door has no effect on colleagues or students (it has been stolen at least twice). Each person coming to my door thinks he or she is the only person asking for a few minutes of my time that day. During my first few years of working I had nightmares of being on vacation and having a student walk up to me and say, "It will only take a few minutes, can I talk with you?"

Perhaps this inability to hide is a characteristic of a regional university. At Michigan State, some faculty had two offices: one for regular work, and one, whose existence they did not disclose, for scholarship. They had "think houses"; I do not.

Three days a week I usually have two morning classes along with office hours. Because I see the graduate students in our clinical program by appointment, I usually see undergraduates from introductory psychology or abnormal psychology courses during office hours. One day a week I devote 3 or 4 hours to supervising graduate clinical psychodiagnostic work and psychotherapy.

Usually I teach introductory psychology in a large (225 students) section. The challenge of teaching large classes is even more difficult by an inadequate sound system and poor acoustics. When I do not recognize students who tell me they had me as a teacher, I know they were in my introductory course.

By late morning I have taught two courses, held office hours and, if I have been lucky, had an hour's worth of focused productive time. At lunchtime I work out at the university gym or eat with colleagues. We talk about teaching, problems with students or lectures, current events, or department or university politics. Often I work through the lunch hour.

In the afternoon I consult with students about their theses or with colleagues on university or department business. When I am in my office, I am often interrupted by phone calls. I teach a night class one semester each year and I prepare for this during part of one afternoon a week.

An average day leaves little time for thinking. I take a full briefcase home each night to grade papers or exams, draft or edit a thesis proposal, read books, and develop lectures. On some days I am so busy I never have time for a single cup of tea. An academic life may appear orderly and smooth, but it is not. Unplanned work is the norm. The department can receive a request out of the blue for information on some topic important to the requestor. Seldom do my responses seem to have any bearing on my work, but the requests must be met.

One day a week I do some work as a practicing clinical psychologist. I have been a consultant to Wisconsin corrections facilities for years. I have spent a decade consulting at a maximum security prison built in the mid-1800s, the same facility in which I was offered a job in 1974. The clinical work improves my teaching and graduate supervision because it gives me a feeling for "doing" and keeps me in touch with what practitioners are thinking, doing, and reading, and the problems they face.

I try to keep two afternoons a week relatively free. Sometimes I use these afternoons to write and explore ideas, both vital pursuits for me. On other days I give up any hope of control and face what comes my way. These days are actually the most fun because there is no conflict between my goals and what the world brings to my office door.

The weeks turn into semesters. In a 14-week semester, I will spend about 125 hours in the classroom, 50 to 60 hours holding office hours, 100 hours or more on scholarship, and anywhere from 30 to 60 hours on department or university business. My past schedule books show there is an unforseen demand or crisis about once each week. I feel stress when I get 2 weeks or 2 months behind in a project. I feel a sense of loss when I am 2 years behind in starting an area of reading or scholarship. There are simply too many opportunities and not enough time to pursue them all.

There are probably five highlights each semester. These can be a lecture which captures the students' attention and was "perfect," a note from a former student, or a piece of writing with which I am pleased.

How Academia Has Affected Me—Some Musings

Academia has given me interesting perspectives on time and work. First, my new year begins with each new fall semester, not January 1. Second, I do not teach in the summer, but I use relatively little of this time for myself. I have not managed this part of my job well. There is always something to do, sometimes a great deal. The 3-month summer vacation for faculty is a myth. It is, however, true that I can develop my own schedule; in summers I often work from 6 a.m. until 2 p.m., freeing up late afternoons and evenings.

Third, because I am a clinical psychologist and have applied, full-time job opportunities, I have sacrificed income. But time with my family and working in a university compensate for this loss of income. I am an academician first, a clinician second. Fourth, university employment is the most intrinsically satisfying work I have ever known.

My work in academia has been a mixed blessing for my family. I have never missed an important event in either of my sons' lives because of work. On the other hand, the full briefcase each night and frequent weekend work throughout the academic year makes me less available than I would like. That is one of the most interesting facets of working in a university. I choose almost all of what fills up my day. I decide to serve on thesis committees, do scholarship and service, work on my courses, and to be current and available, all of which keep me busy. I always bring work home, and sometimes it calls in a loud voice.

If I could go back to the beginning of my academic career knowing what I know now, I would value people and my time with them even more than I did, and I would be less task-oriented. Now, I take pleasure in the company of colleagues at a meeting, knowing that relationships are more important than the topic of the meeting.

Preparing for an Academic Life

If you are interested in pursuing an academic career I have a few suggestions about how to prepare for it. First, attend the best doctoral program that admits you. Second, as a graduate student, prepare for teaching by getting as much supervised experience as possible. Read books on teaching, think about teaching, and get some different teaching experiences. Regional universities have recently placed greater emphasis on scholarship, but teaching is still the heart of what we do. Teaching experience will be of great value when you apply for a job. Third, do not give up who you are. Wherever life takes you, whatever interests you, whatever you do will be useful in the classroom. The more life experiences you have, the more perspectives and depth you can bring to your chosen area of psychology. Next, look honestly at who you are and how you relate to other people. Teaching is an interpersonal enterprise. Ask yourself questions such as "Do I like people?" or "Do I like to be around people?" Last, expect to work hard.

The Present

My inner feelings about working in academia have changed over the years. Being a good teacher has increasing priority. I realize more than ever how lucky I am to be able to work with young people in a university setting. I also accept my role as a teaching faculty in a regional university; I no longer yearn to work in a doctoral program. My soul could still use some of the beauty and magic of a large campus or a small liberal arts school, but it will have to be fed in other ways.

I will probably work at UWO until I retire. The quality of life is good; my family has friends here. A regional university has its attractions: It is large enough to have a wide array of students and programs, small enough that doctoral faculty teach almost all classes. What faculty do at institutions such as UWO set the standard for the value of a college education throughout the country.

But no academic setting is perfect. UWO seldom suffers serious budget cuts, but it seldom seems to move forward. It struggles for symbols of an intellectual climate. Money is difficult to obtain for equipment; we are on the cutting edge of little. Educational and administrative fads come and go; all take time, almost none make a difference. We are at the mercy of legislative bodies and Regents with political aspirations and mind-sets. At times I long to work in a Lawrence University or a Michigan State. But although the grass may be greener, the truth is that I can do my work here.

As I write this chapter, I am on sabbatical, a time of reflection and renewal. I will be doing more undergraduate teaching when I return from my leave and do not regret giving up involvement with graduate clinical teaching. I am spending my sabbatical reading about psychology and thinking about how I want to teach my classes. I feel refreshed after attending a national conference on teaching.

A second focus for my sabbatical is the new teacher. It is estimated that about 40% of university faculty will retire in the 1990s. As a senior faculty I feel a responsibility to mentor and teach new faculty about what it means to be an academician and how to teach. Teaching is a calling and I want my new colleagues to understand what this vocation means to me, and pass it on to them. I am in the beginning stages of another research program, this one looking at the new teacher from a variety of perspectives. I would like to establish a postdoctoral program in college teaching for psychologists to give others what I had at Michigan State years ago.

Who would have thought that I would look forward to undergraduate classes and to working with new teachers? In my academic life so much seems to have been unplanned and unexpected. Scholarship is difficult and time consuming, yet fascinating and fulfilling. Teaching is an act of faith; I seldom know the impact I have or even if I am reaching students. Yet it is one of the most satisfying and important endeavors I can imagine. I have had the opportunity to shape lives and influence how students ask questions and consider ideas. These two dimensions—working with others and the pursuit of knowledge—have sustained me for 20 years and I am confident, will continue to do so. Anyone with the opportunity to work in an academic setting is lucky.

Chapter 8

A Midcareer Perspective: Big City to Small University Town

Patricia Keith-Spiegel
Ball State University

> *In teaching, you must simply work your pupil into such a state of interest in what you are going to teach him that every other subject of attention is banished from his mind; then reveal it to him so impressively that he will remember the occasion to his dying day; and finally fill him with devouring curiosity to know what the next steps in connection with the subject are.*
>
> —William James (1899/1962)

James' description of how classroom time can be elevated to an agent of lifetime influence and impact, neatly penned and framed, sits atop my personal computer. Although he wrote it, and I read it, long before the term *nonsexist language* was a part of anybody's consciousness, I remain attracted to James' ideals. I was aware, even as an undergraduate, that every one of the teachers who had a profound impact on me did reach such a pinnacle—a magic 50-minute production that left me thinking, searching, or expanding my perspective—much of the time.

To this day I still tell, with great gusto, the best stories that my teachers told to me. And of the myriad of professorial duties, carefully crafting classroom presentations and activities has always been my favorite.

My Job According to My Father-in-Law

Trying to explain the job of "professoring" to those totally unfamiliar with higher education is a strenuous and sometimes near-futile exercise. My father-in-law provides the definitive example. "You work part time?" he inquired upon learning that my teaching load was 12 hours a week. "How much do we pay you?" he continued, when informed that in my state-supported institution, 12 teaching hours constitutes a full-time position. After disclosing my salary, he emitted a wheezy little gasp and asked if he had heard correctly about the 16 weeks of vacation time. I tried to explain that preparing lecture notes and exams, grading papers, participating in departmental and university governance and student activities, advising students, keeping up with the literature, and engaging in research and scholarly activity takes another 40 to 50 hours each week. He remained puzzled and, I suspect, unconvinced. "You write these articles, but they are so short," he muttered while thumbing a brief *American Psychologist* article. I described for him the data that took almost a year to collect and tried to explain how scientific writing is very concise and does not reflect the time and effort involved. "Well, how much did you sell this article for?" Another little fluttering sound emerged from somewhere deep in his throat when I told him that it was an honor to have one's work accepted into this journal and that no pay was involved. "Who would read this stuff anyway?" he snapped, "It's not even real English as far as I can tell."

My father-in-law is probably the best, single example of why some taxpayers are not overly sympathetic toward higher education. Although a good and very bright man, he did not pursue a formal education and cannot fathom the joy of scholarship and discovery, or the depth of the far-flung and varied responsibilities professors shoulder, including the services we give to our students and our society that extend well beyond the classroom. College-level teaching is an honorable profession, and although some may abuse its unique privileges and freedoms, most take their calling seriously and dedicate the lion's share of their waking hours to it.

I feel blessed to have been offered, during my midcareer years, a position of the sort I hope becomes more and more available across the country. I am in my fourth year at Ball State University in Indiana, where my title is Reed D. Voran Honors Distinguished Professor of Social and Behavioral Sciences. This is one of a growing number of distinguished professorships being created at my university as concrete testimony of a commitment to, and generous financial support of, quality teaching. Research productivity has traditionally been the standard of prestige and excellence. How one was with students, how one enjoyed teaching students, faded into the background. I hope that the trend I am witnessing at Ball State and elsewhere, indicating a surge of recognition of the importance of the teaching component of the teacher–scholar model, continues to proliferate.

What is especially encouraging about my position, and most of the other similar ones at Ball State, is that the endowments come from local civic and business leaders: town and gown holding hands. Reed Voran, still very much alive, is a brilliant and congenial senior partner in the city's most prestigious law firm. His colleagues contributed to the position I hold as an honor to him.

Early Glimmers Pointing Toward a University Teaching Career

With so much of my current scholarship focused on professional ethics and standards of conduct, it is with a twinge of embarrassment that I confess that, as a child, I consistently disobeyed one of my mother's strictest rules. Despite a nightly attempt to talk her out of the 8 p.m. bedtime hour, which would have allowed me to continue reading a book, I never once succeeded at it. No real problem. The large flashlight, purchased on the sly with hoarded allowance, shed reasonable illumination under the blankets. I used to daydream about someday having a job that paid me to read what interested me. It still seems a marvel that such a career actually exists.

I, and most teaching colleagues with whom I have discussed the matter, loved school from the first day of kindergarten on. Most of us were also fortunate enough to have experienced a number of excellent teachers along the way who helped us cultivate visions of ourselves as potential educators.

As a freshman at Occidental College, I took the introductory psychology course during the "snooze" hour right after lunch. Irwin Mahler, a Stanford-trained experimental psychologist, was an intense professor who glowered at each of us, in turn, as he paced back and forth in front of the class. This technique (or simply personal style, I was never quite sure which) kept us clearly focused and in the moment, but I found that what was going on kept me gladly awake.

A remarkable thing happened one day, and I am sure Dr. Mahler would not himself have remembered it even within hours of its occurrence. He posed a question to the class, and I answered it to his satisfaction. I have no recollection of what the question was, but I remember his response as if it happened 10 minutes ago. He ambled right up to me, bent over into my face, and boomed out, "Are you a freshman?" I meekly responded in the affirmative. "That's really incredible," he announced to the rest of the class while righting himself. "I didn't think a freshman could offer such a fine response. Very good, young woman." He was smiling.

I realized for the first time how powerful even small encouragements from a professor could be. It is an economical way to lift spirits, stretch goals upward, and shoo dreams toward realities.

The only problem I had with my undergraduate psychology career was that I was fascinated with almost every aspect of the field. I had noticed that many professors spent their entire lives delving into one thing. I knew in my heart that I would not be able to do that. This caused a considerable dilemma when it came time to select a graduate program. I did not have a favorite area in which to specialize, and taking a year or two off to "find my niche" held no appeal. I decided to hedge my bets by applying to schools that offered a "general" experimental program.

Making the Decision to Become a Professor

The constant availability of mentors during the undergraduate years was perhaps the single most important factor that influenced my desire to teach. Upper division students who were doing well at Occidental College were informally courted into a daily 3 p.m. coffee/discussion group by three of the five full-time faculty. Although professional boundaries were maintained, this activity provided the opportunity to "feel" the lifestyle of the college professor. We learned that we would not become wealthy in a monetary sense, but that we could have the time and the freedom to explore knowledge and would be able to actually contribute to it as well. (Because Occidental is a small, liberal arts teaching institution, I did not yet realize that I might be required to "contribute to knowledge," whether I wanted to or not.)

All of these men had families, and they appeared to have time to be with them. Summers were often spent travelling (with the whole family) to some intriguing setting, usually partially supplemented by lecturing or consulting appointments. (As an aside, I was later to enjoy that perk as well. For example, I took a terrific Alaskan cruise for the "price" of teaching a class during the mornings while we were so far away from land that there was nothing to see anyway.) Mostly, my professors seemed fulfilled and satisfied with their lives. They laughed easily, argued controversial issues with great gusto, and appeared to genuinely like teaching us as well as our company. The only thing that was missing for me was a professorial model I could more directly identify with—a woman. I did have Lisa Gray-Shellberg, my good college friend, with whom I mused over the future. We talked about teaching, how it might be fun and rewarding, although we did not know any female professors personally.

Lisa and I finally did get lucky in graduate school, only just barely. Our first and only female professor during our entire graduate academic career taught on an occasional, part-time basis at Claremont Graduate School. Margaret Faust, a Stanford-trained developmental psychologist, was a dynamic, brilliant, competent, and caring teacher. She was the model of excellence and dedication that we few female graduate students desperately needed to help nurture our own identities as future professional women. Her title was something like "Visiting Instructor," even though she had been at Scripps College for many years. Her status at that time, then, was so low that the other message we received was, "They'll let you do this, but you have to take what you get, and you don't get much." More than 30 years later, female role models in academia remain too far and few between, especially in senior positions at the more prestigious research universities.

Another very positive role model in graduate school was a young man who was the "super star" among advanced doctoral students. Already an active researcher, he taught a number of classes to the first- and second-year students. Gene ("Jim") Sackett, currently at the University of Washington, was only 3 years older than the members of my class. But he was such a good lecturer, so animated and amusing, and so willing to stick around after class until we "got it," that we admired him as a teacher while also accepting him as a peer. He lavished both criticism and praise.

When admonished, we were not abandoned. I recall sitting at one of those old, bulky, electric calculators doing analyses of variance, summing squares one at a time, with Jim right there every step of the way. His praise was glorious and inspiring. Good work was rewarded. My first publication credit was a *Science* article; a junior authorship for dedicated equipment construction, literature review-ing, and rat-running. When Sackett left to work in Harry Harlow's primate labora-tory at the University of Wisconsin, Lisa and I baked him a giant cake in the shape of a Macaque monkey.

It was clear during the second year of graduate training that I wanted to teach. I took as many courses in as many different areas as I could, and still could not find one I liked better than another. Oddly, my professors were not as supportive of the decision to be primarily a teacher as I had expected. For them, to specialize and focus one's career in research, while holding a position as a professor at a research university (but not doing much undergraduate teaching) was what they wanted for their graduates. I pondered that fate yet again, dedicating my life to the study of one thing, and again it came up way short. I would always love doing research, but my broad interests likely meant that shifts would occur periodically. And then there were those undergraduate students. I wanted to be around them, to expose them to this field that had given me so much joy, and to help them partake of its enchant-ment. It did not matter that they may never major in psychology. I felt there was much that even a single psychology course could give to them.

In order to do both teaching and research, I was attracted to the "comprehensive university" as a target work site. These often large, state-funded schools espouse that professors are paid to teach and that good teaching is important, but they must also produce scholarly work to be retained and promoted through the ranks. This model is not without drawbacks—primarily relatively high teaching loads and limited support for research—but it still seemed my best bet. I had friends at small liberal arts colleges, and most of them were doing no research. Friends (not tenured at that time) at the research universities were mostly unhappy with the pressure and competition for resources and tenure slots and described teaching undergraduates as an inconvenience.

The First Teaching Job

As a new bride, my career site was geographically limited to Los Angeles County. My husband's career was well established and resistant to relocation. I was exhilarated to see an advertisement sporting five openings at San Fernando Valley State College, soon to become California State University, Northridge (CSUN). I was concerned, however, that my chances of being offered a position were slim because I had no teaching experience and had not yet completed my dissertation. What I did have, however, was a strong research record. I had been working at the Veterans Administration Hospital in West Los Angeles as a research assistant during that "lean period" between finishing the doctoral dissertation and getting a career-path job. I had been heavily involved in the projects of several research psychologists and psychiatrists and was also allowed to conduct independent research. These efforts resulted in several more journal publications and a number of presentations at professional meetings. I had no idea at the time that research achievements would dwarf the other rickety features of my vita. I had mistakenly assumed that teachers were hired first and foremost for ability to teach.

An invitation to appear for an interview arrived shortly after submitting my materials. The huge campus was located in the extreme northwest sector of the San Fernando Valley, sprawling for miles in every direction and baking in the California sunshine. I found an affable and gracious group of about 35 full-time faculty members awaiting me for lunch. The interview that followed was actually fun. They had seen some of the cartoons I had drawn for the *Worm Runner's Digest* (the brain child of another of my role models, the late James V. McConnell at the University of Michigan). We chatted extensively about the psychology of humor and my doctoral dissertation, which was in progress, on humor sense and the expression of anger. I hoped that the CSUN psychologists would want me to become one of them during the drive home. The phone was ringing as I entered the house. It was the department chair offering me the position and asking if I had any questions. I accepted without further inquiry.

I was to remain at CSUN for 25 years. The job was what one could make of it. Resources were always scarce. The most difficult feature of the position, for me anyway, was that one got into a niche of teaching the same one or two courses over and over again, often in multiple sections. My teaching specialty was developmental psychology and its attendant laboratory, research techniques in developmental psychology. Although I liked the area, when one has to give the same presentation up to three times in a week, something inside begins to melt down. I wondered how actors could do the same play month after month, and still seem fresh and passionate with each performance. I was to realize much later that although the appearance of passion can be mastered, it is not, in the long run, in the best interests of the performer.

The students, however, were (almost) always a joy, and they provided the variety and satisfaction that kept teaching exciting. California students were fun. They tended to be inquisitive, no nonsense, energetic, and charmingly audacious, more than enough to keep me on fire and hopping.

Because of the high teaching load, however, conducting research was a challenge. We did not receive much research support, so I was to deeply appreciate my graduate school training that taught us, through necessity, to rely heavily on a tiny budget and a big splash of creativity. At Claremont we made our own equipment from scratch with scraps. My heart went out to some of my CSUN colleagues who came from well-funded laboratory training backgrounds. They seemed rather lost and foiled.

I also enjoyed participating in professional psychology organizations. I found the annual meetings to be the fast track to new knowledge, and also realized that being part of the governance of these organizations was a way to expand one's contacts significantly beyond one's own campus. I became active in the state, regional, and national psychology organizations in a wide variety of positions from committee chair (e.g., American Psychological Association [APA] Ethics Committee) to president (e.g., Western Psychological Association). These organizations are as subject to the craziness of political folly as any other grouping of two or more people, but as long as I felt I was doing something positive in whatever position I held, especially if it would enhance teaching (mine or others'), I stayed involved. I am currently the executive director of the Office of Teaching Resources in Psychology, housed at Ball State University and sponsored by the APA's Division of Teaching Psychology.

On Being a Wife, Mother, and Professor

Growing up in the 1940s and 1950s provided young girls with a vision of our futures that considered neither the exercise of intelligence nor serious career planning. "If you must have a profession," my adult family members would say, "teach elementary school like your mother." I considered that, briefly. The idea of fostering the development of younger people was extremely appealing. Yet I had a view of public school teachers, with their overcrowded classes and no support staff, that was hidden from most others. I was the one who greeted a frazzled woman who walked though the door every evening piled with wide-lined papers scrawled with large, wobbly, words of no more than two syllables and often spelled incorrectly. She would spend evenings with these primitive papers, an underutilization of a very bright woman's talents and time, I thought at the time. Bumping up into the higher grades might be more stimulating, but recollections of my own junior high and high school years, and an attempt to empathize from the perspective of my teachers, revealed another variety of horrors.

When I considered the college level, things began to feel much better. A competent, caring professor was given respect. The occasional dolt could simply be asked to leave the classroom if decorum could not be maintained.

I attained maturity at an interesting time. The term *women's liberation movement* was becoming a household word, although often used as a pejorative. I had already bought the "American Dream" of a husband, house, and kids. Yet this new rhetoric, which I boiled down to read "You can do anything you want and are able to do regardless of your plumbing," was exciting. I wanted a piece of this fetching option as well.

The way to be both a career woman and homemaker, simultaneously, was through college-level teaching. Hours could (usually) be finagled to accommodate grade school children's schedules. Vacations and holidays (usually) corresponded. With two salaries, there was enough money to arrange for some of the "traditional women's jobs" to be performed by others. Did this grand scheme work? Mostly, yes. But writing and other teaching-related duties often had to be done after everyone else was in bed. I often envied them because I, too, was tired.

The Great Job: The Move to "Big 10 Country"

Los Angeles was all I ever knew. Diverse, exciting, glitzy, crowded, dangerous. I was born there and it never occurred to me that I might not be buried there. But my husband and I found ourselves getting out of the metropolitan area, if only into the nearby mountains or deserts for a weekend, more and more often. We found ourselves musing about how life might be in a smaller town.

One day, as I walked from the university parking lot to my office with a luggage carrier stacked with papers and books trailing behind me, I had a powerful feeling about doing too much "repeating" in my life. Same two courses. Same walk with the overloaded luggage carrier. Over and over. I could not figure out how I could shake things up, and guessed that I probably did not know how. Funding had become so paltry that we were now dipping into our own pockets for duplicating any handouts other than exams. "Student assistant" was an anachronism. Departmental morale was dragging on the floor, and within 2 years, the bottom was to drop completely out of California's economy.

If it ever got to the place where teaching was not energizing I vowed that I would not inflict myself upon students, even if I had to wait on the tables of others to put food on my own. But the students were not the problem, and I was too young, still bristling with energy, and hardly ready to retire. On the contrary, our children were grown and time to focus on my own career was more abundant than it had ever been before.

Then two events occurred. I was elected president of the APA's Division of Teaching Psychology, and I won the "Trustee's Outstanding Professors Award," a statewide competition, cutting across academic disciplines and all 19 campuses of the California State University system. Although I had been publishing research and books, and had been very active in professional organizations, these two achievements, occurring around the same time, gave my career "longer legs" to move with.

I took to browsing through the *APA Monitor* and the *American Psychological Society Observer*, not really expecting to find much of anything exciting for a middle-aged academic who loved to teach and had been a tenured full professor since 1973. The lists were, indeed, dominated by openings for postdoctoral, temporary, part-time, and assistant professor positions.

In December 1991, however, an ad grabbed my attention immediately. A national search was underway to fill a senior-level distinguished professorship. The best part was that the successful candidate was required to have a demonstrated interest in undergraduate students and undergraduate teaching. I quickly snipped out the ad and showed it to my husband.

Although we had visited many places around the globe, the midwest area of our own country was not among them. "Where exactly is Indiana?" my husband asked while staring at a map of the United States that we had spread out on the dining room table. "Somewhere in here," I responded as I made circles with my hand around the entire middle third of the country. We were to find out soon enough. I submitted an application letter and was invited for an interview. We both flew to Indianapolis and rented a car to drive the 1 hour of nonstop corn fields to the pleasant town of Muncie (population: 72,000).

We were both happy and relieved to quickly learn that the stereotypes Californians hold about the midwest are mostly preposterous. Farm animals are not kept in front yards. Autos on blocks are not in every driveway, and nonfunctioning kitchen appliances are not on everybody's front porch. Rather, beautiful, clean, pride-of-ownership homes on lush, tree-lined streets surrounded a huge, attractive, university complex (half old and traditional, and half new and sleek) with every state-of-the-art technology and service imaginable. The generosity of the Ball family (founders of the Ball Corporation) have provided, among many things, magnificent art collections including numerous "important pieces." Ball State University is higher education's best kept secret. After a 2-day, grueling interview schedule from dawn to late night, sprinkled with elegant dinners and parties, I left daring to feel optimistic. A few days later I was offered the position.

Although I was about to celebrate my 52nd birthday, I sensed a freshness unlike I had felt for almost three decades. Part of the high was a totally new lifestyle, one that was far more involving and intense because of the close community spirit. But much of it was the difference in the mission of the institution. CSUN was one of many campuses, and the game was to remain functional and to scramble for (and then try to hang onto) as many resources as possible. Ball State University, although state supported, stood by itself, and the administration had a vision of excellence and the goal of being known as "the premier teaching institution." Whether such a status can ever be reached by some operationally defined method is irrelevant. What counts is that the campus is on a dynamic pathway, moving forward, and trying new things. Faculty are encouraged to engage in inventive projects, and internal support for such innovations is considerable. The only passion I have not yet kindled is basketball. I am working on that.

A typical semester at Ball State University provides a busy but pleasant variety of academic tasks, scholarly activity, and continuing education opportunities. Each day I walk the block from my new home to my office, past a lovely woods overseen by the Biology Department. This is an exceptionally delightful experience after 25 years of battling back-to-back and belly-to-belly traffic. I decided to take on the introductory class, held in an auditorium to accommodate 225 students, once each year. I had never taught a class this size before. (Whoever designed CSUN had, perhaps wisely, built all small classrooms save for two. My highest class census before coming to Ball State was 78.) I was now on a performance stage with a microphone, an 8' x 10' TV projection screen, and a huge blackboard that can be hoisted up the wall so that everyone can see. I feel like a "one woman show" and am still searching for ways to make more direct contact with students. I have special office hours just for these students. I am available by e-mail (all students at Ball State have user numbers for the VAX system and those without modems can easily locate terminals on campus) and have many high-tech "pen pals" who I would not recognize if I saw them. But it is far different from knowing all the names and faces in the more intimate classroom of 40 students. I am very ambivalent about classes of this size for students new to college life, but I am going to stick with the challenge of getting the hang of it.

I also teach an upper division course once each year entitled Child Experimental Psychology, with about 30 students. This is "the baby" that I had honed for years in California, a piece of cake that I update annually. The most invigorating aspect of my new job is the half-time appointment in the Honors College. Once each year

I teach remarkably bright students in a small, seminar session of my choosing. I developed a course entitled, Ethical Issues in Teaching and Academic Life for aspiring college-level teachers from the Honors College. The unusual feature of this class is that professors are also allowed to enroll, and although they do not take a final exam or hand in a project, they are expected to attend regularly and participate in the discussions ranging from the use of profanity in lectures to how to confront a student suspected of cheating. I have learned that students and professors often view ethical dilemmas and their resolutions differently, and these disparities were the bases of many an electrifying exchange!

The irony of receiving a distinguished teaching professorship is that one of the many "perks" is a lower teaching load! I teach one large or two small classes each semester. However, I am busier than ever with projects related to teaching and education. As examples, I chair a group that is writing the first academic ethics casebook. I created and oversee a graduate school peer advisement office, and am in the process of developing an educational "diversion" program for students who are first offenders of the academic integrity code.

The faculty is smaller (22) in my new department, and we have far fewer (about 700) majors, including graduate students. We all get along quite well, and most of my colleagues are in their offices all day most days of the week. We do most of our socializing, then, in each others' offices or over coffee or lunch. We collaborate on projects. Our after-hour friends, however, tend to be from other circles; usually the wider university community or church. At CSUN, cohesion was generally weak across the whole campus, perhaps because of the larger size in an ever larger community. There were 1,800 psychology majors in my old department, but only one third more faculty positions. Several of these positions were occupied by up to 20 part-time faculty teaching a course or two. Teaching loads were much higher, and faculty tended to disappear once their required duties were performed for the day. Faculty interaction patterns were just the opposite. We rarely interacted beyond quick pleasantries on campus, but subgroups formed close friendships for after-hour expression.

New Joys

University Town Living

Living in a university town often offers the kinds of advantages that the "academic personality" likes about the big city as well as the benefits of a smaller city. A university is a hub of cultural activity and schedules such events as foreign film festivals, musical productions and live theater, road shows and concerts featuring major entertainment personalities, lectures on a wide variety of topics, art shows, special topic "weeks" (women's week, Africa week, etc.), and other attractions (e.g., ethnic cooking demonstrations or antique car shows). The smallness of a smaller city, however, provides a sense of community and belonging, a feeling of safety and peacefulness, space to stretch, and a great place to raise children who won't get lost in the system. Those who want to walk more on the wild side after hours (e.g., trendy night spots or X-rated movies) or who don't want to drive an hour for a Thai dinner will be less content.

One fact that aspiring professors must understand is that salary offers should not be compared using absolute dollars. In some locales, including many smaller college towns such as Muncie, housing and some goods and services offer stupendous bargains.

Continuing Education

An agreement I made with myself since moving to Indiana—one I wish that I had made at the beginning of my teaching career—was to engage in at least one active educational activity (as opposed to passive reading) every week. That is, I would be the student, the recipient of knowledge or wisdom or skill-training. Ball State University has proven to be the perfect setting for fulfilling this pact. Every week there are several guest lectures or interactive teleconferences from which to select, ranging in topics from Bosnia to fractals. Every month mini-courses (one afternoon) are offered on computer applications or other high tech equipment operation. Last year, for example, I learned to take photographs on a floppy laser-disk camera. My "shows," 50 pictures programmed on a tiny disk you can hold in the palm of your hand, can be broadcast to my classroom using our fiber-optical Visual Information System. Although my little disk is a block away, I am in complete control of its viewing on a giant screen.

Almost every week at least one major speaker is brought in from somewhere else, and it is not difficult to wangle a meeting with that person. A rousing, storytelling, Thanksgiving dinner with Sir David Hunt (Winston Churchill's Secretary during World War II) is my favorite event of this sort to date.

Three Challenges

What is unattractive about being a college professor? Typically—after the initial, obligatory grumbling about too little pay and too-large classes, bureaucratic red tape, some inept administrators and colleagues, and students who don't care about learning—the answers must be dug from a deeper place and are more idiosyncratic among us.

Time Management

I suppose that the "time-activity boundary problem" has always been the most challenging problem for me. I have not satisfactorily solved it yet, perhaps because I am not sure an unravelling is possible when one's work has so many facets, and little inflexible routine. I could never get on any kind of schedule. Often I have to work through much of the weekend to meet a writing deadline, grade an exam, or finish a lecture. David Letterman (Ball State University's best known graduate, by the way) is a familiar background companion as I finish up the day's correspondence or make phone calls to the west coast. Sometimes I wake up at 4 a.m. with an idea that just can't wait. Then I'm upstairs at the computer for 3, maybe 4 hours. I take time out to relax, but those variable gaps make my days look like so many slices of Swiss cheese. I don't mind this, but if you asked my husband he would give you a different answer. Long ago we had to compromise. I do not work from dinnertime on Friday nights until noon on Saturday or on Saturday evenings. Ever. Those time slots are sacred. This is not to say that there are not additional opportunities for partner, family and friends. They are just a little trickier to plan in advance.

Student Variability

About 15% of the 225 students in the introductory psychology do not belong in an institution of higher education, at least not at this time. Another 15% are marginal and will not likely make it through a degree program unless substantial changes in attitude or study habits ensue.

So goes the dilemma of teaching in a comprehensive university. At whom does one aim? Students at each end of the pole, and everyone in between, have needs that cannot be met simultaneously. Fortunately, Ball State has many programs for the less able students. I send many students to "University College," a positive, nonstigmatizing label for remedial programs, special tutoring, and advisement. I try to spot and encourage the best and the brightest, and our Honors College has a fine program for them. The ones in the middle, then, are probably the most comfortable with what we pitch, yet we are never fully comfortable with the compromise.

Book Writing

Contrary to popular assumption, academic book writing is not highly rewarded by most institutions. Using merit salary criteria (a commonly used system of financially rewarding productive faculty), senior authorship on a modest research report taking 3 months to run and prepare is worth the same as a 600-page scholarly book that took 5 years to write. Nevertheless, I like to write books. Gathering up literature scattered far and wide, adding in some of my own data and ideas, and organizing and integrating it into a single product caught between two covers is fun for me, despite its requirements to be solitary for several hours a day.

I cannot write one right after the other as some academics do. I would be too lonely. But one every 3 or 4 years works for me. The real thrill is when a book catches on, becomes widely known and used, and appears to have made a positive impact. My ethics textbook, co-authored with Gerald Koocher at Harvard (Keith-Spiegel & Koocher, 1985), reached that level and is currently in revision.

Aspiring academic book writers must also be warned, early on, that this avocation must be motivated by other than the lure of financial gain. Save for the writers of successful, many-times-and-often-revised textbooks for large enrollment undergraduate classes, scholarly book authors could probably have made more money, on an hour-for-hour basis, scrubbing floors! You have to love the process of book writing for itself.

A Final Comment

The discovery of proper balances—between giving to others and getting back, creating and relishing with awe the creativity of others, keeping the fire burning hot without burning out—must be mastered by the veteran academic to remain valued by oneself as well as others. Most of all, the spirit of inquiry and exploration must remain challenged. Christopher Morley is credited with a wise saying: "There is only one success—to be able to spend your life in your own way." College-level teaching in my path to that kind of success, and I anticipate the next turn, and the turn after that.

References

James, W. (1962). *Talks to teachers on psychology*. New York: Dover. (Original work published 1899)
Keith-Spiegel, P., & Koocher, G. P. (1985). *Ethics in Psychology: Standards and cases*. New York: Random House.

Chapter 9

Of People, Places, and Trees: A Varied Career in Counseling Psychology

Ursula Delworth
The University of Iowa

Writing this chapter in my later years as a psychologist presents an intriguing opportunity to reflect upon my 24 years as a doctoral-level psychologist, as well as my earlier careers in teaching, counseling, social work, and school psychology. Since 1984, I have been a professor in a doctoral program in counseling psychology at The University of Iowa. Prior to that, I held a number of service, administrative, and academic positions. I have played a broad range of roles in the profession, yet see four connecting threads of lifelong interests that have somehow held the fabric of my career together.

My first interest was differences in culture or context. Growing up as the child of a U.S. Navy officer, constant moving and adjustment gave me a rare opportunity to be a part of a number of cultures—ethnically, linguistically, and academically. For example, I started first grade in Hawaii, where my classmates represented a diversity of ethnic groups, and all instruction was in French. I learned to view myself in a relative, or "cross-sectional" sense. That is, in some schools I would be one of the top scholars; in others only good average. Thus, my academic self-concept was something like "I am a good to excellent student, depending." I enjoyed this variety and view my peers as well as myself in this nonfixed, more relative way. I developed skills in entering new environments and situations, sizing them up, and adapting quickly. Along the way I also learned a good deal about various cultures, groups, and "ways of being."

My second interest was spurred by a void. Although I could understand cross-sectional development (all of us at this place in time), I experienced a real hunger to understand how one individual (first me, then others) grew and developed. Was there a pattern? Stages? Would my second grade "best friend" still be someone I would like in high school? I explored this interest through literature, preferring books that told stories of individuals' growth to adulthood. Human development, I decided, was an exceptionally interesting subject.

A third interest was writing. Both my parents wrote well and encouraged this interest. It seems I always wrote. As a child I produced stories for my family. As an adolescent, I wrote essays, both for school assignments and for various contests (that I often won!). As an undergraduate, I worked on college newspapers. In my senior year, I edited the weekly *Forty-Niner* at California State University, Long Beach.

A final prevailing interest was in leadership and group activities. My parents were involved in many community activities, especially during my adolescence, so I had a firsthand view of how people, working together, could accomplish positive results. During my undergraduate years, I became active in student government, held a number of organizational offices, and developed skills in working with, and leading, somewhat diverse groups. All of these interests remained alive, in varying degrees, through my early careers, although it has been in my work as a doctoral-level psychologist that they have contributed most strongly to the roles I have played. My undergraduate years set the stage, because it was then that I had the opportunity to "try out" the interests, especially in writing and leadership. I also came to know a group of more diverse peers; friends who varied in ethnicity and age. And I began to understand our development as we moved through the undergraduate years.

Early Career Experiences

My interests, however, did not immediately determine my career. My parents had strong interests in politics and international relations, and this translated for me into a major in political science. My skills in memorizing and debating led toward law school. Unfortunately, in the 1950s there were no student loan programs, and it became clear I would have to earn money if I wanted to go to law school. The one very open profession at that time was elementary school teaching. I took classes to meet credential requirements and began what would add up to 8 years teaching fifth and sixth graders.

I started teaching with few skills and little understanding of what I was getting into. My curiosity and energy, plus my interest in various cultural groups, saved the day. I eventually became a very good teacher. With law school still a goal, I began to take some graduate classes at night in order to better understand my students. I was drawn to counseling and human development courses, enjoying the opportunity to explore many facets of individual growth. Impelled by interests rather than career plans, I completed a master's degree plus work for school counseling and school psychologist credentials at California State University, Los

Angeles. I also found employment as a secondary school counselor in a small school district with a culturally diverse population. Visions of law school were receding, and I began to think of myself as "settled" in a career. I had a satisfying (although somewhat exhausting!) position in the schools, good friends and enjoyable hobbies, and part-time jobs involved with multicultural programs for adolescents.

On to Doctoral Training

I might still be a school counselor had not several psychologist mentors from my masters' program kept urging me to explore doctoral programs. The idea of being fully qualified to deal with the numerous problems that my adolescents faced was very appealing. I began to think seriously of a doctorate in clinical psychology. One of my mentors suggested that I consider counseling psychology instead. She felt the training in counseling programs would be a better match with my interests in practice instead of research, and with my interests in development. I knew little about counseling psychology as a field, remembering only that an undergraduate student advisor had left his position to study for a doctorate in this specialty. By now, law school was no longer a goal, I liked the idea of going to school full time, and of being much better prepared to help. Although I had done well in the master's program, doctoral studies loomed as much more demanding. I dealt with my anxieties by telling myself that I did not have to complete the doctorate degree. I could just take classes, learn a good deal, and have some "time out" from a truly busy job. Thus convinced, I applied to three west coast counseling doctoral programs, was accepted by two, and chose to go to the University of Oregon. This decision was made because Oregon sent me a telegram of admission—my first telegram! Although that was far from the best way to decide on a doctoral program, it worked out well.

Actually, I was better prepared for doctoral training than I had expected. My master's program had been a rigorous one, and I had completed a number of additional classes, some of which fulfilled doctoral requirements. I enjoyed most of the doctoral classes, and did well. But the practice work was my real joy. My internship was very different from the full-time, year-long structured experience that is the current model. Although I accumulated the necessary 2,000 hours, I did so in three very different settings.

First, I spent a semester at a Veterans Administration (VA) hospital, performing the usual testing and therapy work that prior clinical psychology students had done. As the first two counseling interns, however, my fellow trainee and I pioneered services that were more in line with our identity in counseling psychology. For example, we helped several of the younger veterans enroll at the local community college, and worked with them on course selection and requirements. We organized social events, including picnics and basketball games, for the men on the "exit unit." This was a unit where the men lived more independently and held jobs away from the hospital. We were able to counsel them on job-related issues, and also help them deal with concerns about re-entering their families and communities. We also took the opportunity to explore a role common for health psychologists today—consulting with physicians on the general medical ward regarding psychological problems. I learned a great deal at the VA and especially came to appreciate the work and wisdom of many of the aides who carried out the day-to-day treatment plans. In this setting, I found that I could both use well-established skills, such as testing, and also create ways for patients to link up again with the world outside the hospital. Counseling psychology, with its focus on work and development, was feeling more and more like my "professional home."

The second segment of my internship gave me the best opportunity to extend my knowledge and experience with ethnically diverse persons. I served as a training officer for a Volunteers in Service to America (VISTA) project that trained young persons with BAs or MBAs to set up and operate credit unions for low-income communities in mid-California. The initial training was held in Berkeley during the wild and tumultuous summer of 1968. This was a period that witnessed a number of demonstrations concerning both antiwar and racial and ethnic issues. We then moved to the central valley to work directly within communities. My abilities to speak Spanish and work with minority communities, learned on my earlier part-time jobs with adolescents, were important ingredients in my role here. Once again I learned that competencies could be carried forth from old roles, and reshaped to meet the demands of a new situation.

A third part of the internship consisted of providing counseling services at a community college, with a focus on services to ethnic minority and low-income students. In addition to traditional counseling, I organized support groups that dealt with such practical topics as nutrition, for example, how to use and enjoy various unfamiliar foods available through the government surplus program.

Even my dissertation research built on my background experiences, as I explored the effectiveness of paraprofessional counselors in work with junior high school students. I had noted the work of aides at the VA, and of other paraprofessionals in my varied jobs, and I wanted to look more closely at this. And yes, they were effective, but more so in specific environments (one of the schools). Again, I was reminded of my early lessons regarding context, and the "relativity" factor. Interventions clearly worked better in environments that were open to, and supportive of, them!

Postdoctoral Experiences

My first position after receiving my doctorate was at Colorado State University (CSU). By then I was fully engaged in exploring the development of adolescents and young adults, and a counseling center position seemed a perfect match. Some staff and faculty at CSU were also intrigued with development as a guiding principle, and I thought this would be a unique opportunity to work as a member of a team that had similar interests and goals. It was everything I had hoped, and viable models of development and services for college students came out of that work. A part-time academic position was part of the job at CSU. Although I expected to like the teaching, I was surprised to discover how much I liked the scholarship. The writing, although anxiety-producing, was also very rewarding. I found I could reach back to my undergraduate days and hone skills I had learned in journalism. Writing began to become an essential part of my professional identity at that time, and has remained so. The joy of seeing my words and thoughts "out there," in print, offset all the hard work needed to make it happen.

Tensions regarding race and ethnicity emerged at CSU, as they had earlier on campuses on the west and east coasts. Those early 1970s years were also the times of the drug culture, and of antiwar protests. Part of my work was in the counseling center, delivering individual counseling services. But I also became deeply involved in working with students, faculty, and staff colleagues in attempting to address the various tensions on campus. We formed an "interracial unity team" that offered an elective class on racism and consulted with campus and community. I developed and administered a program to train students to work as paraprofessionals in diverse human service roles on campus. We were able to employ some of these students to train and supervise the larger number of volunteers. At one point, we had about 15 employed paraprofessionals, each working about 15 hours per week, and about 100 volunteers, each working 3 to 5 hours per week under the supervision of the student staff.

Our largest paraprofessional program was RoadHouse, a student-operated "hot line" for campus and community. At first, another psychologist and I handled the "go outs" (emergencies that required us to be at the scene, such as a suicide attempt), but soon teams of the most experienced students were handling these tasks as well as the telephones. For a period of time, we provided the only psychological emergency service in northern Colorado, and we developed cooperative relationships with a number of police and fire agencies. For example, the Ft. Collins Fire Department could get any place in the city in a few minutes and would "run cold" (no lights or sirens) to join us in emergency situations. My first book, written with a graduate and an undergraduate student, came out of this experience. (The undergraduate student, an art major, even designed the cover.)

As I worked with the paraprofessional students, many for 3 to 4 years, I had a rich and unique opportunity to both observe and be part of their development. Many still keep in touch. Some are psychologists and counselors, others teachers. Almost all have entered human service careers, although few went on to graduate school immediately after completing their undergraduate degrees. In those days there were a number of jobs in community agencies for persons with their extraordinary skills and experiences, and those provided excellent opportunities for additional service and experience.

I moved a few miles away, to Boulder, Colorado, after 4 years at CSU. Although I was not ready to move, there was a grant director position at the Western Interstate Commission for Higher Education (WICHE) that would allow expansion of the work on development and the environment that we had begun at CSU. The 3 years there were filled with a great deal of writing, reading, consultation, and workshops. It was a fruitful break from the day-to-day work of a busy counseling center. I missed clients, students, and colleagues, and the daily sense of "making a difference." I cherished the opportunity to see and contribute to the "big picture" at WICHE, but as the grant came to an end, I sought a position as a counseling center director with a partial academic position.

I found what I was looking for at The University of Iowa—a counseling center and doctoral program that both required revitalization and refocusing. My appointment was 75% in the center, 25% in the doctoral program. Together with existing staff and faculty, plus the addition of some excellent new young professionals, we were able to conceptualize and implement expanded missions for both units. In the counseling center, we established a predoctoral internship and focused on models of clinical supervision and training. In the doctoral program, we revised the curriculum to ensure a better balance of courses across core areas of psychology and the counseling psychology curriculum. Both units were subsequently accredited by the American Psychological Association (APA), and both retain their accreditation and strong national reputations.

My work in clinical supervision grew from my work with paraprofessional training. I became intrigued with the process of development as a counselor or therapist, and this enthusiasm was shared by a number of staff and doctoral students at Iowa. Through the years our interest has resulted in a number of professional articles, monographs, and in 1987, a book co-authored with Cal Stoltenberg, a former student who is now a colleague at the University of Oklahoma. Throughout this work we used development as the paradigm, seeking to understand how counselors and therapists came to assume this unique identity and integrate it with other aspects of their personhood. We have also attended carefully to issues of context, or the environments in which this development takes place most effectively.

During this period, I also increased my activity in professional organizations, most notably APA. My initial focus was on extending the participation of counseling psychologists in APA, especially in the area of education and training. I served on the Committee on Accreditation, Education and Training Board, and Committee on Graduate Education. I continued to be active in addressing issues of special concern to diverse populations such as women and persons of color, and served as chair of the Committee on Women in Psychology, and as a member of the Council of Representatives. I was also President of Division 17 (Counseling) of APA. As tensions between practitioners and scientists in APA increased, I became part of a group of scientist-practitioners that organized the American Psychological Society (APS). In all of this participation, I reached back for skills developed as an undergraduate, and honed them to fit the new situation.

Throughout the years in Colorado and Iowa, I have identified as a student development/services professional as well as a psychologist. On these two campuses, as on most, counseling centers are part of the Division of Student Affairs or Services. Much of my work, such as the paraprofessional program, has been with colleagues in other areas of student services, most notably residence halls. I have also taught and directed research in the student development program at Iowa, and much of my own work has been published in student services journals. I have also been active in professional organizations in this field, especially the American College Personnel Association (ACPA). It has enhanced my identity to be part of the student services profession as well as the field of psychology, and I have brought traditions and insights from both to my practice, teaching, and scholarly work. With a colleague, Gary Hanson, I conceptualized and edited a book that has become a major text in graduate programs in student development, and is now in its second edition.

New Directions and Meaning

In 1980, four years after coming to Iowa, I began to face a major career decision. I liked everything that I was doing: practice, teaching, scholarship, administration, and involvement in professional organizations. But my energy was no longer quite so high, and at midlife I wanted more time for friends, home and gardening, and my animal companions (currently five cats and two dogs; but just cats in 1980). I also began to get involved in community activities, and had to face making choices about my time more seriously than I had in the past. A major choice was clear. I could pursue administrative roles, moving toward assuming the role of vice president for student services on some campus. Although that was attractive, it would clearly mean less time for the professional writing and involvement that had become important to me. And it would surely mean re-locating away from Iowa City, where I had come to feel at home. I had planted trees and perennials, and I had a strong desire to see them grow and flourish. During this time, I gave a talk at APA entitled, "I Never Saw a Baby Tree Grow Up," speaking to my earlier life of constant moves and my desire at midlife for "rootedness" and an opportunity to see longitudinal development in self, colleagues and friends, students, animals, and even trees.

In the end, the dual pulls of stability and the desire to continue to contribute through professional writing won. In 1984, I left my administrative position, increased my faculty appointment to half time, and increased my work as a therapist in private practice and as a higher education consultant. I also found a new, challenging, and meaningful role. As the farm crisis increased in the midwest, I noted that very little attention was paid to the women involved in this crisis. It was they, it seemed, who carried much of the burden for husband, children, and farm, but they appeared "invisible at the center." First as a therapist, then as an activist and scholar, I have directed a good deal of energy toward these women and their unique situation. In my research I have worked with rural women as co-authors, and our doctoral program has enrolled three farm women as students. Again, I have reached into my background for skills in community networking, and these activities have helped me to feel more "grounded" and at home in Iowa.

The 1980s brought me much professional satisfaction and many awards, but also great sadness. First my father died, and then my younger sister, and I assumed more responsibility for my mother. Frequent trips to California compounded by grief and loss have been very draining. I have cut back once again, this time on practice, consulting, and professional involvement. However, I have also been very fortunate these past few years to be offered an opportunity to edit the APA journal *Professional Psychology: Research & Practice.*

Editing a professional journal, especially this one, is the culmination of my career goals. It is a very special way to influence the field, and to exemplify the importance of the scientist-practitioner model by demonstrating how science aids practice and vice versa. Although giving 15 to 20 hours a week for 6 years is very demanding, it is also very rewarding. My favorite early morning activity in the Iowa winter is to sit with a cup of coffee and edit a manuscript, surrounded by attentive (and sometimes intrusive!) felines and canines. Of course, in the spring and summer editing time must be shared with time in the garden!

I continue to be blessed with excellent colleagues and students who keep me alive and aware. Besides teaching, my favorite activity is supervising the research of my students, and I have gotten much better at it over the years. Fortunately, my many statistical limitations are covered for by our wonderful Iowa statisticians.

At present I teach one graduate course per semester (on my half-time academic appointment). With class time, office hours, and preparation, there is usually 12 to 15 hours of work per week, but more at "crunch" times. There are usually two to three meetings each week, some for student comprehensive or final examinations, others for college or university committees. I spend at least 2 hours per day on journal work at the office (plus all the hours at home!) as well as answering mail. I try to reserve one-half day per week for community work, plus another half-day for my own research. Sometimes the research time disappears!

Where I have ended up is an excellent fit for me at this point in my life. Would I have done as well—or better—in another career? I think not. Psychology has provided a very broad base for me to actualize my lifelong interests in diversity, development, writing, and involvement. I might have found it elsewhere, but this has been a very satisfying choice. Psychology has both molded me, and given me the opportunity to express my own individuality. Such a match, I fear, is rare. I never had a "career plan" per se, but I was always alert to develop my competencies and make the kinds of contributions I could. Each position and role has both taught me much and allowed me to contribute something of my talents and interests. Most of all, the identity of scientist-practitioner fits for me. I could never evolve a theory, or do highly original research. What I can do well is fit practice to theory and develop models that guide toward more effective practice. The models for paraprofessionals, program development, and environmental assessment and redesign, begun at CSU and honed at WICHE, continue to be viable. Hopefully, the more recent work on supervision and rural women will do so as well.

Probably, in the long run, what I am best at is taking skills and experiences from one career or position and integrating those with the unique challenges and opportunities of the next position. In that sense, I have always carried my "home" with me. Sometimes, I did this with full attention. Other times, only a deep pull, not really clear to me, propelled me forward. Only in retrospect, for example, do I understand my career progression of working first with children, then adolescents, young adults, and finally a diverse mix of adults as, in reality, my own personal way to comprehend the sequence of development.

Disappointments there have been, of course. I did not get every position I wanted. Some of my scholarly work missed the mark. Promising relationships, both professional and personal, have sometimes not worked out. I would have liked to have a partner and children with whom to share the journey, and to offer mutual opportunities for growth. There are, as in all lives, some "could have beens . . . ."

Overall, however, it has been fine. The opportunity to utilize myself, with my talents, interests, and areas of needed growth, within my chosen profession has been exceptionally rewarding. The opportunity to write this chapter has stirred many happy memories. Yes, it has been fine, and a good place to be 5 years before retirement. May each of you find such a good fit for your unique talents, interests, and points of development.

Chapter 10

The Evolution of a Feminist Psychologist, Advocate, and Scholar

Nancy Felipe Russo
Arizona State University

Researcher, teacher, scholar, administrator, mentor, editor, leader, policy analyst, and advocate—multiple roles, multiple identities—that is the story of my nontraditional career. Since 1985 I have held the position of professor of psychology and women's studies at Arizona State University (ASU). I write this snapshot of my life during a time of transition from the full-time role of director of women's studies back into the Department of Psychology where I will continue to do all the things that professors do—teach undergraduates, conduct research, train and mentor graduate students, and serve on countless committees! In addition to contributing to my university, I also am very active on the national level in the governance of the American Psychological Association (APA; but more about that later).

About my setting: ASU is the sixth largest university in the nation, 42,000 students strong. An "up and coming" state institution with aspirations of being a top research university, ASU has made a commitment to serving the community, as well as carving out a new definition of what it means to be a university in the 21st century. This makes ASU a very exciting place for a faculty member as well as a student. Although we have had some difficult times with budget cuts and retrenchment (the academic term for cutting back personnel), somehow the difficulties seem less important than the work to be done.

And such a mammoth amount of work it is, particularly in the Psychology Department, where we have 1,600 undergraduate majors (i.e., more students than can be found in whole colleges or schools in some places). In addition, psychology courses are extremely popular with other majors who need general studies credit.

Then there is graduate training that must be done, which involves course work, one-on-one training, and mentoring. As a science discipline, the Psychology Department emphasizes research, and the principle "publish or perish" applies. We have very active researchers on our faculty, and are very proud of our Preventive Intervention Research Center, which is internationally recognized as a place for interdisciplinary research and training related to prevention of mental health problems of high-risk children. All of this makes for a very stimulating setting for me, and I have been able to be very productive at ASU.

One of the features of ASU's Psychology Department that makes it a special place is the encouragement of interaction and collaboration across programs within the department and throughout the university. Graduate training in the department is organized into five graduate programs: clinical, cognitive systems and behavioral neuroscience, developmental, environmental, and social psychology. My primary home is in the social program. As I am also affiliated with the Women's Studies Program, I work with Women's Studies students and teach a Psychology of Women course cross-listed in both the Psychology Department and Women's Studies Program. In addition, I am a member of the Graduate School's interdisciplinary Committee on Law and the Social Sciences, which grants a doctorate in Justice Studies, and am affiliated with the counseling psychology program located in the College of Education. Thus, I sit on committees of students from other programs within the department (especially clinical), as well as from other departments. Even when I'm "only" a professor I still maintain numerous roles.

Early Exposure to and Interest in Psychology

My first exposure to psychology came in an introductory psychology course taught by a Mr. Hardin at Yuba College, a community college located near my home in Oroville, California. Although I majored in biological sciences in junior college, I liked psychology, did well in it, and wanted to learn more about it. When I transferred to the University of California at Davis in my junior year, I majored in psychology.

Throughout my college years, I confess I had no grand career plan (actually, I still don't). My story is more "how not to pursue a career" than how to go about it, and it cannot be understood without understanding my roots. I do not come from a highly educated family—my father, Joseph Felipe, was the son of Spanish immigrants (Basque and Galician, actually), and my mother, Ruby Gould, was the daughter of Mormons who immigrated to California from Idaho. But both sides of the family valued education and were very, very bright. My father could handle a basketball well, which gave him a ticket to a degree at the University of Santa Clara on a basketball scholarship. He was the first person on either side of my family to obtain a college education, and I am the first to obtain an advanced degree. My mother, whose father died when she was 12, lived in a tent when their house burned and worked as a maid to earn money to attend secretarial school after her high school graduation. She knew what it was like to be dirt poor and emphasized the importance of my being able to earn my living. As I was growing up they were both supportive of anything academic (e.g., as long as I was reading or doing homework,

I never had to do household chores). They also emphasized helping other people—for a time my mother worked as a social worker (in the days before social workers had degrees), and as a little girl I used to go with her to visit "her families." My father, who was a coach for a time before going into business, was constantly doing something for "his boys." Watching them instilled a family ethic of service to others that has guided my career.

Had I been a boy, I probably would have followed in my father's footsteps and gone into business, working in the local lumberyard (which he managed when I graduated from high school). But as a girl, at the time, that male-dominated world was closed to me. I had no real female career models in my family, other than secretary or social work, and those roles just did not seem right for someone who loved science, thirsted for knowledge, and had as many interests as I did. The only other career women I knew were teachers, so I figured I would do something academic and scientific, but did not know what.

Thus, although I never had a career plan, I always had career ideals. That is, I have always wanted to do something meaningful with my life; to solve problems and to help people; to use my knowledge and skills to get people to work together and to build something lasting; to leave this earth just a bit better than when I came into it; to have an impact, to make a difference. I'm still working at it.

It was in this context in 1963 that I embarked on a psychology major at the University of California at Davis, where I met Robert Sommer, my first real mentor in psychology. He is an environmental psychologist, interested in "off-beat" applications of psychology, like how to design buildings to serve people's needs rather than architectural esthetics. He got me involved in research that resulted in an undergraduate honors thesis exploring responses to invasion of personal space (our work made it clear that the norms governing interpersonal distance were powerful but unspoken—when they were invaded, the response was to flee rather than to say anything about their violation). That research (Felipe & Sommer, 1966) became highly cited and stimulated a host of articles on personal space around the world. It engendered my interest in nonverbal communication that I pursued in my dissertation and maintain to this day. He also left me with a vision of the usefulness of psychology for asking real world questions and solving real world problems, and a good start on a track record of research publications.

Sommer encouraged me to go on to graduate school and so I applied—to Cornell University because my only female teacher, Marion Prentice, had gone there; to the University of California at Berkeley, because it was close and I could be near my boyfriend; and to the University of Minnesota, for what reason I cannot now fathom. Again, I had no plan and did not have any idea of what I was doing. But I was on top of the world—Phi Beta Kappa, top scores on the Graduate Record Exam, a budding research track record, top letters of recommendation—I figured I could go anywhere, do anything. Unfortunately, it was 1965, when sex discrimination was common practice, and the only place I was accepted was at Cornell University in upstate New York. So here I was, a small town girl, destined for the East Coast and Ivy League—it was only then that I found out that Ivy League was more than a brand for clothes.

I mention brushes with sex discrimination not because they were important to me at the time. I hardly noticed them and when I did notice them, I processed them with "oh, they don't take women," as if that were acceptable and natural. It was only after the women's movement in the 1970s that I realized how much sex discrimination in the larger context had shaped my options and opportunities and how it was definitely not acceptable or natural. This knowledge, combined with my desire to serve others, has forged a commitment to eliminating gender bias in psychology and society, a commitment that must be understood in the context of my personal experience with that bias.

Entry Into and Exit From the Academic World

In addition to earning a doctorate at Cornell, I acquired a husband, Thomas A. Russo, which meant that after graduation I did what wives typically did in that era: followed him and his job to Washington, DC. Jobs for women in academe were scarce in 1970. Consequently, my first job was in a nonprofit research corporation where Henry P. David, my second career mentor and another lifelong friend, gave me my first full-time professional job, at the American Institutes for Research (AIR). There I worked on projects related to population, family planning, family formation, and wantedness of children. Working with Henry David required reading several different literatures related to population, family planning, and women's roles, which engendered insights and interests that continue to shape my life.

But I didn't stay at AIR long. Federal grants, the life's blood of a nonprofit corporation such as AIR, were being cut back. After a year, I took the plunge into academia, in a tenure track assistant professor position in the Department of Psychology at American University. My role there was pretty standard, teach two courses and carry out research. But I was only there a year when my husband got a fabulous job in his native New York, and off we went (it was 1971—I, of course, followed my husband). Fortunately, I was able to obtain a position at what was then the Richmond College Campus of the City University of New York. It was an experimental campus, located on Staten Island, where my husband's parents lived. The institution was new, and there weren't any senior female role models or mentors there either—the young faculty sort of felt our way together, and I confess that I still had not really developed a conception of the professorial role beyond what I had seen as a student: holding classes and doing some research. I cannot say that I learned much about psychology from my time at that institution, although I did develop a lasting friendship with Sandra Tangri, a psychologist whom I continue to admire.

Nonetheless, this was a very critical period in my life, for it was during these years that I consolidated my burgeoning interest in public policy. My father-in-law, Lucio Russo, served in the New York State Assembly for 20 years, and my mother-in-law, Tina Russo, was active in the community, particularly with the March of Dimes. She was a powerful role model and mentor for me. I got involved in politics and policy advocacy, and even ran the Walk-a-Thon on Staten Island for the March of Dimes (I still have my "Order of the Battered Boot" plaque on my wall). One of my most treasured accomplishments during this period was using my research skills to synthesize and organize background material to argue for a law to prohibit sex discrimination in mortgage banking. The law, which was known as "the Russo credit bill" after my father-in-law, was a model for later legislation on the national level. My work on sex discrimination in credit-granting later led me to organize the first Women's National Bank, which opened in Washington, DC, in 1978 (now called the Adams National Bank after Abigail Adams).

Such community involvement was in keeping with my career ideals, but it took time that could not be used to establish an academic research record. Overloading on service activities is not a wise thing for an assistant professor to be doing if she aspires to obtain tenure, but who knew? During graduate school at Cornell, I never really had a mentor to explain the academic ropes to me. My new husband studied hard during his first year of law school, and I spent as much time drilling him on his work as I did on my own. I did not become very involved in departmental activities nor did I have many close friends who were graduate students (Jeannette Desor and Raymond Yang being noteworthy exceptions). No one impressed the importance of such activities on me for the development of future professional contacts and recommendations for jobs.

Although I learned an awful lot about the law, which has served me well in my public policy activities over the years, my focus on my marriage meant that I missed out on the informal professional socialization that communicates the norms and values of the profession. Thus, I had never heard the phrase "publish or perish" and did not realize the importance of establishing a research program and publishing in peer-reviewed journals if I wanted a research-oriented academic career in the discipline. I thought that if I were an outstanding teacher and took on a lot of service tasks I was doing my job. Fortunately, I did not stay in academe long enough for lack of research publications to catch up with me. After 2 years at Richmond College, my marriage broke up and I went back to American University on a 1-year appointment to regroup. Although I divorced Thomas Russo after 7 years of marriage, I had strong ties with the Russo family which continue to this day.

In 1974, my 1-year appointment was up at American University, and I had few prospects. Fortunately, I learned of another 1-year replacement position in the Educational Affairs Office of the APA. At this point in my career I exited academia for the life of an APA staff member. One thing led to another, and I spent the next 11 years of my life at APA (except for a 15-month stint in government as a health scientist administrator at the National Institute of Child Health and Human Development—a horrible experience and another, nonacademic story).

Life at APA

This account of my life is supposed to focus on the academic aspects of my career, so I won't go into lots of detail about the exciting times I had at APA—that would take a whole book to relate (and what stories I could tell). But my nonacademic experience at APA does deserve some attention, because it was there that I learned what it truly meant to be an academic psychologist and why a "publish or perish" norm is important because it ensures that research universities will produce and disseminate new research knowledge. As the largest and oldest scientific society for psychology in the world, APA was a gathering place for some of the best psychological minds in the country. The Educational Affairs Office dealt with all aspects of educational training in psychology, from precollege to undergraduate, to graduate and even postgraduate levels. I was able to meet psychologists from every kind of setting, inside and outside of academe, to learn about their values and activities, and to attend meetings where they discussed and debated roles for psychologists. It was at APA that I first worked with senior women in psychology, and felt what it was like to have women mentors. Florence Denmark, who eventually became the fifth women to serve as APA president in the 100-year history of the organization, was and remains a particularly important role model and mentor for me.

Through that experience I learned about unspoken norms in the discipline that had never been explained to me, and I came to understand the importance of mentoring young people in psychology to make such norms explicit. My eyes were opened to opportunities that I had missed. For example, I had not sought out a mentor in graduate school (I even had rebuffed an offer of mentorship because I thought that working with someone was something undergraduates did and that I was supposed to work as an "independent researcher"). I hadn't raised an eyebrow when my major professor had told me that a fellowship was going to another student because he had a wife to support and I had a husband to support me. I considered it reasonable when someone encouraged me to go into developmental psychology "because women were naturally good with children." I could go on. . . . It is fascinating to me that I never noticed the sexism in the messages at the time—I didn't think twice about the fellowship opportunity (how was I to know that holding that fellowship was an honor that would have given me an edge in the job market).

I liked developmental psychology and so I double-majored in it and did my thesis on the development of nonverbal communication in children. And every once in awhile I still wonder what that famous psychologist thought when, in response to his invitation to be one of the few students to work closely with him, this naive, small town, first-year graduate student replied "thanks, but I have my own research program." How was I to know that working with an internationally renowned psychologist can open numerous doors to jobs and other opportunities? It wasn't until my experience at APA that I learned that there were things to learn that weren't in the books and there is a social side to achievement in addition to the traditional factors of "ability and effort." I began to devote a substantial part of my professional career spreading the word about survival strategies in academe, so that others will be able to learn more quickly what I missed. These activities included updating APA's most popular publication, *Careers in Psychology*, and editing a newsletter for high school teachers of psychology.

Most importantly, I began to work on women's issues in psychology during this period. The women's movement of the 1970s was having an impact on all areas of society, and psychology was no exception. The Association for Women in Psychology had created such a stir at APA's 1969 annual convention that APA had established an ad hoc Committee on the Status of Women in Psychology, and by 1973, a permanent Committee on Women in Psychology (CWP) was established. Tina Cummings and Martha Mednick got me involved in CWP activities to enhance women's status in psychology and encourage research and applications of psychology related to women's lives. This, of course, fit right into the interest in women's roles that I had developed during my stint at the American Institutes for Research. Spurred on by CWP, women psychologists organized to establish the APA Division of Psychology of Women to promote research on women's issues, which was established in 1973 as the 35th division of the association, and is therefore known as "Division 35." In 1977, after concentrated lobbying by women and men who cared about these issues, APA established its first Women's Programs Office. Women psychologists now had an institutionalized power base for their issues, and I was the lucky one to head it. I served as head of the office from 1977 to 1985, when I left APA to head the Women's Studies Program at ASU.

It was during my time at APA that I began to establish a publication record that would one day enable me to return to academe. I began to write about women's lives in earnest, for I now understood the need to create such knowledge and the importance of publishing such information if it is to be used and have an impact. I had an interest in the history of psychology from an incident in my graduate school days at Cornell. A memo by a male graduate student that was distributed to all faculty and graduate students raised concerns about the number of women accepted for graduate study at Cornell and asked "Besides, what have women ever contributed to psychology, anyway?" I was incensed. Not being able to answer the question, I began to comb my books for women's names, which I placed in my own memo to be distributed in all of the mailboxes. The matter was dropped. Ironically, Eleanor J. Gibson, one of the most distinguished psychologists in the world (indeed, one of the few psychologists to be admitted to the National Academy of Sciences), was an adjunct faculty member at Cornell at the time (she wasn't allowed to be a tenured faculty member because anti-nepotism rules meant that only her husband, J. J. Gibson, could be hired).

This critical incident led me to begin writing about women's history in psychology when I was at Richmond College (Bernstein & Russo, 1974), and at APA promoting and preserving women's contributions to psychology became a major project. I worked with Agnes O'Connell, who had headed a Division 35 Task Force on Women Doing Research that emphasized the importance of role models. We organized symposia at APA conventions that brought eminent women together to tell the stories of their lives that we later published in books of autobiographies (O'Connell & Russo, 1983, 1988). Through this and several related works (e.g., O'Connell & Russo, 1990, 1991), we wanted students and colleagues to understand that psychology and the people in it (women and men) both reflect and shape the larger social context. My hope in studying women's history and participation in psychology has been to change the circumstances of women in the field and to develop a psychology where men and women can work together on a mutual, equal basis. A look at the current status of women in psychology suggests that things indeed have changed, and I would like to believe my work has had some part in making such change happen (there is still a way to go, however, so nobody get complacent!). In addition to writing about women's status in psychology, I joined with women in other disciplines to work to change women's status across the disciplines. The passage of legislation to establish a Committee on Women, Minorities, and the Handicapped in Science and Technology in the National Science Foundation, was a particularly satisfying success (the story is told in Russo & Cassidy, 1983).

Another big change in my intellectual development during this period was engagement in mental health issues. A large proportion of APA members are in clinical fields, and my social network became populated with feminist clinicians. My work on family planning and unwanted childbearing brought me into touch with mental health issues, and my social-psychological perspective was of interest to feminists who wished to consider therapeutic issues in their sociocultural context. In 1977, I was appointed to the Subpanel on the Mental Health of Women of the President's Commission on Mental Health, established by then-President Jimmy Carter. There I met psychiatrist Elaine Carmen and sociologist Patricia Rieker, and I became intensively involved in efforts to change the male-dominated mental health establishment (particularly centering on the National Institute of Mental Health [NIMH]). I began to write and publish on the relationship between women's roles and status and mental health, and roles for mental health professionals in dealing with women's issues.

In 1980, the commission had completed its work and we were ready to implement its recommendations, when Carter lost the election. It became imperative that women's mental health issues become "laundered" so they would look like the Reagan administration's idea. I got the idea to identify a women's mental health agenda, and obtained funding from the Ittleson Foundation for a conference to develop it. We invited women leaders from the various mental health disciplines to the conference, and afterward released the conference report on Capitol Hill in a meeting that included speeches by such dignitaries as Representative Patricia Schroeder (Russo, 1985). We were successful in stimulating NIMH to establish a women's mental health research agenda, and I am told this effort was a model for current efforts to develop a national women's health agenda. In addition to being highly successful policy advocacy, this effort has led to numerous publications related to women's mental health that have helped to change how women's mental health issues are defined and addressed, and continues to be a major interest of mine to this day.

Another critical incident during this period that bears on my academic career is my involvement with ethnic minority women's issues. I had long been concerned with civil rights issues and had been a great admirer of Martin Luther King, Jr. during the 1960s. During graduate school I had worked as a psychological assistant in a Head Start Program that included a center in Harlem, and had always included African-American women's issues in my work. One of my most satisfying accomplishments has been preserving the autobiographies of African-American psychologists Mamie Phipps Clark, Ruth Howard, and Carolyn R. Payton. One of the major points of my empirical research has been that patterns of usage of mental health facilities differed for African-American women compared to White women. My work shows that failure to separate the data simultaneously by gender and race distorts our understanding of factors affecting utilization.

But I was never involved in Hispanic women's issues until the day that Hortensia Amaro walked into my office at APA and asked me to become involved in Division 35's Task Force on Hispanic Women, which she chaired. When I told her that I had never felt discrimination in my career because I was Hispanic, she responded, "But you are one of the few senior women role models we have and we need role models. Are you ashamed of being Hispanic?" Taken aback, I replied, "Of course not!" And I remembered my high school days in Santa Clara, which I hadn't thought about for years, when many of my friends were of Mexican ancestry and where a color line was drawn between "Mexicans" and "Spanish." I always thought that was ridiculous, for my Spanish ancestors could have just as easily gone to Mexico (several went to other countries in Latin America). Besides, I had thought, weren't we all Americans? I also remembered Danny and Anita, who had to date in secret because Anita's mother (who claimed Spanish ancestry) wouldn't let her go out with a Mexican (we covered for her). I also remembered an incident on Staten Island that didn't mean much to me at the time, when someone asked me about my ancestry and I replied, "my father's Spanish and my mother's from Idaho—probably Irish." Their response: "Oh—just say you're Irish." By the time Hortensia left my office, she had signed me up for the Task Force and we embarked on what has become a lifelong friendship forged in our work to enhance the status of Hispanic women in psychology and promote psychological knowledge about Hispanic women's lives. I am also proud that my work has preserved the autobiography of the first Chicana to obtain a doctorate in psychology, Martha Bernal.

The final big change I will mention that began during this period was a new marriage. In 1975, I married Allen Meyer, which makes us partners for more than 18 happy years. I tell students that marriage is not for everyone, and it is better to have no marriage than an unhappy marriage—but there is absolutely nothing better than a happy marriage. Allen is a wonderful source of support in good times and bad. When I had a major accident, he stayed by my side in the hospital and helped me adjust to the fact that I would have a permanent disability (I can walk, but my days of racquetball are over; the ankle is unstable and I will never have another pain-free day). In 1985 he left his position in the Senior Executive Service at the Office of Management and Budget, and came with me when I got a job in Arizona (how times do change). We have published together on women and economic issues, and he is a withering critic of my initial drafts, enabling me to polish my work before offering it to public view (an absolute necessity for success in psychology—it can be a colleague instead of a spouse, but having a constructive critic is a must). He brings me coffee when I am writing on a 12-hour-a-day schedule, and makes sure I take my vitamins. I could not be happier.

People sometimes ask me why I still have the name Russo rather than go back to Felipe or take the name of Meyer. It is difficult to explain to young people how disruptive a change in name can be to one's professional (as well as personal) identity. Let me just say that I learned a lesson in disruption and invisibility when I changed my name to Russo after publishing under Felipe, and I was not about to go through that again. I do regret that I changed my name in the first place, but I wasn't aware that I had an option. Today's women do have an option, and I am constantly urging my students to be aware of it.

How My Views Have Changed

My undergraduate days with Robert Sommer had given me a deep concern about human-made as well as natural environments. Through my work with Henry David, it became clear to me that environmental problems could never be solved as long as population issues were ignored, and in fact, population pressures underlie most of our human problems. The truth of the slogan "Whatever your cause, it's a lost cause, as long as there's overpopulation" came home to me.

I came to understand the pervasive destructiveness of unwanted childbearing to the child, the family, and society. I became extremely interested in family planning and abortion issues, and a substantial portion of my research, writing, and policy advocacy continues to concentrate on these issues (e.g., Russo & Zierk, 1992).

Through this experience, it became clear that helping people to have only wanted children would help with overpopulation, but would not eliminate the problem. Too many people want too many children. For many cultures, where few children live to adulthood, where children are critical for the economic health of the family, and where the society needs more people to survive, desiring large families and proceeding to "go forth and multiply" is an important adaptive strategy. Hence, the evolution of pronatalist norms and pressures is understandable. But in the modern world, where public health and medical interventions have lengthened life spans all over the globe, high fertility norms threaten the survival of the human race, not to mention other species. Why do people still want to have so many children in today's world? That question led me to issues of gender, which in turn, led me to women's roles, the status of women, and the women's movement.

Focusing on women's roles and status, in psychology and society, brought the global problems of environmental devastation and overpopulation down to manageable size for me. As long as women are defined in terms of motherhood and told that to be valued they must be mothers (i.e., as long as there is what I call a *motherhood mandate*—Russo, 1976), asking them to limit their family size is futile.

Empowering women, widening choices beyond motherhood, helping people plan and control childbearing—these were areas where psychological knowledge could contribute and perhaps I could help make a difference. In addition to my work to empower women in psychology and to promote research on women's mental health, I have focused on the problems of teenage pregnancy, closely spaced childbirth, large family sizes, and access to family planning and abortion. For more than 20 years I have argued that as long as women hold a disadvantaged status and are socialized to seek male approval, they would not be able to "just say no" to unprotected intercourse and family planning programs will not be fully effective.

More recently, my work on the women's mental health research agenda (Russo, 1990), has led me to focus on violence against women (Goodman, Koss, & Russo, 1993a, 1993b). I became involved in APA's Task Force on Violence Against Women (co-chaired by Mary Koss and Lisa Goodman), and immersed in the literature on rape, battering, and sexual harassment (Koss et al., 1994).

This work on male violence implicates rape and sexual coercion in problems related to unwanted pregnancy. It also confirms the importance of empowering women, promoting social and political equality, and enhancing mutual communication between women and men as strategies for prevention of a host of psychological and social problems. We have yet to appreciate fully the impact of physical and sexual violence on women and children. For example, research stimulated by and conducted with my colleague Sara Gutierres, has shown how a history of physical and sexual abuse in the clients of drug treatment centers (male and female) undermines their response to treatment. Thus, we argue, drug treatment personnel must be trained to deal with psychological effects of such abuse if treatment for drug abuse is to be successful.

How I Use My Time

For the past 8 years I served as director of women's studies, which involved substantial administrative responsibility. In addition to administrative duties, my time has been distributed between teaching (one class per year), research, committee work for the College of Liberal Arts and Sciences, and the university, outreach to the community, and service to the discipline. I never really have a "typical day." I try to get up early (5 a.m.) so I have time to write before the hustle and bustle of the day begins. In addition to my work at the university, I do considerable work for APA. For example, I am on the APA Council of Representatives, the Board of the Advancement of Psychology in the Public Interest, and the Task Force on Male Violence Against Women, which means that I spend a lot of time on the telephone conferring with people about APA business and travelling to Washington, DC for meetings. I may work with students from counseling psychology, justice studies, and psychology on research or writing projects—joint publication with students is one way that I contribute to their training.

My biggest project at the moment is an introductory psychology textbook with Lyle Bourne and Bruce Extrand. I took on the project because it was a chance to write a textbook that I wished I could have had, one that conveys a broad vision of psychology as a science and profession, that celebrates and communicates gender and ethnic diversity in psychology, and that shows how useful psychological knowledge and skills can be in dealing with the problems that will challenge students in the 21st century. We are still working on it, and I am very excited about what we have accomplished so far.

Rewards and Discouragements

I have been truly fortunate in the many recognitions I have received in my field, which include being elected to the office of president of two APA divisions (Division 34—Population and Environmental Psychology and Division 35—Psychology of Women) as well as the Rocky Mountain Psychological Association. My awards include a Distinguished Leadership Citation from APA's Committee on Women in Psychology (1986); a Distinguished Career Award from the Association for Women in Psychology (1991), and a Heritage Award for Distinguished Contributions in the Area of Public Policy from Division 35 (1992). My most special honor—special because it is in memory of someone I greatly loved and admired—is Division 35's Carolyn Wood Sherif Award (1993). And for someone like me who has devoted so much of her career trying to ensure that women's contributions to psychology do not become invisible, it was quite a kick to find myself listed among the 100 most prominent living women in psychology in the English-speaking world (Gavin, 1987). My election to Fellow status in six different APA divisions (Divisions 9—Social Issues; 26—History, 34—Population and Environment, 35—Psychology of Women, 38—Health Psychology, and 45—Ethnic Minority and Cross Cultural Psychology), reflects my broad ranging interests and recognizes "sustained and outstanding contributions" to these subfields of psychology. I am also a Fellow in the more recently formed American Psychological Society. Like anyone, I take pleasure in receiving such honors. They are also an important source of self-validation, particularly when times get rough—advocating change in one's field takes a certain amount of intestinal fortitude, for it is not always welcomed. I also keep in mind one of the major points made in our work on psychology's history—that is, accomplishments and deeds are never done by one person alone. All that I have accomplished reflects teamwork. Whenever I accept an award, it is on behalf of the team, and all of my colleagues and students who have worked with me share in the rewards and recognition that I achieve.

As for discouragements, there are some, but my style is not to dwell on them. After all, if you are optimistic about achieving your goals, you are halfway there. Perhaps my greatest disappointment has been in the lack of commitment and motivation of some of my undergraduate students. In all of the thousands of students I have met over the course of my career, only a few fall into this category. But those few students who cheat on exams or lie about their absences are long remembered and can take the joy out of a class. They dilute the meaning of the college degree, which hurts all students graduating from the institution. Even though they may graduate from college, I suspect they will encounter a lifetime of disappointments and frustrations in their careers because of their failure to learn basic reading, writing, and thinking skills.

When asked what I would do differently, nothing major comes to mind. I have had some miserable experiences, but all of my experiences, good and bad, have made me what I am, and I love my life. For example, if I had spent more time networking with psychologists in graduate school rather than studying with my law student husband, I might not have developed my interest in the law and public policy. If I had concentrated on research in my first faculty position, I would have never gone to APA and been able to have such an impact on psychology. If I had stayed married to my first husband, I would never have experienced the joy of being married to someone who is a true partner. And so on. . . . My motto is "learn from your experience, but never look back."

What Does the Future Hold

I am looking forward to the fall of 1994 when I complete my sabbatical and begin my role as full-time professor. My textbook will be completed, and I plan to work on my introductory psychology course, to make it a model for how such courses should be constructed. I will also have completed a book on the impact of feminism on psychology, which I hope to use in a new course in feminist psychology that I want to develop. I want to spend more time working on research with psychology graduate students, exploring how our social identities and interrelationships affect our mental health and well-being. One of my roles will be the new editor of the *Psychology of Women Quarterly*, so I will be spending a substantial amount of time developing the lead research journal in my field. My big project, however, will be an update of the *Women's Mental Health Agenda*. It is time to evaluate how far we have come in the past 20 years since the first one was developed.

Advice to Future Generations

Carpe diem! The world is open to you as it has never been. I try to impress on my students that a degree is sometimes a ticket to a job—but to keep a job and get ahead, you must have the knowledge and skills that the degree represents. If you are working for grades and not for the knowledge, you are facing some major disappointments in the years ahead. Learn to communicate in writing and orally— this requires practice. Learn to read and understand the complexities of what is being said. Learn to think critically. Be able to identify assumptions that lie behind arguments and expose gaps and errors in reasoning. Learn mathematics, including statistics. In addition to being able to balance your checkbook, mathematics is a language that will enable you to manipulate abstract ideas, solve complex problems, analyze your data, and critique research on the leading edge of your field. Learn technology—today it is computers. Who knows what will evolve tomorrow? The problem is, you never know what the future will bring, so you must prepare yourself to be flexible by learning to learn, and learning as many skills as possible.

Develop your interpersonal skills so that you can understand issues and situations from diverse perspectives, including the perspectives of another culture. Remember that behavior is a joint product of the person and the situation, and sometimes situations are unjust and unhealthy. One of the things that makes human beings so unusual is our incredible capacity to act on our environments and create culture. Develop your ability to adapt and adjust to changing circumstances, yes—but also be prepared to join with others and change those circumstances if they are unhealthy or unjust. And remember that all of this should be fun, at least some of the time.

Most importantly, however, be clear on your values. What are the things most important to you? In addition to my feminist value of social and political equality for women and men (we are all in this together), some of mine include commitment, compassion, community, courage, creativity, excellence, gentleness, health, honesty, integrity, justice, knowledge, rationality, service, strength, and tolerance. Figure yours out. Then live your life in the service of your values. Sacrifice to maintain them (for me, this once meant leaving a well-paid job with the federal government because I would not behave in a manner that I considered unethical, and it was clear I would not get a promotion unless I changed my mind). Live your values and you will have a sense of purpose and meaning wherever your career path takes you, and whether or not you ever achieve what other people define as "success."

If you want to be a psychologist who does research related to the psychology of women, take anthropology, biology, sociology, and women's studies courses in addition to those in psychology. Learn quantitative techniques—some of the most interesting questions about women's lives cannot be answered by experimental designs, so knowing how to design studies that can use statistical controls is essential. Volunteer in settings that will expose you to the realities of diverse women's lives: rape crises hotlines, battered women's shelters, Planned Parenthood. Know that to understand the psychology of women, you have to be broader than the usual psychologist. You will at least need to study developmental, social, and clinical approaches to understanding women's lives, and be aware of how other social categories, such as age, ethnicity, sexual orientation, and able-bodiedness interact with gender. It's a challenging task, not for everyone—but I have found it to be a source of meaning and satisfaction, well worth doing.

References

Bernstein, M., & Russo, N. F. (1974, February). The history of psychology revisited or up with our foremothers. *American Psychologist, 29*(2), 130–134.

Felipe, N. J., & Sommer, R. (1966). Invasions of personal space. *Social Problems, 14*, 206–241.

Gavin, E. (1987). Prominent women in psychology determined by ratings of distinguished peers. *Psychotherapy in Private Practice, 5*, 53–68.

Goodman, L. A., Koss, M. P., & Russo, N. F. (1993a). Violence against women: Physical and mental health effects. Part I: Research findings. *Applied & Preventive Psychology: Current Scientific Perspectives, 2*, 79–89.

Goodman, L. A., Koss, M. P., & Russo, N. F. (1993b). Violence against women: Physical and mental health effects. Part II: Conceptualizing post-traumatic stress. *Applied & Preventive Psychology: Current Scientific Perspectives, 2*(3), 123–130.

Koss, M. P., Goodman, L. A., Browne, A., Fitzgerald, L., Keita, G. P., & Russo, N. F. (1994). *No safe haven: Male violence against women at home, at work, and in the community*. Washington, DC: American Psychological Association.

O'Connell, A. N., & Russo, N. F. (Eds.). (1983). *Models of achievement: Reflections of eminent women in psychology.* New York: Columbia University Press.

O'Connell, A. N., & Russo, N. F. (Eds.). (1988). *Models of achievement: Reflections of eminent women in psychology* (Vol. 2). Hillsdale, NJ: Lawrence Erlbaum Associates.

O'Connell, A. N., & Russo, N. F. (Eds.). (1990). *Women in psychology: A bio-bibliographical sourcebook.* Westport, CT: Greenwood Press.

O'Connell, A. N., & Russo, N. F. (Eds.).(1991). *Women's heritage in psychology: Origins, development, and future directions.* New York: Cambridge University Press. (Special Centennial issue, *Psychology of Women Quarterly*).

Russo, N. F. (1976). The motherhood mandate. *Journal of Social Issues, 32,* 143–154.

Russo, N. F. (Ed.). (1985). *A women's mental health agenda.* Washington, DC: American Psychological Association.

Russo, N. F. (1990). Overview: Forging research priorities for women's mental health. *American Psychologist, 45*(3),368–373.

Russo, N. F., & Cassidy, M. (1983) Women in science and technology. In I. Tinker (Ed.), *Women in Washington: Advocates for public policy* (Vol. 7, 250–262). Beverly Hills, CA: Sage.

Russo, N. F., & Zierk, K. L. (1992). Abortion, childbearing, and women's well-being, *Professional psychology: Research and Practice, 23,* 269—280.

Chapter 11

Playing the Hand That's Dealt You: My Life and Times (So Far) as a Psychologist

Robert Perloff
University of Pittsburgh

Prologue

In 1991, forty years after receiving my doctorate from The Ohio State University, I became an emeritus professor at the University of Pittsburgh. What transpired during these four decades? What were my professional and scientific activities, the disappointments and frustrations along with satisfactions and successes? Would I have done anything differently? The answer, given my style, interests and abilities, is probably no, I would have behaved more or less in the same way. Are there lessons or clues from these 40 intensive years as a scholar, scientist, practitioner, consultant, and teacher, of possible value to young people making decisions about career opportunities? The answer is yes.

What follows is primarily an effort to answer the foregoing questions, but also, immodest as this may sound, here is an archival account of "what makes Sammy (Bob, in this instance) run," resulting, I believe, in a better understanding of who I am in light of what I did and did not do, and how a recollection of these experiences will help me understand myself somewhat better than I now do, and help me, therefore, come to grips with how I should spend the remaining years of my life.

Before the Beginning. My formal education began in February 1946, when I entered Temple University as a freshman, graduating with a bachelor's degree in August 1948. At that point I started my graduate education at Ohio State University, receiving my doctorate in August 1951.

(During my last year at Ohio State I was an instructor at Antioch College, in nearby Yellow Springs, Ohio.) This autobiographical odyssey covers the years from 1951 until the present time (1994), but my perceptions, drives, and various career pathways will be better understood by first providing a brief account of my 25 years in life preceding the formal intellectual exposure and training commencing with my first year as an undergraduate at Temple University in Philadelphia.

I was born on February 3, 1921, in Philadelphia, Pennsylvania. The years before high school were happy ones, even though our family had limited means. I have vivid memories of being a hustler of sorts, looking for ways to overcome my modest material resources, these ways being hard work, fast talking, supreme confidence that I could make it and would therefore prevail, and rarely accepting a "no" or refusal of any kind. From around age 8 or 9 until about 13, I was preoccupied with collecting autographs of famous figures in or visiting Philadelphia (athletes, movie stars, politicians), peddling magazines at busy downtown street corners, engaging in fantasies with boys my age as we pretended that we were battling rival gangs, and by selling junk perfume at a profit to people of quite modest means. I am not especially proud of this latter exploitative huckstering episode, but neither does it drown me in paroxysms of *mea culpas*. I was a defiant type, but very likable because I was a generous kid with a strong sense of invincibility. This phase of my early years came to an abrupt end at age 12 when my father died, and my mother, an aunt, my sister, and I moved from our apartment near the center city to an apartment in a "better" neighborhood, West Philadelphia.

I went to high school in West Philadelphia and, because my mother was the family's sole breadwinner, I worked after school and for 3 or 4 years after graduating until I was drafted by the Army. Every day and most weekends I gained experience at soda fountains, as a door-to-door salesman, parking cars in public garages, distributing handbills, as a stockboy, movie usher, and toy salesman in a downtown department store, delivering dog meat to wealthy residences in Philadelphia's "mainline" suburbs, as a driver lugging boxes and boxes of shoes from a store's main location to its branch stores, as a clerk-typist for the U.S. Signal Corps, and as a trainee in Cincinnati learning how to assemble engines for the airplanes that played such a prominent role in America's battles and ultimate victory in World War II.

Then came World War II. I was drafted into the U.S. Army in September 1942, at age 21, and there I stayed until I was honorably discharged, 3 years later, in November 1945, having served 8 or 9 months at military installations on the west coast and the remaining 2½ years in the Pacific Theater of Operations as one of General Douglas MacArthur's GIs, where I received a Bronze Star in 1945 for performance on Luzon, in the Philippines.

This "before the beginning" interlude is intended to lay the groundwork for understanding a bit the restlessness I experienced in my four decades as a professional and, according to most measures, as a highly successful and visible psychologist. I was able to weather many storms in my career, some of which were of my own creation, because I never, at any time, entertained the idea that I would fail (Albert Bandura's perceived self-efficacy), having been bolstered and strengthened by memories of overcoming adversity as a boy and managing my life as a noncommissioned officer overseas in Hawaii, New Guinea, Indonesia (Morotai, Netherlands East Indies), the Philippines, and Japan. (Hell, after surviving the war anything else would be a piece of cake—or so I thought back then.) The anxieties of college exams; of graduate work and the dissertation; of early jobs as a newly minted doctorate; of reorganizations and other uncertainties and challenges in one's career; of paper rejections and other disappointments and distressing experiences including the early and unexpected deaths of my father (when I was 12) and of a daughter (when she was 2); of the normal ups and downs in family life including living beyond one's means and being penniless before the end of the month; and the shocks large and small of living in a society peppered with the great depression, wars, AIDS, and you name it—all these assaults upon and disturbances of normal everyday living and the good life are, I am convinced, sustainable and conquerable, thus enabling one to become even stronger because of adversity.

So, the justification for this early section is to advise one to inoculate him or herself with a few toughening journeys throughout one's life, particularly the early, formative years. I encourage one to avoid risk-aversiveness, a continuing dose of which may lead to fecklessness and a soft, overprotective existence that is the bane of hardy survival in, let's face it, a cruel and troubling world. A life, any life, yours and mine, is, in a real sense, a continuous battle to cope, to overcome adversity, to compete, to survive, to muddle through hostile environments offered up by a malignant mother nature as well as by dispassionate political, social, and economic forces. This must not be interpreted as nay-saying or as a wallowing in *Weltschmerz*, because I am by nature a cockeyed optimist. It should be interpreted, rather, as a warning that to succeed, to overcome, to compete successfully, one must have practice in being buffeted about, including in one's professional life as a psychologist.

My Present Position

I joined the faculty of the (then) Graduate School of Business of the University of Pittsburgh in 1969, as director of the Management Research Center. My title changed a few years after that to director of Research Programs. My last official administrative post at the school, before returning to full-time faculty status, was as director of the Consumer Panel. The courses and seminars I taught—more or less dovetailing with my research and scholarly activities—were in organizational behavior, consumer behavior, research methodology, and evaluation research.

Business School Versus Psychology Department. I have often been asked to comment on the environment and collegiality of a business school versus that of a psychology department. This is a fair question, because for a decade preceding the Pittsburgh appointment I was a psychology professor at Purdue University, and it is also an important question as the vast majority of applied (industrial or personnel) psychologists now ply their wares in business schools rather than in traditional psychology departments, a state of affairs that I am convinced is a loss for the latter and a gain for the former.

But before addressing this question, let me share with you some of the strains a psychologist might endure—I did—in his or her early years in a business school. At first it appears to be an alien environment for the psychologist, what with accountants, operations researchers, economists, finance professors, marketing mavens, industrial relations specialists, and other business types populating and whizzing within the corridors, offices, and classrooms.

In a psychology department you are juxtaposed with rat labs, clinical or counseling cubicles, the apparatus and other trappings of psychophysiology (now called neuroscience or biopsychology), tachistoscopes, and all the rest. Here in a business school, there may be a computer lab and a behavioral sciences lab, but little else reminding one of the scientific desiderata of one's discipline. As a matter of fact, although psychology is in fact a discipline, business administration or management science are not disciplines, being loose collections of several disciplines, where for the most part the subject matter is not as fundamental or "pure" as it is in an arts and sciences department. For example, organizational behavior in a business school is, for the most part—and it could and should be no other way—not as broad or as basic as, for example, social psychology or industrial psychology, or psychometrics are in a psychology department. Getting used to these differences, as well as accepting and respecting them is no easy matter, or at least it was not for me when I joined the business faculty at Pittsburgh after having spent 18 postdoctoral years in settings more fundamental than the heavily applied use of psychology in a business school.

The question arises, then, given the truism (in my view) of the fact that it is more efficient and effective for an applied psychologist in academia to be in an applied setting than in a pure psychology department, how can business school psychologists stay close to their disciplinary roots and guard against becoming stale and out of date? I attempted to do this by "hanging around" psychologists and immersing myself in the psychological literature, perhaps even going somewhat overboard through my lengthy involvement in a number of leadership roles in U.S. psychology. In a word, I stayed close to psychology by becoming very active in professional associations, notably the American Psychological Association (APA), on committees, boards, and in various leadership capacities. I did not necessarily choose to do this because I was in a business school. It simply happened, or at least I made myself available and soon discovered that, gee-whiz, this is great, I am mingling with psychologists while at the same time fulfilling myself vocationally, if you will, in a business school.

Benefits of Being in the Business School. Business school faculty, deriving from many disciplines or fields of study (accounting, administrative science, economics, finance, human resources, marketing, mathematics, operations research, political science, psychology, and sociology), are broad-gauged men and women with a considerably more expansive view of the world of the mind as well as of the practical world than that of psychology department faculty. Thus, the prospects of interdisciplinary interactions are considerably greater in a business school than in a psychology department. It follows from this that from the vantage point of a business school the professor has greater access to research populations, support, and consulting opportunities than one's colleagues in a psychology department. Business schools tend to have more and better resources and amenities, such as fewer restrictions on the telephone, photocopy facilities, computers, overnight-mail means of communicating, and other coveted resources. Salaries and travel budgets are more munificent in business schools, along with secretarial and other support personnel. Because the business school is a professional school (along with, e.g., law and medicine), I do believe that the business school professoriate takes its teaching responsibilities more seriously and may well perform better in the class-room. Finally, and this is awkward to express fully in a few words, because the problems and missions inherent in business schools are broader and less parochial than in psychology departments, the psychologist on the business faculty is considerably more in touch with the critical problems facing society (e.g., reces-sion, inflation, unemployment, mergers and acquisitions, discriminatory hiring practices, fraudulent practices such as insider trading, world markets, industrial competitiveness, environmental pollution, international conflicts) than is the psy-chologist on a psychology faculty.

Benefits of Being in the Psychology Department. The psychology profes-sor, although more insular, is closer to his or her disciplinary roots, quite probably enabling him or her to make more penetrating contributions to the theory and science of psychology per se. There are exceptions, of course, where business school professors have indeed become celebrated psychologists, but these are the exceptions, not the rule. Although the bread-and-butter students of business schools are those pursuing the master of business administration (MBA) degree, students who are very serious and work hard in order to land good jobs in Fortune 500 corporations, I must acknowledge that, at least in my limited experience, the psychology doctoral student on average is "a cut above" the business school doctoral student. It used to be the case that the business school professor, in the eyes of academics across the board, was regarded less favorably than was the psychology professor, but I believe this is changing so that over time they will be viewed as being on par with one another. Methodologically and theoretically, it is my impression that the research outputs originating in a psychology department are, on the margin, better than in a business school but that business school research tends to be less shackled by unnecessary intellectual constraints and is therefore more flexible and intellectually risk-taking.

How I Became Interested in Psychology

My interest in psychology became sharpened after I decided to major in it following the first two semesters of college. The choice then was among economics, mathe-matics, and psychology. I selected psychology as my major because it appeared to have greater breadth and opportunity for intellectual nourishment and satisfaction than either economics or mathematics. It is interesting to note, however, that my early specialization in psychology was quantitative psychology (my master's thesis and doctoral dissertation were purely quantitative) and now I have gravitated to a business school, where more than half of my postdoctoral years are in a milieu heavily saturated with economics. Indeed, my APA presidential address (Perloff, 1987) was, at least conceptually, an argument (the pervasiveness of self-interest in our lives) at the core of fundamental theory in economics. My point is that, more often than not, our career choices may not be as haphazard and accidental as they appear on the surface.

Finally, whether it was by design (subconsciously at least) or happenstance, psychology was a happy career choice for me because it offered greater opportunities for breadth of activities than I suspect most other fields would have. For me, this breadth was essential for minimizing job dissatisfaction if not for maximizing job satisfaction, because I am an inveterate generalist, psychology having allowed me to cover the gamut of interests from measurement and statistics to a nagging preoccupation with civil liberties, which turn out to be, whether the humanistic psychologists admit it or not, at the core of humanistic psychology. By this I mean that humanistic psychology, promoting as it does growth and change and encouraging individuals to express themselves freely and openly, at its core is a manifestation of the first amendment of the U.S. Constitution: "Congress shall make no law. . .abridging the freedom of speech, or of the press, or the right of the people peaceably to assemble, and to petition the Government for a redress of grievances."

My Early College Exposure to Psychology

Much to the credit of Temple University's philosophy of undergraduate psychology education and consequently to my good fortune, the 30 or so hours prescribed for the major were saturated with fundamental courses in laboratory psychology, the history of psychology, schools of psychology, and psychological measurement. My initial exposure to formal psychology served me extraordinarily well, not only in allowing me to compete favorably with the excellent cadre of doctoral students with whom I interacted at Ohio State, but throughout the first decade or more into my active professional years as a working psychologist.

At Temple, the two mentors who were the most inspiring and encouraging included, first, a psychology professor (Richard Harter) who was a gifted teacher and who did no research and no publishing. His intimate knowledge of the contributions by psychology's luminaries, from Wilhelm Wundt on to the hotshots at that time, such as Clark Hull, Edward Tolman, L. L. Thurstone, Rensis Likert, Kurt Lewin, and others, stirred my intellectual juices to the point where, right then and there, I knew I had to pursue psychology in graduate school. The second influential mentor at Temple was a French professor (Henry Dexter Learned), with whom I studied 3 years of French. He saw in me, I suppose, a returning GI ("Government Issue," referring to ordinary enlisted men, by and large infantrymen, who symbolized America's servicemen in World War II), who had an insatiable appetite for learning and a voracious sense of wonder and awe when confronted with new ideas. So Harter, the psychology professor, propelled me into further study in psychology, while Learned, the French professor, awakened in me a deep hunger for stretching my mind in many ways, but I cannot vouch for how much French I learned!

My Entrance into the World as a Professional

Department of the Army. My first 8 years postdoctorally were in the "real world," not academia. In my first professional job, I was a research psychologist with the Department of the Army, an organization now called the U.S. Army Research Institute for the Behavioral and Social Sciences, located in Washington, DC. This agency was concerned with personnel research on Army enlisted and officer personnel. We were engaged in research on selection, classification, and evaluation of the performance of uniformed personnel. A watershed event occurred while working for the Army, moving my career in a new direction. On the second day of my 4-year tenure there, a well-known personnel research psychologist, E. K. Taylor, announced his departure for a new job, with (then) Western Reserve University in Cleveland, before that institution merged with the Case Institute of Technology. Taylor was the contract research officer. I was then asked to be the assistant contract research officer, in which capacity I remained for a couple of years. That activity and responsibility gave me a taste of administrative and supervisory work, laced with power and prestige, which nudged me in that direction on several occasions during my career, and away from substantive research or scholarly work. Who knows, were it not for the kind of "Potomac Fever" that assignment flaunted, I might have more single-mindedly pursued a career more immersed in a research and scholarly direction than in other supervisory positions which, truth to tell, may have spoiled my focused ardor for research and similar activities that would have insulated me against the more heady involvement with policy makers and other bureaucratic swingers.

At the Department of the Army I became conversant with the processing of enormous—in size and complexity—data sets analyzing biographical, attitudinal, aptitude, personality, some physiological, and leadership variables. The statistics and distributions thus generated formed the basis of much of the military's policy vis-à-vis the recruitment, selection, evaluation, and utilization of the men and women in the armed forces.

Military Psychology. At this juncture I must comment on the undeserved image that many psychologists have about military psychology. Military psychologists, and I was among them for 4 years as a civilian (and for 3 years as an Army Reserve officer), are not belligerent demons scheming to blow up the whole bloody world. Rather, they are a conscientious, hard-working, and talented group whose expertise forms the basis of decision-making affecting the satisfactions and lives of millions of men and women. Their dedicated blood, sweat, and tears have been responsible in no small measure for the success of our military establishment in efficiently, effectively, and, yes, even humanely, deploying the abilities and personalities of uniformed personnel in military operations mandated by civilian authority. The skills and training of military psychologists have saved lives and helped our nation perform its military mission more wisely, less expensively, and more safely than would have been possible with the uninformed but benign guidance of good intentions and the sometimes fuzziness of data-free judgment. Military psychologists, in a word, enable military organizations to perform their duties and execute their missions with considerably more success than would be possible bereft of the brains and devotion of psychologists.

Science Research Associates. My second early position was as director of research and development at Science Research Associates (SRA) in Chicago. SRA was a commercial publisher of testing and guidance materials, among whose leading psychometric instruments were those by John Flanagan, Frederic Kuder, and L. L. Thurstone. I loved Chicago as a city, but found my duties at SRA stressful because of the need to constantly be on the hustle for grants, contracts, and other soft money. But my duties at SRA opened up, as was the case, too, with the Army job, a very wide circle or network of professional colleagues whose association stood me in very good stead in later years, particularly the quarter of a century at Pittsburgh during which I held numerous leadership positions. At SRA I was associated with large-scale test development projects for such agencies as the Navy, Coast Guard, Air Force, and the Selective Service System.

Professional "Street-Smarts." From SRA I learned about profit-making organizations or, if you will, the private sector, its leadership, operations, balance sheets, bureaucratic procedures good and bad, and their place in U.S. society. I learned something of office politics and how to position one's self favorably in the pursuit of self-interest. I learned, too, and this is certainly not an unarguable truth, that with protection of some sort, certification, status, or what have you, of the PhD or of some other professional designation, you are far less vulnerable than "uncertified" people lacking the imprimatur of a degree and of the "cover" that that degree provides. I am sure that on more than one occasion I would have been unceremoniously booted were it not for my protective academic armor. This is not to say that PhDs cannot be fired. However, I believe that organizations may be wary of rocking this boat to avoid criticism and public relations headaches. My counsel, then, to young people on the threshold of career decision making is to give damned serious thought to adorning themselves with protective, certification-linked armor. It will serve them well for the rest of their lives.

Finally, at SRA I learned that equivocation and ambivalence are the enemies of success and achievement. If you take a job you must do what the job requires. Very few of us are free to define the job as we like or to enjoy the fruits of the job without doing the hard work of earning those fruits. Specifically, in the case of SRA I was uncomfortable in chasing the dollar—although there is absolutely nothing wrong with doing this. (I'm in love with dollars, but not with the grubby effort their acquisition requires!)

On the other hand, had I talked myself into accepting the fact that hustling for grants was in many ways desirable, I could have avoided a lot of grief and at the same time earned a pile of money. But I was spared from making this decision because in the spring of 1959 I was visited by a long-time friend, Ben James Winer, then a professor in the psychology department of Purdue University, who convinced me to become a colleague of his at Purdue. I left SRA on June 30, 1959, thence inaugurating my career as an academician, first at Purdue University and later at the University of Pittsburgh. Throughout my academic career I have had the opportunity to visit nearly 100 universities and colleges, giving talks, recruiting, or making accreditation site visits, and that many or more public and private organizations beyond academia.

My Years as a University Professor

My 10 years in the psychology department at Purdue University, in West Lafayette, Indiana, were very fruitful. Our children grew up amid Indiana's fabled Hoosiers, near the banks of the Wabash river and in the thicket of midwestern conservatism, family values, and reverence for the flag, and it was at Purdue that I learned about and engaged in faculty politics. It was at Purdue that I learned, alas, that teaching, although important, was "More honor'd in the breach than the observance." At Purdue I breathed the fresh, clean, exhilarating air and the joys and satisfaction of scholarship, spending countless hours in my beloved carrel at the Purdue main library. In the carrel I had a cot, my typewriter, books, paper, and 3 x 5 cards. Heaven could not be better than that!

The love of learning fostered by Henry Dexter Learned at Temple University flourished bountifully at Purdue, reminding me that this is probably what I should have done all the while, instead of being wooed off track by the Washington and Chicago jobs, and maybe even by Pittsburgh. At Purdue, my wife, Evelyn, and I hosted multitudes of dinners and cocktail parties for students, faculty, and visiting colloquia speakers, including, among others, Leon Festinger, Patricia Cain Smith, and "visiting firemen" from all corners of the globe. At Purdue, located in a provincial small town, I settled in comfortably. I grew to like and respect the people there, the merchants, the professional cadre of doctors and lawyers, and the livestock and farms, just minutes away from our residence with a basketball backboard on the patio (after all, this was Indiana!).

At Purdue, I mused over and was rarely irritated by the freight cars holding up traffic as they meandered through downtown streets. At Purdue, during the turbulent 1960s, when the university was dubbed "a hotbed of student rest," I acquired and satisfied an all-possessing need to write letters to the editor of the local newspaper, and it was there that my staunch belief in individual rights and liberties—the Bill of Rights, the U.S. Constitution—flowered. At Purdue, in a word, from approximately ages 38 to 48, I grew up intellectually and began to have a better feel for who I was and what I wanted to do with the rest of my life. Unfortunately my old nagging infatuation with being an administrator, a wheeler-dealer, along with (a) growing dissatisfaction with local sentiments and values antagonistic to the restlessness and malaise of youth in the 1960s, and (b) our family's desire to locate in a less-insulated environment than Lafayette in Tippacanoe county in Hoosierland, awakened my interest in leaving Purdue. An opportunity that seemed ideal, and in many ways proved in fact to be comfortable and suitable if not ideal, was with the Graduate School of Business at the University of Pittsburgh. Several years later, through a generous endowment, we became the Joseph M. Katz Graduate School of Business, the school's current designation.

The Pittsburgh Years

Earlier in this chapter I made a few comparisons between business schools and psychology departments. These comparisons and adjoining comments are in Perloff (1992), along with related observations and biographical data, where they are presented somewhat differently.

But there are several cogent insights that may be instructive to fledgling psychologists. First, let it be said "loud and clear" that business school environments are intellectually enriching and amenable to impressive productivity; besides, business school faculties, doctoral students, and MBA students are decent people hardly in the mode of greedy materialistic nerds popularly depicted by the media, and by snobbish colleagues in the arts and sciences. Naturally, I cannot speak for all business schools, but the anecdotal evidence along with my observations at many other "B schools" I have visited or heard about confirms my conclusion that even though a business or management school is a professional school, like law, medicine, engineering, or social work, it is essentially a unit of a college or university. As such, the B school is not particularly different than the disciplines in the arts and sciences concerning its dedication to excellence in teaching, scholarship, and research. Business school professors are no different than their arts and sciences colleagues with respect to their attitude (contempt, maybe, or condescension) toward deans and university administrators. The one difference that is apparent—other than the fact that business school professors are often better paid than their arts and sciences counterparts, and that business school deans have deeper pockets for photocopying, travel, and the like—is that business school professors, unlike, by and large, the arts and sciences professoriate, despise faculty unions more vengefully than President William Jefferson Clinton eschews healthy snacks.

From a substantive point of view, at Pittsburgh my interests evolved into two areas, first in program evaluation or evaluation research, and next, in knowledge utilization. I should add that for a variety of reasons the number of graduate students whose theses or dissertation committees I chaired dropped from around 40 at Purdue to 8 at Pittsburgh, although I was at Purdue for just 10 years and now I am in my 25th year at Pittsburgh. One of the more conspicuous reasons for this is because at Pittsburgh my involvement in outside activities, including professional organizations and consulting, flowered.

Leadership Positions for Professional Associations and Societies

While I assumed the presidency of the APA's Division of Consumer Psychology in the late 1960s, during the Purdue years (where my substantive area was consumer behavior), my efforts with the other organizations I was honored to lead occurred when I joined the Pittsburgh faculty and continued thenceforth. I would like to make a few comments about this aspect of my professional life, but it may help the reader if I identify the organizations whose affairs I was entrusted to handle during the periods indicated.

Association and Society Presidencies. I was elected and served as president of the APA (1985–1986); the American Psychological Foundation (1990–1992); the Association for Consumer Research (1970–1971); the APA Division of Consumer Psychology (1967–1968); the Eastern Psychological Association (1980–1981); the Evaluation Research Society (1977–1978); Sigma Xi, The Scientific Research Society (President of the University of Pittsburgh Chapter, 1989–1991); the Society of Psychologists in Management (1993–1994), and the Knowledge Utilization Society (1993–1995). (I also was treasurer of APA, 1974–1982, and served on dozens of APA's boards, committees, and task forces.)

Time is, of course, a zero-sum game. Hence, my activities over the years with the aforementioned organizations severely ate into my time at Pittsburgh, not only my university duties, but publishing, research, and all that jazz. So the benefits, honors, and status conferred upon me by serving in leadership positions with these associations and societies came at a price, the price or cost being not only in terms of less scholarly output, but also at the cost of annual salary increases that would have been higher had my outside activities been less intrusive and demanding than they were. As someone once said, if you dance you have got to pay the band (or, put less delicately, if you don't pay the loan shark, he'll break your legs!).

Additionally, I have served, for example, on the boards of the Archives of the History of American Psychology, the California School of Professional Psychology, and of Recorded Psychological Journals, as well as on several community organizational boards and how many university committees at Purdue and Pittsburgh I have long since stopped counting. (Even as we speak, I have just accepted an invitation by Pittsburgh's Chancellor J. Dennis O'Connor to serve on the University of Pittsburgh Task Force on Intellectual Property Rights in a Networked Environment.) One receives enormous clues regarding organizational structure, leadership problems and opportunities, and management practices as a result of service to these organizations. This certainly is also true for experience with government agencies, corporations, and community groups, where one has the opportunity to become engaged consultatively.

Yes, I have given a larger chunk of time to professional and scientific association leadership functions than many of my wiser friends and colleagues might have chosen to devote to these activities. Maybe I am a professional society "groupie" or "junkie." Obviously, I was not forced into these pursuits. Apparently, I had a need for, or at least a strong interest in, this kind of involvement. A rationalization is that one is helping other individuals in their own careers, not to mention the advancement of scholarly and practitioner-oriented fields through a variety of organizational initiatives, the totality of which helps solidify a field; earns it recognition by other professional and scientific fields; adds credibility to it in the eyes of employing organizations, such as universities and corporations, among others; and produces visibility for it to receive funds from a variety of sources. Besides, this has enabled me to hobnob with the "right people," eat in fancy restaurants, and engage in retreats at opulent resorts. I never had it so good!

Consulting Activities

I have rendered consultative services for 20 academic institutions, including the Baylor College of Medicine, Cornell University, Harvard, and the University of Illinois; for 15 corporations, including Bell Telephone, Fisher-Price Toys, Procter & Gamble, and Westinghouse; 13 government agencies, including the Air Force, Federal Trade commission, the Food and Drug Administration, the National Institute of Mental Health, the National Research Council, the National Science Foundation, and the Peace Corps; for 8 nonprofit organizations, most of them being local community agencies; and for 8 research organizations, including the Educational Testing Service.

Among the benefits of consulting are the opportunity to try out your ideas in the employment setting, the marketplace, or elsewhere beyond the protective walls of the groves of academe; the income; a particular organization may allow you the opportunity to gather data, for example, on its employees, thus enabling you to test out your ideas, or to obtain data a student might use for his or her dissertation; to gather experience or illustrations useful for giving your lectures more credibility or for making them more interesting; or for acquiring that variability in one's daily routine that serves as a healthy intrusion upon what Henry David Thoreau called our "lives of quiet desperation." Variability makes life less desperate.

Consulting is, therefore, a useful diversionary activity, not to mention a satisfying and remunerative full-time pursuit for many psychologists and other professional men and women. It has served me well for all the reasons suggested in the preceding paragraph. But I must issue a word of caution (please forgive the sermonizing): You should guard against putting the cart before the horse, becoming excessively involved or occupied in your client's behalf so that your efforts for the client seriously impair your effectiveness in discharging your regular duties, for example, as a university professor. Another and equally damaging consequence is when you have committed yourself for a period of time to a client but learn that what you are asked to do is tedious, of questionable morality professionally, or is on behalf of or working with client personnel who are oafs, sleazy, or otherwise undesirable. A problem I have encountered on more than one occasion is the client who is ill-equipped to use my services—such as they were—appropriately, asking me to do things that his own subordinates, whose pay is less than mine, should be able to do, or the client who hasn't really thought out how the consultant's talents and expertise should be deployed, and leaves the consultant dangling, for weeks at a time, doing little or nothing in return for the retainer the consultant receives.

What Stresses Have Been Experienced in My Career?   How many ways have I been stressed? Let me count the ways. First, and a continuing problem with me, even now that I am an emeritus professor spared from the obligations of *schlepping* (a Yiddish word meaning "to proceed or move slowly, tediously, or awkwardly") in and out of classrooms and of attending exasperating committee meetings and of being bombarded by faculty meeting screeds, is that I still have not disciplined myself to the point where I am able to resist undertaking more than I can reasonably accomplish or deliver. But I am improving, I think. It will take time. . .what's left of it. Where did it all go? Why did I let it slip by so quickly and, more often than not, as a temporal spendthrift who did not know the value of an hour, a day, a week, or months?

Another stress, not unrelated to the foregoing character flaw, is starting more projects than I can possibly finish, leaving me in a perpetual state of nearly always being behind in meeting my deadlines and keeping my promises. Similarly, I have "big" ideas that I drop like lead balloons when I must get into the details. (The devil, they say, is in the details.) Along the same vein, I find myself putting off doing easy but wearisome tasks even though they are capable of completion without breaking a sweat.

Finally, I am generally bothered by the way I am universally praised, as being a nice guy, a thoughtful person. To hell with that. I would rather be known for having done some noteworthy things in my life. Hey, maybe I am not told about these noteworthy accomplishments, because there haven't been many, or any! Say it ain't so.

What Might I Have Done Differently?

Exorcise myself from being a generalist so that I could do one or two things well, and in depth, rather than a multitude of things more than satisfactorily but not really with distinction. Well, this is what I would desperately seek to do, assuming that this new me were equipped with the genes requisite for such a transformation.

I also would have liked to make up my mind with respect to the professional track I wished—or ought—to follow, full-time professing including a tunnel-visioned preoccupation with research and scholarly activities, or following my natural bent toward being a wheeler-dealer, whereupon I might have positioned myself for positions of considerable responsibility in universities or federal agencies, or whatever. Hey, maybe a university presidency or Secretary of Health and Human Services (HHS)? Well, why not? Many psychologists have held university presidencies and one psychologist was Secretary of Health, Education, and Welfare (before it became HHS)—John Gardner of self-renewal fame.

Advice to Others

Experiment. Innovate responsibly. Take risks judiciously. Do not shrink from new ventures for fear of failure. No one is immune from adversity. The hallmark of a successful achieving person is his or her ability to snap back after misfortune, and to benefit from and not be immobilized by failure. Also, the following:

1. "This above all: to thine own self be true, And it must follow, as the night the day, Thou canst not then be false to any man."—Shakespeare: Hamlet.
2. "Never explain; never complain."—Author unknown.
3. "Don't make predictions, especially about the future"—Yogi Berra.
4. "Watch the turtle. He only moves forward by sticking his neck out."—Author unknown.
5. "I can't. I can't go on. It goes so fast. We don't have time to look at one another."—Lines spoken by Emily Webb, Act III, *Our Town*, by Thornton Wilder.
6. "Play the hand that's dealt you."—Author unknown
7. "There are two tragedies in a man's life. The first is to have failed to have reached your goal. The second is to have reached it."—Nietzsche
8. "If one advances confidently in the direction of his dreams, and endeavors to live the life which he has imagined, he will meet with a success unexpected in common hours."—Henry David Thoreau

But the way I counsel myself is with these lovely words of Robert Frost: "The woods are lovely, dark and deep. But I have promises to keep, And miles to go before I sleep. And miles to go before I sleep."

References

Perloff, R. (1987). Self-interest and personal responsibility redux. *American Psychologist, 42*, 3–11.

Perloff, R. (1992). The peregrinations of an applied generalist in government, industry, a university psychology department, and a business school. *Professional Psychology: Research and Practice, 23*, 263–268.

Chapter 12

*Building Safe Environments
for Children and Families:
The Integration of Research,
Teaching, and Public Service*

Gary B. Melton
University of South Carolina

Politics—both international and domestic—has always fascinated me. By the time I was in the second grade, I was an avid newspaper reader (beginning with the editorial page). In high school, I became an equally ardent debater, in both informal discussions and forensic competition. Reaching adolescence during the tumultuous 1960s, I served as district press secretary for a candidate for the U.S. Senate, I campaigned actively for a populist gubernatorial candidate, and I wrote political columns and many editorials and related news stories for my high school newspaper (judged at the time to be one of the best in the country) and a national underground newspaper. For my labors (notably including a front-page editorial advocating busing in order to integrate the all-White high school that I attended), my family was sometimes rewarded with a late-night splattering of our house and cars with raw eggs, and at times I found myself taunted by other students and occasionally even teachers.

During a time in which the world was being turned upside down, I found high school to be oppressive in most respects. While Rome was burning (a metaphor that became a close analogue in much of the country), high school was long on rules and short on either social relevance or intellectual stimulation. I was a high achiever and I always complied with the rules, but I felt frustrated by an educational setting that seemed often to punish and rarely to stimulate careful thought and action about matters of great moment and social concern. Although a few courses were broadening and challenging (notably a tutorial in world history and a seminar in 19th-century European history), I longed to be able to explore the issues of the day—especially the forces that seemed to be in the way of a lasting peace—in greater depth.

In retrospect, what really bothered me about high school was a sense that neither my peers nor I were being taken seriously even though our concerns were serious ones, even if they sometimes were expressed with undiplomatic adolescent bravado. In that regard, I am forever in the debt of my parents, who enabled me to express unconventional beliefs without becoming alienated. They often did not agree with the political stances that I took, and even my religious views were at variance with theirs. (As the great-grandson of a Methodist circuit rider, I was the product of many generations of devout Protestant faith and active participation in small town Southern churches, but my intellectual skepticism and social concern led me to Unitarianism.)

Although the specific content of my beliefs differed from my parents, they respected their four children as individuals and encouraged us in our own interests and convictions. Accordingly, my parents shared the aggravation that came with early morning washing of egged cars and, although not without some ambivalence, supported my political, social, and religious involvement. I know now that my parents were unsure whether they (and I) were doing the right thing, in that they worried that I would be swept up and away by the turmoil of the times. Ultimately, however, they recognized what I knew from the beginning: My social concern emanated from the values that they had taught and the sense of caring that they had modeled. Now as an adult, I have no doubt that my professional and personal involvement as an advocate for children reflects the respect that my parents showed for the dignity of children as people.

My Undergraduate Years

I did not start my university studies, however, with the intention of such a focus on children's issues. As I began the search to decide the college that I would attend, I was single-minded in my approach. My future course in life had been set (or so I thought) for almost as long as I could remember. Wanting to make the world a more peaceful place, I had long planned to be a foreign service officer with a specialty in Eastern Europe. Consistent with that goal, I had taken Russian all the way through high school, I had spent a summer in the Soviet Union near Leningrad (now St. Petersburg), and I had even attended a Boy Scout world jamboree.

With such well-established interests, it should come as no surprise that I diligently sought a college with a strong program in Soviet studies and an atmosphere that would foster independent thinking and scholarly debate. After carefully narrowing the list of colleges to which I would apply and receiving notices of admission and financial aid, I accepted a scholarship to attend the University of Virginia, where (so I thought at the time) I would major in Soviet studies.

Today, however, the Soviet Union has ceased to exist, and even more to the point, my studies and career obviously took a different direction; otherwise, this tale would not appear in a book of autobiographies of psychologists. There may be some instruction in knowing how that detour occurred—and also in considering the ways that my work as a psychologist has reflected, perhaps to an ever greater extent, the concerns that underlay my childhood and adolescent interests and plans.

The detour occurred as a result of a chance event. I was searching for a summer job prior to entering college, and I had not been successful in obtaining the unskilled laborer jobs that seemed to be standard for teenage boys in the summer workforce. As the summer began, I changed strategies and began to seek jobs consistent with my interest in community service. When I visited the state Easter Seal Society office just before summer activities were to begin, I learned that a camp counselor had been forced to withdraw because of an emergency appendectomy. I was offered the position and accepted.

Very shortly I was off to the mountains of Virginia. My work as a camp counselor in a large Easter Seal camp—work that I repeated during my later collegiate summers—was truly a life-changing event. In a physically isolated setting that fostered intense identification with the campers—"us," who were stigmatized by "them" (cf. Dibner & Dibner, 1973)—I met my future wife, and I had experiences that substantially altered my educational and career plans. I was struck by the degree of variation among children's functional disabilities, even when their physical handicaps were objectively similar. I began to understand reactions to physical disability as normal consequences of an abnormal situation, to consider the ways that the social environment could be altered to mitigate maladaptive reactions, and to recognize that I had both a commitment and a talent for alleviating children's concerns.

Quickly my major shifted to psychology, with a special focus on children. Although this change may seem abrupt, it reflected the same social concern that had led initially to my interest in Soviet studies. At that time, Virginia's psychology department was rigorously experimental, with (unlike today) few faculty on the social-science side of psychology. Although the major gave me little substantive background in the area of most interest to me (I did not know, for example, that the area that interested me was community psychology, which was never mentioned directly in my undergraduate classes), it did instill an appreciation for the scientific study of human problems.

At the same time, I was able to take advantage of an honors program that resulted in a waiver of all course prerequisites and residence with other honors students. Both the intellectual opportunities and the sense of community were liberating contrasts to the stultifying high school environment that I had experienced. I broadened my substantive knowledge about social policy, especially in regard to children and families, by enrolling in advanced undergraduate and graduate courses in education, government, foreign relations, and religion, and by working as a counselor in a group home for delinquent boys. While working full time in the group home, I also carried heavy courseloads (at one point, 22 credit hours) that enabled me to graduate in 3 years.

My Graduate and Early Career Experiences

With the same single-mindedness that drove my college application, I applied to graduate programs (mostly in clinical child psychology) that would enable me to learn about the social psychology of childhood disabilities and to develop social and psychological supports to mitigate their effects. That search led me to Boston University (BU), where Andrew Dibner and Frances Grossman had conducted studies of community and family factors in adaptation to physical disabilities and mental retardation.

The key fact that I did not realize when I applied was that the clinical-community psychology program at BU was strongly psychoanalytically oriented. Indeed, BU's clinical program in the 1970s could be fairly described as having been somewhere to the right of Vienna, with even ego psychology not yet embraced by several senior faculty members who had been trained as classical Freudian psychoanalysts. Not only did that orientation not easily match my community interests, but it also created considerable cognitive dissonance with the emphasis on empirical research that I had developed during my undergraduate program.

To make matters a bit more complicated, I apparently was the first White student from the South whom BU had accepted into its then-30-year-old clinical training program. I was stereotyped by some professors as in "cultural shock" and forced for the first time to make "Southerner" a part of my identity.

Boston offered rich opportunities, however, and BU had few requirements that constrained my taking advantage of them. Dibner encouraged my continuing interest in the social context of childhood problems, and a then-junior faculty member, Verne McArthur, introduced me to community psychology and the use of psychology in social change. Both provided support for my breaking the mold that typically resulted in conservative clinical practitioners.

In my first practicum placement (in the Developmental Evaluation Clinic at Children's Hospital), I was fortunate to be involved in a setting that was interdisciplinary in both philosophy and organization. Not only were the insights from more than a dozen disciplines integrated in the evaluation of children with developmental disabilities, but the clinic was so self-consciously interdisciplinary that the chairperson-ship of case conferences was rotated without regard to discipline or seniority. In general, the clinic was focused on developing plans that would meet the needs of children and families, regardless of whether those plans met the usual compartments of disciplines and agencies. The case coordinators were charged with ensuring that the resulting plans were implemented in the clients' home communities and, when necessary, greasing bureaucratic wheels to turn accordingly.

In that context, I was able to learn from another then-junior psychologist who was a master in child advocacy, Gerald Koocher. As a supervisor in the Develop-mental Evaluation Clinic, Koocher tutored me in building family and community support for individual children with complex needs and, in so doing, changing service systems. I later recruited Koocher (who was not a regular faculty member at BU) to supervise my dissertation on *Children's Concepts of their Rights* and, after I completed my doctorate, to collaborate in a series of research projects on issues in child policy.

With McArthur's help, I was able to develop my own internship that integrated clinical and community training. Doing so was an internship in itself. The program was designed from scratch, contracts were negotiated among multiple agencies that had little or no history of work together, and finally approval was secured from the BU graduate program. The last step was not an easy one in a program that had always placed its students in traditional, typically psychoanalytically oriented, clinical internships in Boston, often with supervisors who themselves were BU graduates.

In the internship I divided time between the Boston regional office of the Office for Children, a state child advocacy agency, and the Solomon Carter Fuller Mental Health Center, a community mental health center serving several predominantly African-American neighborhoods. With primary supervision by William Malamud, a psychiatrist who is a community-oriented psychoanalyst (yes, such a person does exist), I developed a concept of *clinical child advocacy* that blended help for individual children with change of political systems. That idea and the experiences in my internship served as the foundation for one of my first books on child advocacy (Melton, 1983a).

The chief psychologist in Children's Services at Fuller, Judith Singer, was also chief psychologist in Children's Services at another mental health center in Boston, Dorchester Mental Health Center, which also served a predominantly African-American community. On Singer's recommendation, I went straight from my internship to directorship of Adolescent Services at Dorchester, which included a staff of 25 clinicians and paraprofessionals in a variety of clinical, consultive, and therapeutic educational programs.

In my 2 years at Dorchester, a combination of events led to my growing up professionally in a hurry. I entered a set of programs that had been merged involuntarily, that had a number of serious personnel problems, that were often in conflict with the central administration of the mental health center, and that were supported by a creative but fragile blending of funding streams and bending of civil service rules. Meanwhile, Boston was racked by racial tension and intermittent violence as it complied with—and resisted—federal court orders to desegregate its schools. Reflecting the prevalent intrapsychic focus of the Boston mental health community, the other five community mental health centers in Boston remained largely removed from the crisis. Therefore, we not only moved our services into the junior and senior high schools in our catchment area, but we also followed youth from our catchment area as they were assigned to schools throughout the city. We consulted with school staff about ways to respond to the students' concerns.

Through this baptism by fire and tutelage by Louise Wylan, then the director of Children's Services at Dorchester, I honed skills in program design and administration. At the same time, I taught two courses a semester at various colleges and universities in the Boston area, and I worked on my dissertation.

I knew that I wanted to become a professor when I completed my doctorate, because such a position would give me the freedom to blend research, teaching, and clinical and community service. These functions usually are considered to be distinct elements of higher education. It is common for faculty to have more or less explicit contracts that indicate how much effort they will devote to each function, with the proportion dictated by whether the institution defines itself primarily as a "teaching college" or a "research university." (Unfortunately, service tends to be a poor third in the priority list regardless of the nature of the institution.) I have never been able, however, to write such a job description, because almost everything that I do integrates research, teaching, and public service.

Moving on to Academia

Although the optimal venue for my work was clear from the beginning, finding a suitable academic position was not easy. Coming from BU, I did not have the level of research training and publication history that many of my peers in the job market did, and I also was stamped (to what would have been the amusement, I'm sure, of my professors at BU) as too Freudian.

My soft Southern-American style also did not match the demands of the academic interview. The "interview" in most academic psychology departments is not really that. Rather, it is a multiday process that more closely resembles rush week in a college fraternity or sorority than a typical job interview. It typically involves relatively formal individual conversations with many of the faculty members and some of the graduate students, relatively informal conversations in a plethora of social situations, and an "audition" in which the candidate presents a research colloquium or a sample lecture.

Although this process may illuminate a candidate's current level of expertise, it also favors gregarious, assertive individuals, and it probably is not a highly valid process for assessing candidates' motivation or ability to work independently, or even their likelihood of fit into the university's social environment ("collegiality"). As a result, the predictions made by senior faculty in the departments where I initially interviewed were far off the mark. One well-known professor concluded and convinced her colleagues that I would never publish. Fifteen years later, I have about 200 publications. In another department, the conclusion was drawn that I was too soft-spoken to be successful in applied community psychology. Fifteen years later, few psychologists have been as active or influential in public policy or large-scale program development.

With persistence after completion of my dissertation, I did obtain a faculty position at Morehead State University in eastern Kentucky, where I was on the faculty of the Department of Psychology and Special Education. Morehead serves a particularly impoverished region of central Appalachia with an especially low median educational level. Unsurprisingly, Morehead is self-consciously "Appalachian." At least at the time that I was employed there, however, this perspective was expressed largely through an occasional folk festival and an ideology that seemed to deny the need for special attention to the needs of the students or the communities from which they came.

I was shocked by the lack of systematic attention to child development and family life in Appalachia. In response, I organized a network of social scientists interested in children and families in the region. We began to sponsor annual conferences that brought together scores of scholars who typically were unfamiliar with each other's work. I also edited a book on rural psychology (Childs & Melton, 1983), a theme of which was the need to differentiate the demands of rural life in general from those that are specific to particular regional cultures. Having spent my childhood (prior to high school) in small towns in North Carolina, this focus was not foreign to me. Nonetheless, it is useful to note that it emerged from a concern with a desire to be helpful in the particular community in which I was working—not a previously established program of study.

I stayed at Morehead only a year. Because of a 15-hour teaching load at that institution, I did not have the time that I wished for activities outside the classroom. Recognizing the constraints that such a teaching load placed on research and public service, the department of which I was a part had developed a policy of recruiting the best young scholars that it could and accepting that they would stay only a short time.

I had not planned to leave quite so soon, however. Consistent with the department's general approach, I received reasonably strong administrative support for my work. I did not send out many resumés, but I left because an unusual opportunity arose at the Institute of Law, Psychiatry, and Public Policy at the University of Virginia, where I became the research director—the first psychologist to be hired in the Institute.

Developing a Specialization in Psychology and Law

A couple of points about this career shift are noteworthy. First, chance was again a significant factor. I had seen the ad for the position in the *APA Monitor* but had decided that I had insufficient background in forensic psychology to be a serious candidate. When I called Dick Reppucci, a community psychologist whom I had met when I had interviewed unsuccessfully in the Department of Psychology at Virginia (prior to taking the job at Morehead), to discuss his ideas about the Appalachian network, he mentioned the position and his belief that I would be appropriate for it. Without that incidental discussion, I never would have applied for the job, and I may never have become a specialist in psychology and law.

Second, although I was a member of the faculty, the position at Virginia fulfilled the function of a postdoctoral fellowship for me. The Institute had a number of bright young faculty and fellows, and it offered the possibility of involvement in a first-rate law school. However, the Institute ran on grants, so that the positions that we filled were not tenure-track (permanent lines), and the focus of our work was dictated in part by the funding agency's needs. Accordingly, the Institute has provided a training ground for psycholegal scholarship for several individuals who have become major scholars in the field. With the lack of tenure-track positions, however, all left Virginia before we became widely known, but we have continued our collaboration (e.g., Melton, Petrila, Poythress, & Slobogin, 1987).

While at the Institute, I learned law by auditing a few classes, mastering use of the law library, and having my writing critiqued by excellent legal scholars who filled the margins between paragraphs with "Transition?". This experience convinced me that development as a psycholegal scholar does not require formal legal education—at least not at the level of a JD—but that it does require facility in "thinking like a lawyer," a cognitive style that is effectively socialized in the first year of law school or, in my case, in the critiques by my colleagues and the independent study of legal treatises and judicial opinions.

By the same token, formal education in both psychology and law does not guarantee their integration, as I subsequently learned in reviewing applications for faculty positions by JD–PhDs who were psychologists by day and lawyers by night or vice versa. Moreover, neither a JD nor a history of research on psycholegal issues necessarily results in an appreciation of the unique culture of law schools (see Melton, Monahan, & Saks, 1987), the special problems involved in bringing psychological research to the attention of legal policymakers (see Melton, 1987), or the philosophical, practical, and evidentiary issues in application of psychological research to specific cases in the legal system (see Monahan & Walker, 1993).

Those lessons were applied when I moved in 1981 to the University of Nebraska–Lincoln, where I directed the law/psychology program for more than a decade and where I created a Consortium on Children, Families, and the Law (a network of 11 interdisciplinary policy research centers around the United States) and a large Center on Children, Families, and the Law. In the graduate training conducted by the law/psychology program, we have emphasized careful legal analysis, application of empirical methods to empirical questions in the law, and sophistication in knowledge diffusion, public administration, and policy reform (Melton, 1990).

We also have emphasized the need for a normative perspective with which to select questions for study and variables for analysis, whether in empirical psycholegal research or in legal decision making and scholarship. Developing an approach that I have termed *psychological jurisprudence* (see, e.g., Melton, 1992), I have argued that such an inquiry should rest on the quest for protection of human dignity, a journey that requires psychological-mindedness. Such an approach diverges from conventional law-related studies in psychology, which typically have focused on topics, like eyewitness testimony and jury process, that have superficial resemblance to areas of psychology (respectively cognitive and small group research) but that for the most part do not relate to core problems in law. It also deviates from conventional legal scholarship and judicial decisions, but the focus is on the subjective meaning of legal constructs and the social consequences of legal policy.

The psychological–jurisprudential perspective provides a systematic framework for selection of issues worth empirical scrutiny. It also offers a coherent approach for jurists seeking to apply concepts that are recognized as fundamental but that have been notoriously slippery. For example, a psychological–jurisprudential perspective provides jurists with a focus on the *experience* of invasion of privacy in deciding whether the Fourth Amendment's prohibition of unreasonable searches and seizures has been violated (Melton, 1983b). (By contrast, judges typically undertake arcane logical analyses of whether there is the same expectation of privacy in a closed paperbag as an unlocked suitcase and whether there is the same expectation of privacy when the paperbag is on a car seat in plain view as when it is on the seat under a blanket or it is on the windowsill of a house.)

Applying Psychology to Current Problems

In my own work, I have applied the psychological–jurisprudential perspective to the creation of safe environments for children—in effect, the theme that began my work in psychology. In the past several years, I have had a series of remarkable experiences that have convinced me of both the growing possibility for such a safe society but also the growing threat to children around the world (Melton, 1993). I have served on the U.S. Advisory Board on Child Abuse and Neglect (U.S. ABCAN) and developed a proposed new national strategy to end the social isolation that breeds child maltreatment (U.S. ABCAN 1991, 1993), but I have watched public officials consumed with bureaucratic trivia as the number of reports of suspected child maltreatment climbs to a stunning figure (about 3 million in the United States in 1992) and as the failure of the current child protection system becomes more and more catastrophic. I have lived in Norway and observed the remarkably rapid development of the office of the first ombudsman for children in the world, but I also have heard about the sense of crisis in family life in that country (Melton, 1991). I have conducted surveys showing a similar sense of isolation rampant in both inner-city and suburban communities in this country, and I have participated in mostly unsuccessful efforts to build a new child and family service system in several states. When I have sought help for my own family, I have felt the frustration inherent in a system driven by perverse fiscal contingencies (frustration that is undoubtedly multiplied for families living in poverty and facing multiple serious problems) and ill-suited to the cost-effective delivery of help to people where they need it, in the form that they need it, when they need it.

I have observed the concern for children manifest in some of the more than 170 nations that have ratified the U.N. Convention on the Rights of the Child since 1989 (unfortunately not including the United States), but I have yet to see a government implement the convention fully in spirit. I have visited Central and Eastern Europe and observed both the possibility for greater attention to child and family welfare and the inattention in most of the region to the "people problems," including a skyrocketing infant mortality rate, that have accompanied the fall of the Soviet empire. Amid the Gulf crisis, I visited Jewish and Druze, Christian, and Moslem Arab leaders in Israel and heard such divergent tales of the reasons for their families' anxiety that I could conclude only that everybody was right and everybody was wrong.

I share anxiety about the future of the family as an institution and the support available to parents and children, but I also have hope. At midlife, as I look back at my own career, I am struck by the number of times that a chance event has led me in a new direction—indeed into psychology itself. I also am impressed, however, by the constancy of perspective and goals across my life—indeed back to a specific concern with Eastern Europe. More fundamentally, my work has been governed by the conviction that the protection of human dignity is a serious matter—perhaps the *most* serious matter—that requires serious effort in thinking as well as doing.

"Being nice to kids," for example, is not enough to build a society that is safe for their development. Neither is conventional application of professional skills. To make a difference in social conditions, one must learn by whatever means to do careful policy analysis and research and to communicate the results clearly and persuasively to diverse audiences. One must be thoughtful but grand in developing a vision of how the world might be, open to new ideas and methods (whatever their disciplinary origin), creative in their application, and diligent in seeking opportunities for teaching and change.

A Day in the Life of an Institute Director

A final point that did not occur to me until writing this autobiography is that I have never worked in a setting that was not interdisciplinary (note that I did not say "multidisciplinary") or even nondisciplinary. All of the core faculty other than me in the center that I created at Nebraska have formal training in multiple disciplines. There is no disciplinary hierarchy or even a disciplinary perspective in the center. Rather, we are committed to doing what makes sense: Using social science methods and legal analysis to discover ways of fulfilling our normative goal of a family-friendly society respectful of children.

As I write this chapter, I am about to move to the University of South Carolina (USC), where I will direct a new interdisciplinary entity, the Institute for Families in Society. Both the Nebraska Center and the South Carolina Institute are exemplary of a growing phenomenon: university-based centers that blend research, teaching, consultation, and advocacy in support of a *mission* (with all of the surplus meaning of that word) of development and implementation of policies supportive of strong families and healthy, happy children.

Although somewhat more intense than a typical day, a recent day that I spent in the Institute at USC illustrates the operation of centers and institutes on children's issues. I began the day with a 7:30 a.m. breakfast meeting with a dozen faculty members from several departments about implementation of pending legislation to support comprehensive, school-based mental health services. Implicitly, the legislation will demand that the Institute:

- develop school-based programs that are of broader scope than any that have been attempted anywhere else;
- select and supervise practicum students, who will accrue payback requirements for ultiamte professional work in the schools;
- redesign graduate training programs to provide the skills needed for school-based services;
- consult with and provide continuing education to mental health professionals in the schools;
- design and implement research to test the effectiveness of the programs and to provide the foundation for fine-tuning the programs and adjusting both graduate and continuing education accordingly;
- consult with program administrators and agency executives about the administrative and financing mechanisms needed to support the programs; and

- ultimately, educate agency executives and legislators about the potential for expansion of the programs.

I went from the meeting with the various faculty to a 2-hour meeting with the director of the state Department of Social Services (DSS) and one of his principal staff to propose several research demonstration projects to test the effectiveness of novel approaches to foster care and family services—ideas that I had proposed in my federal work to develop a new national strategy for child protection (U.S. ABCAN, 1993). We also discussed structures and practices within both DSS and the university that might interfere with implementation of the proposed projects.

I then drove from DSS back to campus for a luncheon with about 20 legislators to discuss ways that the university could assist them in developing child and family policy and to inform them about the forthcoming visit of about 30 experts from around the world (a visit that may include a joint session of the General Assembly), most of whom I know from various consultation and research projects abroad. I left the luncheon a bit early to hurry down the street to the state capitol, where I made an hour-long presentation to the House Judiciary Committee on research about the operation of the juvenile justice system and alternative programs that might better respond to the problem of youth violence.

After talking with the House Judiciary Committee and making arrangements with the committee's staff for follow-up communications, the staff director drove me back to campus, where I was late for a meeting that my colleagues and I had convened of the media coordinators from every state human services agency. That meeting was the first step in the design of a statewide, year-long observance of the International Year of the Family, with a focus on educating the public about policies needed for support of the family in a rapidly changing world. That media campaign also will include community surveys, focus groups, town meetings, and interactive broadcasts to generate information and coalesce community concerns.

Immediately after the meeting with media coordinators, I went to a monthly dinner with several of their bosses (state agency directors), where we engaged in a spirited, off-the-record discussion about the goals of state-agency programs for families and the means of stimulating related community involvement. After the dinner, I had an informal conversation with the mental health director about the choice of counties to participate in the school-based programs discussed at the beginning of the day and about provision of information to one of the legislative committees considering the relevant bill.

When I returned to my hotel room at about 9:30 p.m., I prepared a presentation that I was to make the next day to deans of schools of education in the state about ways that undergraduate service learning objectives could be integrated into the initiative for school-based mental health centers, and I reviewed my notes for a conference on African-American families at which I was to speak the next day. I also reviewed a memorandum that had been sent to me about a proposed Medicaid standard for therapeutic day school programs—the focus of my dinner meeting the next evening.

The Need for an Interdisciplinary Approach

The range of activities involved in that day's schedule indicates why centers and institutes have arisen. Participation in such diverse activities would be suicide in most traditional academic departments, which generally look to discipline-based measures of productivity (in psychology, publication in APA journals), which commonly reward laboratory research with pristine controls, and which are organized around formal classes conducted on campus. To get the work done, one must be able to move outside traditional academic structures and to take a problem-, rather than discipline-centered approach. Center faculty must be able to respond quickly to emerging issues and grant opportunities—to act more like "Beltway bandit" consulting firms (referring to the Beltway around Washington, DC) than university departments.

At the same time, it is instructive that centers and institutes generally have arisen inside universities—not in private firms or state agencies. It is not accidental that the dinner meeting with the human services cabinet was in the Faculty House; the university culture promotes free thinking in a way that agency cultures typically do not.

Centers permit scholars from diverse perspectives to join with policymakers and practitioners for relatively unconstrained policy analysis and planning. Centers also enable linkages to be made among global concerns, national issues, and local programs in ways that inform analysis at each level (e.g., testing assumptions underlying prospective national policies through local demonstration projects).

Although potentially much more useful than traditional practice or scholarship, the integration of research, teaching, and public service is both intellectually and emotionally demanding. Doing it well requires that one work far more than 40 hours a week, do so in diverse settings, travel frequently, interact regularly with the media, tolerate the ambiguity and volatility of the political process, and accept a low success rate in even getting the message to those who could use it.

I worry that conventional graduate education in psychology is increasingly unlikely to socialize scholars and practitioners with such a broad approach. By their nature, the regulatory structures of professional guilds and the narrowness of discipline-based—or more commonly, subdiscipline-based—education lead to solutions that often have little relation to the problems that they are purported to address.

Psychology has much to contribute when psychologists put people—not their profession—first. Too often, however, the questions that are asked start from a desire to apply and expand existing psychological knowledge and methods, not the need to respond to problems with optimal solutions. The results are overattention to trite questions (e.g., eyewitness reliability) and implementation of professional practices (e.g., growing use of hospitalization, residential treatment, and foster care) that are contrary to our stated values, outcome research, and common sense.

We can do better. We need a vision, careful planning, a little luck, and the creativity and diligence to take advantage of opportunities when they arise.

References

Childs, A. W., & Melton, G. B. (Eds.). (1983). *Rural psychology.* New York: Plenum.

Dibner, S. S., & Dibner, A. S. (1973). *Integration or segregation for the physically handicapped child?* Springfield, IL: Charles C Thomas.

Melton, G. B. (1983a). *Child advocacy: Psychological issues and interventions.* New York: Plenum.

Melton, G. B. (1983b). Minors and privacy: Are legal and psychological concepts compatible? *Nebraska Law Review, 62,* 455–493.

Melton, G. B. (Ed.). (1987). *Reforming the law: Impact of child development research.* New York: Guilford.

Melton, G. B. (1990). Realism in psychology and humanism in law: Psycholegal studies at Nebraska. *Nebraska Law Review, 69,* 251–275.

Melton, G. B. (1991). Lessons from Norway: The children's ombudsman as a voice for children. *Case Western Reserve Journal of International Law, 23,* 197–254.

Melton, G. B. (1992). The law is a good thing (psychology is, too): Human rights in psychological jurisprudence. *Law and Human Behavior, 16,* 381–398.

Melton, G. B. (1993). Is there a place for children in the new world order? *Notre Dame Journal of Law, Ethics, and Public Policy, 7,* 491–532.

Melton, G. B., Monahan, J., & Saks, M. J. (1987). Psychologists as law professors. *American Psychologist, 42,* 502–509.

Melton, G. B., Petrila, J., Poythress, N. G., & Slobogin, C. (1987). *Psychological evaluations for the courts: A handbook for mental health professionals and lawyers.* New York: Guilford.

Monahan, J., & Walker, L. (1994). *Social science in law* (3rd ed.). Westbury, NY: Foundation Press.

U.S. Advisory Board on Child Abuse and Neglect. (1991). *Creating caring communities: Blueprint for an effective federal policy on child abuse and neglect.* Washington, DC: U.S. Government Printing Office.

U.S. Advisory Board on Child Abuse and Neglect. (1993). *Neighbors helping neighbors: A new national strategy for the protection of children.* Washington, DC: U.S. Government Printing Office.

Chapter 13

Change, Persistence, and Enthusiasm for Ethnic Research

Stanley Sue
University of California, Los Angeles

I consider myself to be quite lucky. Over the past two decades, I have immensely enjoyed my work. After receiving the PhD degree, my first position was at the Department of Psychology, University of Washington where I was assistant and associate professor. I then went to the University of California, Los Angeles as a professor of psychology. Along the way, I have served as director of an American Psychological Association (APA)-accredited clinical psychology internship program, associate dean of the UCLA Graduate Division, and director of the National Research Center on Asian American Mental Health.

Each of us has a story to tell about our careers. I first want to indicate how I became interested in psychology, then how I developed my line of research, and finally what my work is like.

Chance Factors in Life

My story begins early. I enrolled in an all-boys technical high school in Portland, Oregon, in order to become a television repairman—for reasons I can no longer remember. After a year of machine shop, electric shop, and automotive shop, I found little interest in what I was learning and decided to change high schools and prepare for college.

A couple of years later, I developed great fascination with psychology, especially clinical psychology. I was intrigued with psychotherapy and with the opportunity in psychology to help emotionally disturbed individuals. I told my parents that I wanted to become a clinical psychologist, not fully knowing what a clinical psychologist did. My father, who was born in China, said, "What is that?" He couldn't believe that people would pay me to listen to their problems—indeed, he wondered if I could make a decent living. His reaction and that of my mother partly reflected some cultural differences. Even now, many Chinese and other Asians are unfamiliar with the profession of psychology, preferring their sons and daughters devote their careers in the fields of medicine, law, engineering, or physics. In any event, I persisted in pursuing a career in psychology. Then my second oldest brother decided to become a psychologist; my oldest brother became a psychologist and married a psychologist; and my youngest brother also became a psychologist. In fact my father refers to us as "psychiatrists," perhaps still harboring an unconscious wish for us to be physicians! In any event, my mother and father are proud that we all received our doctorates, but they still wonder what we do as psychologists.

Why did I develop an interest in psychology? Bandura (1982) argued that chance encounters play a prominent role in shaping our lives. Although we would like to believe that life is predictable, that life paths are consciously and deliberately planned, and that aptitude, skills, and motivation determine our lives, fortuitous events can often explain much of what we become. In retrospect, I believe that two fortuitous encounters strongly affected my choice of careers. The first encounter came during high school when I happened to see a book on psychoanalysis at a book store. After reading about five pages, I bought the book and was fascinated by the notions of the unconscious, ego, defense mechanisms, and so on. This led me to the second experience.

My oldest brother was attending Portland State University and was enrolled in an introductory psychology course. I saw his textbook and wanted to read about psychoanalysis. There was a section on psychoanalysis but the book contained much more exciting materials on cognitive, social, developmental, and other areas of psychology. Because I was enrolled in a high school science seminar class that required a research project, I asked the instructor if I could conduct a psychology experiment. Students in the course typically devised and conducted physics experiments. The instructor was quite encouraging and indicated that a psychology experiment was permissible, as long as "scientific methods" were used. I then proposed an experiment involving learning and retroactive and proactive inhibition that was essentially a replication of a study in my brother's textbook. I ran the experiment on fellow students. To my amazement, the results came out as hypothesized! I was hooked on psychology and attended the University of Oregon, and then UCLA, where I received a doctorate.

Development of My Research Interests

During my initial years as a graduate student, I had considered a career as a clinician. I rather enjoyed psychotherapy and working with clients. However, my interests changed after gaining experience in research and teaching. Through clinical–community research I could help people and satisfy my own curiosity about human behavior. The problem was that unlike some students who developed a clear line of programmatic research during their graduate days, I was not sure of what I should do. Many areas of research seemed fascinating. In fact, my dissertation research, under the supervision of Professor Bertram Raven, was in the area of social rather than clinical psychology—it dealt with processes involved in the reduction of cognitive dissonance. What sharpened my interest in ethnic research was the turmoil I observed at many universities. In the late 1960s, the civil rights movement and Vietnam war were on the minds of many students. Personal and societal values were being challenged, and I experienced some personal conflicts. I felt committed to civil rights, but it did not initially occur to me that my chosen profession could address ethnic minority and cross-cultural issues or that a career could be built on researching such issues.

Then I started to read literature on ethnicity. It struck me that much was unknown about identity development, mental health, and means to structure our intervention and prevention efforts with respect to ethnically diverse populations. I then began to study mental health problems among Asian-American clients at the UCLA Psychiatry Clinic, where I was working as a graduate student intern. The research found that Asian Americans tended to underutilize mental health services in comparison to their population, and the relatively few clients who used services were severely disturbed (see Sue & Sue, 1974)—findings that persist even today. Why did Asian Americans underutilize services? Did they have a low prevalence rate for mental disorders? These questions aroused my curiosity.

Although the research was personally interesting and important, I was still uncertain as to whether an academic career could be built on such research when I joined the psychology faculty at the University of Washington. Ethnic research was considered by some psychologists to be the study of a population rather than the study of a phenomenon. As a consequence of ethnic and racial tensions in society, others thought that the research was not really "science" or "psychology" because ethnic investigators were often polemical or interdisciplinary in approach. Then too, because ethnic populations such as Asian Americans were rather small in number, there were frequent difficulties in finding adequate sample sizes on which to base research.

I persisted in the research for several reasons. First, I believed that science was defined not by the population of study but by the methods of inquiry and by a way of thinking. As long as hypotheses or theoretical propositions were tested, or knowledge was being contributed using appropriate methods, this was science. Furthermore, some colleagues conducting survey research and psychophysiological research also complained that their work was considered by others as being outside of psychology. It occurred to me that what is considered the proper domain of "psychology" was debatable. Second, at UCLA and the University of Washington, many faculty were supportive of my interests and encouraged me to pursue ethnic research. Particularly important in my development at Washington was the support of Nathaniel Wagner, Director of the Clinical Psychology Program, who, himself, was interested in ethnic research. Third, I felt I had something important to say and that I could satisfy my curiosity about ethnic issues through research. Although there were very few colleagues with whom to discuss Asian American research, a small group of us did establish the Asian American Psychological Association in 1972, which enabled us to have collegial support for the work.

After spending about 10 years at the University of Washington, I joined the faculty at UCLA in 1981. Although my wife and I enjoyed living in Seattle, and we found it difficult to leave colleagues and friends, I felt that my Asian American research would be enhanced in California. California was becoming more and more culturally diverse, and I would have better opportunities to study Asian Americans and other ethnics. Indeed, as of 1990, 43% of the population of California was composed of members of ethnic minorities (i.e., 57% are non-Hispanic Whites). About 10% of the population was Asian Americans, and at UCLA the entering freshman class was nearly 40% Asian American.

Academic Life

As mentioned earlier, I thoroughly enjoy my work teaching, conducting research, and consulting. I cannot imagine retiring. Ironically, because many faculty at research universities find their work satisfying and meaningful, we are often publicly stereotyped as not doing much work. Several of my friends outside of the university joke about how university professors are in the classroom only a few hours of the week; and because I like my job, they assume that it must be because I do not do much work. To the contrary, I spend 50 to 60 hours a week teaching, conducting research, or giving talks. It is true that professors can often create their own schedules, rather than working from 9 a.m. to 5 p.m.; it is true that we have a measure of autonomy in choosing the kinds of courses to teach and of research to conduct; it is true that variability exists on the amount of work that individual faculty perform; it is true that, unlike a corporate environment with a strong hierarchy and chain of command, faculty are given considerable freedom to speak their minds; and it is true that many of us receive "highs" from writing good papers or making good presentations. These "psychic benefits" from work have been used to justify budget cuts to universities and increased public scrutiny of the work of faculty. Perhaps, we have neglected to adequately convey to the public what our work entails. Nevertheless, as a group, we tend to work long hours and to be extremely productive.

The work is enjoyable largely because I find it meaningful and important. Through research I am able to contribute to new knowledge. This is gratifying because research allows me to express myself, to satisfy my curiosity, and to contribute findings that have theoretical and applied meaning. As mentioned earlier, I was curious about the mental health and utilization of mental health services among Asian Americans. The popular belief years ago was that Asian Americans were fairly well adjusted, because of their relatively high levels of education and occupational attainments and relatively low rates of juvenile delinquency, crime, and divorce. Although it is beyond the scope of this chapter to critically examine this belief, I was interested in mental health issues. We found that Asian Americans tended to underutilize mental health services. Among those who used services, Asian Americans tended to exhibit greater severity of disturbance. This led me to think that perhaps Asian Americans with serious disorders were relatively more likely than those with moderate disorders to utilize services. Although all groups may underutilize services in that not all who need mental health care seek services, Asian Americans may be especially prone to avoid and delay mental health care until the problems are highly disruptive.

We began to study why Asian Americans use different sources of help for emotional problems and conditions that would enhance favorable outcomes from treatment. We concluded that for cultural reasons (e.g., shame and stigma, having different conceptions of mental health, and the unavailability of bilingual and bicultural therapists), Asian Americans tended to avoid using services. Only the most severely disturbed, who lacked other resources or who posed management problems for the family or community, tended to enter the mental health system. The work illustrates the systematic investigation of issues, starting with one basic question and then following up on the possibilities raised. The work also sheds some light on the role of culture and on means for improving the utilization and treatment outcomes of services. Over time, the research has gained more salience. Because of the increasing numbers of ethnic minorities and ethnic researchers in our society and the growing recognition of the importance of culture, research and training on cultural diversity issues have become more of an integral part of psychology. Years ago, I would not have predicted this.

Although I have primarily focused on research, I also enjoy teaching and working with students. In 1988, we received a grant from the National Institute on Mental Health (NIMH) to establish the National Research Center on Asian American Mental Health. Because of the center, a large number of students who are interested in Asian American research have applied to our PhD program in clinical psychology. We have been able to offer undergraduate as well as graduate students a unique opportunity to conduct ethnic research. What has been gratifying is to see some of my former students now pursuing distinguished careers of their own.

Academic life also offers opportunities to do a broad range of things. In addition to teaching and research, I became an administrator—associate dean of the Graduate Division. My responsibilities included academic affairs (degree requirements, evaluation of the quality of departments and programs offering graduate degrees, etc.), student affairs, and graduate admissions for the university. The work was quite different from what I was used to. There was an opportunity to help strengthen and create programs and to work with faculty and other administrators. I enjoyed the work but discovered that administration is not easy. Faculty have very strong egos and speak their minds freely. It is often difficult to achieve consensus and there are the usual "politics" going on: hidden agendas, personal goals, clashes of values, and so forth. Such political maneuverings are not unique to the university and they occur in all organizations and occupations. But administration was a radical departure from my usual role as researcher and teacher. Despite the fact that there was an opportunity to rise in the administrative ladder, I found that administrators must sacrifice their research interests. Although I was determined not to let my productivity suffer, it was simply not possible to maintain my research and I finally made a decision to return to research and teaching.

Possibilities to serve in national organizations (e.g., the APA and American Psychological Society), on journal editorial boards, on research review committees (e.g., National Institute of Health and National Science Foundation), and in government agencies point to the incredible opportunities that are available to academics. Many faculty are asked to consult with community agencies, other universities, and private corporations. These opportunities do not occur simply because one is an academician but are based on one's accomplishments. Faculty who become experts in their areas of research and who are nationally recognized find that they are in great demand for services.

In my case, I served on various governance structures within the APA—member of the Board of Social and Ethical Responsibility in Psychology and chair of the Board of Convention Affairs—as well as within APA divisions (president of the Society for the Psychological Study of Social Issues and co-chair of the Ethnic Minority Task Force for the Society for Community Research and Action). Other activities have included membership on an NIMH review group and on various editorial boards of journals: *American Psychologist, American Journal of Community Psychology, Journal of Community Psychology, Hispanic Journal of Behavioral Sciences*, and *Psychological Assessment: A Journal of Consulting and Clinical Psychology*. Involvement in these activities was highly meaningful to me. I was able to meet other psychologists, whom I had read about, and to have some degree of influence in the direction of psychology, research, and funding. Meeting and working with others are also important because it provides an opportunity to learn from others and for one to gain visibility.

Challenges and Problems in Academic Life

Academicians often complain of serving on countless committees, having too many things to do and not enough time to do them, an inability to meet multiple deadlines, and so forth. In my experience, these complaints have some validity because of the varied demands and opportunities that are always present. In addition, university life is not for everyone. Professors are subject to intense peer evaluations. A faculty member is constantly judged in his or her area (e.g., clinical, social, and experimental), department, and university. One's research is also evaluated by journal peer reviews or research granting agencies. Students provide input into teaching effectiveness. Thus, academicians must be open to constant criticism (as well as praise!) from others. The most important periods of evaluations occur when one is considered for tenure and promotion. Tenure is intended to provide some assurance that faculty have academic freedom and can speak their minds. It also allows one some assurance of continued employment. Thus, tenure is important. However, it also means that faculty members are essentially on a probationary status for 4 to 6 years. This is much longer than the probationary periods for civil servants or union members, which can be 1 year or less in other occupations.

Work does dominate my life. As in all careers, if you want to get ahead and achieve, you must put in the work. Ambition in advancing one's career is not the only reason why professors work hard. I have always found that faculty are overstimulated. We are often asked to take on one more project or to engage in another activity. The ability to manage time must be acquired if one is to avoid the reputation of never being able to complete assignments on time. Fortunately, my wife Sophia also has a strong work orientation and has been very supportive of my career, so my time on the job has not created personal problems. However, I know of many colleagues whose devotion to work has created family problems. Again, the conflict between career and personal life is not unique to academia. I cannot imagine how anyone who has led a distinguished career in business, the arts, law, medicine, politics, and so on, can avoid putting in long hours of work.

I get upset when I do not do well. For example, I am frequently asked to give lectures or to hold seminars at other universities or institutions. My estimate is that up to 20% of my presentations do not turn out as well as I would like them to. This usually occurs when I do not know the audience. The presentation may be too technical and specialized for a general audience, or too general for a sophisticated audience. This bothers me greatly, and I constantly try to gather as much information on the audience as possible. Furthermore, presentations regarding ethnicity are likely to generate a great deal of emotions in the audience. Dealing with issues of cultural differences, prejudice and discrimination, and so forth, challenges long-held values. Some in the audience want me to bring out issues of racism; others want me to address themes of racial harmony. Some want my talk to be highly research-based whereas others may want me to make critical social commentaries. I, of course, have my own agenda—to be research-based and challenging, and to be able to provide an effective message that makes people think.

Academic life requires that one perform regularly in front of audiences (students and colleagues) and others. Perhaps it is not apparent from my behaviors, but I consider myself to be a rather shy and anxious person. To this day, I feel anxious getting in front of a class or making a professional presentation. Some of the anxiety is helpful: It energizes me and forces me to be well prepared. On the other hand, there are some situations that I would rather avoid but cannot. This may sound strange, especially because I am a clinical–community psychologist who helps others to overcome their anxieties and emotional problems. In any event, my anxiety is not overwhelming or I would have changed my career.

Recommendations on Developing a Career in Academia

When I graduated with a doctorate from UCLA in 1971, I knew I wanted to teach and conduct research. However, I was not sure how "marketable" I was. Unlike recent doctorates today who often have 5 to 10 publications as graduate students, I had only 1. In 1971, there were relatively few academic positions, so I began to apply for many positions throughout the United States, regardless of whether they were primarily research or teaching institutions. Research institutions stress research productivity and have fewer teaching responsibilities, whereas teaching institutions require a great deal of teaching relative to research. Out of the many applications that I made in response to job advertisements, only two teaching universities showed some interest in me. Because I wanted to enter a research university, I delayed visiting the two universities for job interviews. Then Ned Wagner from the University of Washington contacted Eliot Rodnick, director of the Clinical Psychology Program at UCLA, about a faculty position at Washington. Rodnick recommended me, and within several months I had accepted the offer from the University of Washington. Earlier, I spoke of chance factors in life. To this day, I wonder what my career would have been if I had gone to a teaching instead of a research institution or if I had focused on a different area of research. I suppose that I would have been happy anyway, but the question does occasionally cross my mind.

Over the years, I have encountered many graduate students who want to enter academia. What advice do I have? Let me indulge a bit and offer some recommendations for advancing one's career as a faculty member.

In terms of teaching, I find it ironic that students are exposed both to inspiring and uninspiring teachers from kindergarten through graduate school. Yet, we often fail to model the behaviors of good teachers when we begin teaching. I believe that we are often so concerned about learning and achieving a high grade that we fail to recognize or focus on teaching styles. Once one decides to enter academia, one should begin to systematically note and model characteristics of good teachers. We should observe characteristics involving knowledge of subject matter, organization of ideas, clarity, presentation styles, and openness to students. This can also be accomplished by attending talks of outstanding lecturers at conventions. Rehearsing talks and gaining experience as teaching assistants are also critical, as is having a graduate program that will help one learn how to teach effectively.

With respect to publishing one's research, few problems exist in finding an abundance of journals in psychology and related fields. Of course, the most important journals are those that have rigorous peer review standards, include the works of the best respected psychologists, and have a wide distribution. Although some specialized journals are considered very prestigious, wide distribution or circulation increases the likelihood that a broad audience will be exposed to the research findings. In the early stages of one's career, it may be difficult to know which journal is the most appropriate outlet for one's research. Over time, most scholars pretty much know if the research question, methodology, and results merit publication in top journals. I have found that it is very useful to develop in my mind a template for writing journal articles. The template is a mental prototype or model to guide my writing. It includes visualizing the introduction, methods, results, and discussion sections of a paper, once the results have been analyzed. Constantly reading journal articles and writing papers for submission (and taking to heart reviewers' comments) enable one to develop a template. Collaborating with senior colleagues who can serve as mentors is also helpful. There are other avenues for publishing, such as books and book chapters, but for psychologists at research institutions, journal articles are still the bread-and-butter of the profession. Another important scholarly activity is applying for research grants. Funding for research is extremely helpful and, for some researchers, essential in order to conduct meaningful and systematic investigations. Therefore, developing good skills in writing for research grants is an integral part of scholarly activities.

Finally, it is also important to have contact with colleagues who are experts in one's area of research. Attendance at conventions, volunteering for national boards and committees, serving as a journal or research grant reviewer, and so on, can provide opportunities to meet and work with more senior colleagues. These activities are important in establishing national visibility and learning from colleagues.

What does the future hold? My interest in research has not at all diminished, and I want to continue with my research work and teaching. Outside of that, I am not able to make many predictions. Presumably chance will continue to play a role in the opportunities that arise.

References

Bandura, A. (1982). The psychology of chance encounters and life paths. *American Psychologist, 37,* 747–755.

Sue, S., & Sue, D. W. (1974). MMPI comparisons between Asian- and non Asian-American students utilizing a university psychiatric clinic. *Journal of Counseling Psychology, 21,* 423–427.

Chapter 14

The Autobiography of a Social Psychologist: Scholarship, Advocacy, and Leadership

Dalmas A. Taylor
University of Texas at Arlington

Personal history always brings us into confrontation with the arithmetic of life. Life is essentially a series of movements from one stage to another. Several theories in psychology treat development in a stage framework. Most notable among these, Erikson (1975) and others showed life unfolding in observable sequences in which each stage is marked by a crisis, or turning point, a crucial period of increased vulnerability, and heightened potential. Likewise, in *Passages: Predictable Crisis of Adult Life*, Gail Sheehy (1976), writing for the public, described salient passages and crises in moving from dependence on one's family constellation through successive stages of growth and development into the full maturity of one's adulthood. According to Sheehy:

> We are not unlike a particularly hard crustacean. The lobster grows by developing and shedding a series of hard, protective shells. Each time it expands from within, the confining shell must be sloughed off. It is left exposed and vulnerable until, in time, a new covering grows to replace the old.

> With each passage from one stage of human growth to the next, we, too, must shed a protective structure. We are left exposed and vulnerable — but also yeasty and embryonic again, capable of stretching in ways we hadn't known before. These sheddings may take several years or more. Coming out of each passage, though, we enter a longer and more stable period in which we can expect relative tranquility and a sense of equilibrium regained. (p. 20)

Sheehy's popularized application of development theory in psychology influenced the organization of this chapter. As I employ the concept of stages, my focus is on ways change heightens the potential for positive outcomes.

I began my professional career as a psychologist, primarily as a researcher in a nonacademic setting where I had an opportunity to study the impact of stressful environments on men working in isolated and confined situations. From that experience I moved into an academic setting where my activities were broadened to include teaching and service. Eventually I yielded to calls for academic administration in which I still find myself involved. Another stage or phase of my career includes service outside the academy— contributions to professional associations, churches, and other academic institutions. Throughout each of these stages I have experienced the stress and anxiety associated with the sloughing off of the old, but, equally, I have benefited from the opportunities to grow. I am persuaded that the choices I have made about being a research psychologist, pursuing an academic career in administration, and providing community service are deeply rooted in my family environment and inextricably related to the events visited upon me by the larger U.S. society.

Early Family Experiences

My parents, who married in 1926, exemplified the tensions of change when they migrated north in search of greater opportunity. My mother was an educator as were all of her family, and my father was a barber (who at age 93 continues to practice his trade). They settled in a ghetto community of Detroit where I was born in 1933—the third of eight children. Those were hard times economically and you did not need "smarts" to feel the ill effects that I experienced. More challenging was the experience of living in a nearly 100% African-American community that was entirely White-controlled—school teachers, merchants, landlords, policemen, postmen were all White. Barriers created by chain-link fences permitted African-American children and the White children of resident merchants to see each other and to occasionally talk and touch, but our commerce was strained and unreal. Wooden frame houses, two and four units each, were dilapidated and barren of lawns and other vegetation. An occasional tree seemed an accident of nature. A retrospective glance easily reveals the unconscious messages and lessons imparted by that environment. This condition is made dramatically worse when I think back to other nearby neighborhoods with single-family dwellings and tree-lined, sprawling green lawns.

We moved from the ghetto to a middle-class neighborhood when I was 8 years old. My parents, through sacrifice and clever economics, had beaten the odds and positioned us for promised opportunities. We had crossed the coinciding "maginot" lines of income, educational opportunity, and residence that separate the poor from the middle class. My father's dominant theme to us was (I can hear it now), "Stay in school; so long as you stay in school, I will support you." Our family saw education as the key to success.

In a knowledge-driven society such as ours, class warfare is inevitable when the political economy only rewards the skills of the highly educated. The highly educated people of my childhood, however, were White. Witnessing a riot in Detroit as a 9-year-old African American helped motivate me to move beyond that environment of poverty, violence, and limited opportunity, even at the risk of possibly having little material or social reward. The 1942 race riot in Detroit was only part of a historical stream that has repeated itself at regular intervals, as Clark's testimony to the Kerner Commission reveals:

> I read that report . . . of the 1919 riot in Chicago, and it is as if I were reading the report of the investigating committee on the Harlem riot of '35, the report of the investigating committee on the riot of '43, the report of the McCone Commission on the Harlem riot. I must again in candor say to you members of this Commission—it is a kind of Alice in Wonderland—with the same moving picture re-shown over and over again, the same analysis, the same recommendations, and the same inaction. (Clark, quoted in the U.S. Kerner Commission, 1968)

This observation is made more poignant when one hears the words of Henry Johnson, a manager of communications at Polaroid, who took the morning off after the Rodney King verdict in Los Angeles to write a poem that concludes:

> Today I know that I am not an American,
> Today I know that I am a Black man,
> living at the margin
> of a place called
> America
> Damn! Damn!
> Damn! Damn! Damn you America!
> Once more you have lied to me.

I mention these persistent themes in history, as disturbing as they are, because they have made an impression on me—and continue to do so. Segregation, violence, poverty, and poor educational opportunities frame the context and backdrop for a thought process that has followed me throughout my career. I will always be concerned with issues of justice.

As an upwardly mobile and mildly curious African-American male in pre-affirmative action America during the 1940s and 1950s, there were only two career paths available to me. First, I could choose to be a blue-collar worker (and that meant becoming a factory worker or garbage collector at best), but that would have been to trap myself in the fate of most youth in the urban ghettoes even today. Or I could choose to be a professional—a choice that offered the promise of a different life and the opportunity to be all I could be and to help others do the same. But even the choices in that professional world were severely limited for African Americans. As a young African-American teen pondering a career of intellectual pursuit and service, for instance, I knew nothing of the world of geology, or of engineering, forestry, architecture, or even psychology. My high school and college years occurred at times when state laws and customs precluded entry into many predominantly White institutions. These exclusions raised the social and economic calculus of remaining in the comforts of where one is versus taking the risk of seizing opportunity for growth. Nonetheless, I have always felt the push and the pull to move to the next level.

Throughout the years of public school education, I remained faithful to lessons learned, and drew regularly upon coping skills developed early in life. Race prejudice was ubiquitous then as now and has followed me personally and professionally. Even as that child of 9, I recall sitting on the curb with my brothers watching looters breaking into stores and stealing food in the Detroit race riots of 1942, soldiers with bayonets in my schoolyard, and the anger of my father at the childish insensitivity to the dangers we faced from that curb. From that experience, I would later be able to put in context the brutality of the internment of Americans of Japanese ancestry and the cruelties suffered by Native Americans that were so successfully hidden by distorted messages in the media and the classroom.

As an adult, the many manifestations of racism would become only too clear. Throughout the development of my career, I would experience the tension of the irresistible pull to turn an intellectual interest or scholarly focus to problems of race prejudice, but first I needed to gain the education I sought, that I believed would equip me to confront racism in U.S. society. It was not easy to leave the familiar and the comfortable to go away to school. My parents' attempts to get me to stay at home and attend school locally added to the difficulty of the decision to leave. Leaving, however, was both an emancipation and a foray into the unknown of my future. The mixture of emotions that I felt addressed both ends of this pole.

Undergraduate Studies

I set out to conquer an intellectual world that, up to that time, had primarily been reserved for Whites. As an undergraduate student I had several interests before accidentally settling upon psychology at Western Reserve University in the 1950s. The Western Reserve campus, located in the University Circle area of Cleveland, was a short distance from a prominent African-American middle-class neighborhood. Cleveland was dramatically different from Detroit. African Americans were not only prominent in the traditional professions of education, law, medicine, and dentistry, but they also held positions on the school board, in city government judgeships, and owned and operated a variety of businesses. Additionally, there was the nationally prominent Black theater—the Karamu—and a host of other classical institutions that were not a part of my recollections of Detroit. There were more "I can" messages in these observations than I had ever before experienced. Cleveland seemed to be free of the racist practices I had experienced in Detroit, and this city had an important impact on my life.

In addition to my schooling, I became involved in Cleveland's cultural, social, religious, and political life. During these years I contemplated careers in law, philosophy, ministry, and finally, psychology. I chose psychology because it seemed more practical and offered a greater variety of opportunities than the other considerations.

By my senior year at Western Reserve I had developed a curiosity about research as a discovery process. The methodologies in psychology afforded me opportunities to ask and answer questions regarding issues about which I was curious or concerned. I was fascinated by psychopharmacology, physiology, and personality. My earliest research project was an investigation of the pharmacological properties of LSD. I was proud, as were my professors, of the shuttle box apparatus that I designed and built. The proverbial white rat was my subject, and simple statistical analyses revealed predicted differences between experimental and control subjects. I was now convinced that psychology was the right choice for me even though there were no role models for me to emulate or consult.

Graduate Study

As a beginning graduate student at Howard University in the late 1950s, I conducted research using the Wisconsin General Test Apparatus to study the concept of upside-downness in monkeys. Leslie Hicks, who was then in California studying "split brain" procedures with Sperry, acquired the apparatus and subjects from his work with Harry Harlow at Wisconsin. Subsequently, however, my major research focus turned to an interest in authoritarianism. I was thoroughly fascinated with the social psychological studies of the fascist personality and its pernicious effects in human behavior. Following the completion of my masters degree on this topic, I had an opportunity to work with Herb Lansdell in the clinical center at the National Institutes of Health on brain localization of function. Through a battery of pre–post paper-and-pencil psychological questionnaires, we were able to demonstrate deficits in human behavior specific to the area of the brain in which tissue was removed. Findings confirmed the lateralization of function and an asymmetry of function between males and females.

This research experience fueled my conflict over the area of psychology I wanted to study, and also created anxieties about leaving employment to pursue further graduate study. After much deliberation I was convinced that returning to graduate school was the right thing to do despite the loss of a reasonably good salary, a nonemployed spouse, and a newborn daughter. I was not, however, sure of which field of psychology to study but enrolled in personality and social psychology. I have never regretted that choice.

In 1962 my decision to pursue doctoral studies at the University of Delaware brought me into contact with people who would have a lifelong effect on my career. I was a research assistant assigned to the project on groups under stress at the Naval Medical Research Institute in Bethesda, Maryland, where Irwin Altman and Bill Haythorn happened to be directing Project ARGUS—an acronym for Advanced Research on Groups Under Stress. A key feature of this research involved the manipulation of environmental variables and personality effects on pairs of men working in isolation and confinement. In a serendipitous result, we observed that men in confinement seek a variety of stimulus opportunities, including self-disclosure, to combat the monotony and stress of their condition. Dyadic pairs found relief, and occasionally stress, in disclosing to one another as they attempted to cope with the anxiety and boredom brought on by their confinement. Their disclosure of personal information to each other, often expressed at rapid rates and at deep levels of intimacy, violated the pace of normal social interactions. Later, Altman and I published a theory of "social penetration" in which we described interpersonal development as movement through layers of the personality from the superficial to deep-seated intimate aspects of the self. We were able to relate the observation of accelerated disclosure to our interest in the development of interpersonal relationships in which persons in a disclosure exchange tend to match each other in intimacy and amount. This dyadic effect was one aspect of the motivational dynamics that propels relationships from early to late stages. For approximately 20 years I pursued a program of research on self-disclosure as a personality construct.

For all of my intellectual growth and excitement in these years, there still was little I could do to escape the impact of racism in my life. I had been one of three African-American doctoral students admitted to the psychology program at the University of Delaware in 1962. The university was making an effort to integrate its student population, but the town of Newark was not. I could not rent an apartment for my family. Bars, barbershops, and drugstore lunch counters were still segregated, which for the most part restricted any social life for African Americans to the campus. In addition, graduate student life has its own tensions, stresses, and sense of unreality. The long hours of study, the grueling array of comprehensive exams, the seemingly endless drafts of research papers, the necessity of covering multiple fields, the agony of proving language fluency, and the constant pressure to perform left most of us anxious for some small respite.

The University of Delaware was experimenting with a Foundations of Behavior program in which I was involved. Participants were doctoral students from sociology, education, and psychology engaged in intense proseminars and exposed daily to massive amounts of new material. The stress and intensity of this curriculum brought us together regularly to study in groups and to engage in the kind of intense intellectual discussions and rehearsal of anxieties that most graduate students experience. Similarly, we became part of each other's research. The Center for Research on Social Behavior became our home away from home. However, when the group went off campus to relax in a local bar or restaurant, I could not join them.

The Martin Luther King, Jr. march to Selma took place during the spring of my final year in Newark. Although my studies interfered with my direct participation in the march, I knew many who went. When Jim Reeb was bludgeoned to death (hammered right in the head) in Selma, I felt the pain of the death of someone I knew and respected. I had met Reeb, who was then the assistant minister at All Souls Unitarian Church in Washington, DC, while I was a graduate student at Howard University. I knew of his commitment to social justice and admired his willingness to bear social witness. I was delighted to learn that he had gone to Selma and angered that he had been martyred there by hatred.

Two influences from graduate school that began to gel in my mind even as I explored more traditional pursuits were Myrdal's (1994) *An American Dilemma* and Allport's (1958) *The Nature of Prejudice*. Myrdal's comprehensive analysis of the contradiction in America's promises of liberty and freedom by the denial of rights to persons of color reverberates with as much force today as it did in 1944. The persistence of prejudice was, and is, paralleled by increasing militancy on the part of people of color and shifting trends in research productivity by behavioral and social scientists. In seeking ways to focus my attention on issues of prejudice and racism, I began introducing these themes into the scholarship of my teaching. I produced several conceptual pieces on prejudice, discrimination, and racism in the United States. Chapters in textbooks on prejudice and racism followed.

The 1950s and 1960s represented a flowering for race relations research in psychology. Social scientists, especially psychologists, also became committed to changing prejudicial attitudes with a focus on behavioral indices, as well as verbally expressed attitudes. Some increased their activism against segregationist practices by testifying in the courts and legislative arenas as expert witnesses. The political and philosophical activism of Martin Luther King, Jr., heightened the salience of the dilemma cited by Myrdal a decade earlier. King's leadership challenged us all to a higher level of social and ethical criticism. Profound positive changes in attitudes, laws, and institutions began to occur. Yet as Katz (1976) observed, we must be leery of three disparate trends:

1. Things are now better than ever.
2. Things may look better, but under the magnifying glass . . .
3. Things may be better now, but there's still a long way to go. (pp. 12–13)

In absolute terms, many positive changes occurred following the social upheavals of the 1960s. Most of the positive change was in the form of policy shifts and laws designed to combat de jure discrimination. Due to entrenched institutional practices, however, relatively few ethnic minority individuals were able to take advantage of the new opportunities. Many who were able to pass through the portals of newly opened doors experienced new forms of prejudices from within a system that had previously excluded them. For example, minority students on White campuses faced open hostility and new stigmas based on some Whites' perceptions of inequitable treatment resulting from affirmative action programs. African Americans who crossed once-restrictive boundaries that kept them out of certain neighborhoods experienced new tensions as some found their newly purchased homes fire-bombed before they moved into them. These experiences heighten feelings of exclusion from mainstream America. On many occasions I felt qualified for and able to afford financially situations that were denied to me for reasons designed to mask racist motives. But I have refused and will continue to refuse to submit to defeat.

In relative terms, things got worse as revealed in comparative statistics in employment, income, and other indices of well-being. For example, African-American family income rose, but the disparity between African-American and White income widened. These comparisons, coupled with resistance associated with a conservative drift in the country, left little doubt that despite our gains much of the racial justice agenda remained incomplete. The ever present struggle to prove one's self in a White world coupled with a constant fear of assault to one's person or career inevitably leads to lifestyles that work against racial inclusiveness. To combat these tendencies I have committed myself to fight oppression wherever it exists in my personal and professional life.

Early in 1974 I was invited to write a chapter summarizing the status of social science applications to racial integration. Because I was driven by a passion to challenge traditional notions of integration I accepted the invitation. The idea of integrating U.S. institutions by this time provoked skepticism in a large number of circles among African Americans and others. Nonetheless, no one had worked harder toward the attainment of integration in this society than African Americans who did so with much pain, personal sacrifice, and great danger to life and limb. I felt a compulsion to examine the apparent contradiction of striving to move into mainstream America and simultaneously challenging the efficacy of integration. I worked from the premises that dependent people cannot be integrated into an egalitarian society and that the social, political, and economic institutions in the United States were not being used to reduce the dependence of African Americans and other victims of prejudice and discrimination. By the 1960s more strident and aggressive strategies were employed by African Americans and other oppressed groups. These strategies, not well understood or accepted by many, called for self-determination, empowerment, and control over the racial justice agenda.

The basic element missing in the conceptual approaches offered in most social science remedies for prejudice was the concept of power and the concomitant strategies essential to that quest. Hence, our social science conceptualizations and research were not addressing a significant aspect of the racial justice agenda. Simply put, I reasoned that racial justice, not integration, should be the goal of our society, and we needed social science theory and research on these issues if our disciplines were to be relevant. Racial justice, I argued, meant intergroup harmony predicated on the concepts of equity and fair play irrespective of racial identification. In a racially just society, all individuals would have power over decisions that directly affect them, and individuals from diverse ethnic and racial backgrounds would maintain their identities. The empowerment conceptualization acknowledges that status equilibration is a necessary precursor to any oppressed group's effort to move from its existing situation to the desired goal of pluralism and racial justice where differences are valued and appreciated. The empowerment conceptualization also implicitly transmits the idea that desegregation, in which racial barriers are relaxed or substituted by token integration, is inadequate and rarely involves the transmittal of power.

The advantage of the empowerment conceptualization was that it did not preclude multiple strategies, nor did it prejudge the character of any strategy. More importantly it acknowledged that some strategy was necessary to move from a condition of oppression to one characterized by racial justice. I have taken the time to delineate this analysis of integration and racial justice because it is central to a next important phase in my career.

Leadership for a Minority Fellowship Program

Not long after I had completed the publication of my ideas on racial justice and empowerment, I was asked to consider the directorship of a newly conceived Minority Fellowship Program at the APA. The goal of the program was to provide fellowship stipends to students of color for doctoral study in psychology. In December 1974, I became the first director of the APA Minority Fellowship Program and embarked upon this assignment fresh from my own analysis of the role of empowerment in preparing individuals for future citizenship and productivity. The new challenge seemed ideal and offered a relatively easy transition for me.

The principle strategies of the program were to facilitate the recruitment of students of color into doctoral-level psychology programs, to aid in their financial support, and to provide guidance and counseling in their training and entry into professional life. At that time students of color constituted less than 5% of all psychology graduate majors. Yet, we were provided only a $6 million grant to be allocated in $1 million installments over a period of 6 years—a drop in the bucket in terms of the magnitude of the problem. In order to gain an increased leverage on the situation, I initiated the concept of cost-sharing with host universities that were training minority fellows or willing to do so. The program paid the stipend support, and the school contributed to the student's expenses for graduate training. The cost-sharing arrangement, which continues to this day, had the advantage of stretching Minority Fellowship Program funds to support additional students and allowing host institutions to demonstrate their commitment toward the support of students of color. Additionally, we were able to use the cost-sharing partnership to introduce new ideas to psychology departments regarding ethnic minority recruitment at the student and faculty levels, curricular modification to include multiculturalism, and ways of providing social support to students facing an alien and sometimes hostile environment. Our suggestions to introduce multicultural themes into the curriculum antedated current efforts to do so and were met with resistance not unlike objections that continue today. Gains have been made, however, and today there is more sympathy for multiculturalism in curriculum than could have been expected in the 1970s.

An advisory committee of ethnic minority psychologists not only participated in the screening and selection of the fellowship finalists but also made campus site visits to engage in a series of support activities on behalf of the students. As an empowering strategy students were asked to arrange the site visit itinerary for their respective campuses. This experience provided opportunities for them to learn how to gain access to university administrators, and how to identify and pursue institutional resources. During the visit we held open seminars with other students on the host campus to explain and promote the program, and to recruit applicants. Throughout my tenure with the program three important objectives were prominent in the messages we delivered during a site visit: (a) We believed a critical mass of ethnic minority students within the student population was essential. Students can be very supportive of one another. (b) A critical mass of ethnic minorities within the faculty ranks was equally important. Students need role models, and ethnic minority faculty could bring perspectives to the curriculum which were sympathetic to ethnic minority student concerns. (c) A modification of the curriculum to include other perspectives and assumptions was not only necessary but would logically follow from the interaction of students of color with faculty of color. We urged university officials toward these objectives and offered assistance when possible.

A number of other innovations, such as mentoring and activities that provided empowerment for the students, made this program not only unique but probably became the key to its success over the years. Finally, the program provided funding for students to attend annual meetings of the APA to present their dissertation and other research, and a job locator, to ease their transition from graduate school into the professional world. The majority of the graduates have assumed professional and leadership positions within their respective fields.

Academic Leadership

A phase of my career that has been central since the late 1970s is academic administration. When I think back to the day that David Sparks, the graduate dean at Maryland, first asked me to become assistant dean, I think of the irony of my posture. My refusal was based on my emphatic opinion that I already had the best position in the university—a tenured full professorship. Two years later I succumbed to yet another call. After serving a year as chair of the Afro-American Studies Program and 2½ years as director of the Minority Fellowship Program, I had not only come to like administration, but also to see it as an opportunity to serve and provide critical influence in the university community.

The mission of universities is multifaceted. They promote the generation and dissemination of knowledge on the one hand and, on the other, train practitioners to solve problems. Both scholars and practitioners are admonished to serve or administer. The role of the administrator is to promote a sense of community, pride, and mission among the faculty, staff and students. Included in this view of the administrator's role is the empowering of others to achieve greater quality and effectiveness in their work. My motivation for continuing in administration, first as a dean of a college of liberal arts and now as provost and senior vice president, is exemplified in the concept of the leader as servant, which conveys the notion of representational leadership in which the leader is "first among equals." There are very few ethnic minority persons in academic administration, especially in line positions. I am persuaded that this outcome represents another instance, and a last holdout, of Whites' willingness to share power with persons of color. Opportunities to provide critical influence in academic policymaking and implementation are enhanced by one's presence and participation in various board meetings, and as a senior level administrator. We very much need an ethnic minority presence at these levels, yet there is an inadequate sensitivity to this deficiency in much of higher education despite protestations to the contrary and pronouncements regarding affirmative action and diversity.

In his book, *The Psychological Sense of Community: Prospects for a Community Psychology*, Sarason (1974) urged those whose work purports to inform social policy to spend time working in a policy arena. The arena of action allows one to implement the connection between theory, data, and action. According to Sarason this experience creates a healthier balance between the overvaluing of ideas and the undervaluing of action. This perspective on the "cash value" of ideas has sustained my commitment to academic administration, but simultaneously fuels a concern that our academic enterprise bridge the gulf between the laboratory world and the world external to the university. The virtues of university governance include a respect for facts and analysis, civility in debate, and a tolerance for opposing arguments and solutions. These virtues, I believe, transfer to the policy arena where ideas and action provide the strongest connection to society. Before assuming my present position I spent a year as a policy fellow with the APA where I was involved in the intersection between scholarship and action. I am encouraged that more and more academicians have come to view this level of involvement and participation as legitimate.

As my personal story has unfolded here, I have glossed over the lines of demarcation or boundaries that separate the stages in my life. The focus has largely been on distinct and overlapping phases of my career. It has, however been the case that passage through these phases has been accompanied by the psychological tensions alluded to by the stage theorists I cited at the beginning of this chapter. There was always ambivalence in moving from the comfort of the known and the anxiety associated with change and uncertainty. Prejudice and racism have followed me as uninvited companions, and I have summoned from within whatever it took to overcome their pernicious objectives. This overview has permitted me to see the integration of my scholarship of research into pedagogy and service, and how these themes were influenced by my early environment. Things have gotten better, but we still have a long way to go. When I find myself engaged today with issues, albeit in different form, I encountered 20 years ago, I wonder how long it will take.

The integration of the personal and professional for me began with my father's admonition and my mother's example about education. Their courage and insight sustained me as I pondered the professional paths before me. Along the way my mentors have been many, and I trust I have passed on to my students the good counsel with which those mentors blessed me. My scholarship on prejudice and racism has been fueled by my personal experience, but more importantly it has been verified and sustained by colleagues who have had the insight to understand the relationship between scholarship, policymaking, and life. Through my work on the theory of social penetration and prejudice and racism, I have tried to contribute to our ever-gowing understanding of communication and interpersonal relationships and the dynamics of prejudice and racism in our ever-changing and more complex world.

References

Allport, G. W. (1958). *The nature of prejudice*. Garden City, NY: Doubleday.
Erikson, E. H. (1975). *Life history and the historical moment*. New York: Norton.
Katz, P. A. (1976). *Towards the elimination of racism*. New York: Pergamon Press.

Myrdal, G. (1944). *An American dilemma: The Negro problem and modern democracy.* New York: Harper & Row.

Sarason, S. B. (1974). *The psychological sense of community: Prospects for a community psychology.* San Francisco: Jossey-Bass.

Sheehy, G. (1976). *Passages: Predictable crises of adult life.* New York: Dutton.

U.S. Kerner Commission. (1968). *Report of the National Advisory Commission on Civil Disorders* (special introduction by Tom Wicker. The complete text of the U.S. Riot Commission reports). New York: Bantam.

Author Index

Page numbers in italics indicate complete bibliographical references

A

Allport, G. W., 165, *169*

B

Bandura, A., 150, *157*
Bernstein, M., 111, *118*
Browne, A., 115, *118*

C

Cassidy, M., 112, *118*
Childs, A. W., 141, *147*

D

Dibner, A. S., 137, *147*
Dibner, S. S., 137, *147*

E

Erikson, E. H., 159, *169*

F

Felipe, N. J., 107, *118*
Fitzgerald, L., 115, *118*

G

Gavin, E., 116, *118*
Goodman, L. A., 115, *118*
Gordon, R. A., 33, *37*

J

James, W., 81, *93*

K

Katz, P. A., 165, *169*
Keita, G. P., 115, *118*
Keith-Spiegel, P., 92, *93*
Kilburg, R. R., 4, *14*
Koocher, G. P., 92, *93*
Koss, M. P., 115, *118*

M

McGovern, T. V., 47, *49*
McKeachie, W. J., 29, *37*
Melton, G. B., 139, 141, 142, 143, *147*
Monahan, J., 142, *147*
Myrdal, G., 164, *170*

O

O'Connell, A. N., 4, 8, *14,* 111, *118*

P

Perloff, R., 126, 130, *134*
Petrila, J., 141, *147*
Pittenger, D. J., 35, 36, *37*
Poythress, N. G., 141, *147*

171